BONATTI

ON

BASIC ASTROLOGY

Treatises 1-3
of Guido Bonatti's
Book of Astronomy

THEORY, SIGNS, HOUSES,
PLANETS, CONFIGURATIONS

Translated by Benjamin N. Dykes, Ph.D.

From the 1491 and 1550 Latin Editions

The Cazimi Press
Minneapolis, Minnesota
2010

Published and printed in the United States of America
by the Cazimi Press
621 5th Avenue SE #25, Minneapolis, MN 55414

© 2010 by Benjamin N. Dykes, Ph.D.

All rights reserved. No part of this publication may be reproduced, stored in or introduced into a retrieval system, or transmitted, in any form or by any means (electronic, mechanical, photocopying, recording or otherwise), without the prior written permission of both the copyright owner and the above publisher of this book.

The scanning, uploading, and distribution of this book via the Internet or via any other means without the permission of the publisher is illegal and punishable by law. Please purchase only authorized electronic editions and do not participate in or encourage electronic piracy of copyrighted materials. Your support of the author's rights is appreciated.

ISBN-13: 978-1-934586-12-9

PUBLISHER'S NOTE:

This reprint of Treatises 1-3 of Guido Bonatti's *Book of Astronomy* has been excerpted from the out-of-print 1st edition, published in 2007. The text reflects the original pagination for each Treatise, and has not been revised or updated to reflect new translation conventions or citations in more recent translations. The Table of Arabic Terms has been removed (a more recent version can be found at: www.bendykes.com/reviews/study.php).

Students should also consult *Works of Sahl & Māshā'allāh* (2008), which contains much material on basic concepts and delineation, now translated into English.

Dr. Benjamin N. Dykes
The Cazimi Press
May, 2010

TABLE OF CONTENTS

Book Abbreviations: vi
Table of Figures vii
TREATISE 1: DEFENSE OF ASTROLOGY 1
    Chapter 1: On the usefulness of astronomy in general 1
    Chapter 2: That the stars imprint in inferior bodies, and that the changes which come to be in this world come to be by means of their motions 2
    Chapter 3: How we arrive at the science of the judgments of the stars, and how it is that it can be excused 3
    Chapter 4: Against those who say tha the knowledge of the stars cannot be known by anyone 4
    Chapter 5: Against those who said that the planets or other stars do not signify anything about generation, nor about corruption, nor about any of those things which come to be on this side of the globe of the Moon 7
    Chapter 6: Against those who said that the planets have signification only over something universal 7
    Chapter 7: Against those who said that the stars signify only two things, namely the necessary and the impossible; but not the possible 8
    Chapter 8: Against those who speak against the judgments of astronomy, and who condemn it, not knowing its dignity because it is not lucrative 9
    Chapter 9: Against those who said that the knowledge of the stars is not useful, but rather harmful because it induces sorrow and distress to those who would have foreknowledge of future accidents, whence they are made sad for that reason before the impediment comes 12
    Chapter 10: Against those who said that the judgments of the stars are not of value, nor are elections of value, saying that it can be elected for the enemy just as for him for whom it is elected 18
    Chapter 11: Against those who said generally that astrology was not anything; [and] to show that it is, and what it is 20
    Chapter 12: What astronomy is, which is the active part 21
    Chapter 13: That this science should not be rebuked, since the Holy Fathers used it 24
    Chapter 14: To show that astronomy is an art and one of the four mathematical ones, namely with the theoretical sciences 25
TREATISE 2: SIGNS AND HOUSES 27
    PART 1 27
    Chapter 1: On the division of the orb of the signs, and that the signs are only twelve, and that they are neither more nor less 27

Chapter 2: In what way the signs act in the elements, and in which elements every sign acts 29
Chapter 3: Why the elements are so disposed and ordered 38
Chapter 4: To show that the elements are only four, neither more nor less 38
Chapter 5: Why the signs are so ordered or disposed 39
Chapter 6: Why the denomination of the signs begins from Aries, and not from any other of the signs 41
Chapter 7: Why the signs were named by these names 43
PART 2: On the Nature of the Essential Circle 46
Chapter 1: On the division of the orb of signs into twelve signs, and of every sign into thirty degrees, and of every degree into sixty minutes, and of every minute into sixty seconds 46
Chapter 2: To show which signs are northern and which southern 47
Chapter 3: Which signs are of direct ascension, and which of crooked [ascension] 47
Chapter 4: On the order of the circle of the seven planets, and the disposition of those seven planets, and their courses, and in what times they perfect their courses 49
Chapter 5: What powers the planets have in the signs 50
Chapter 6: On the domiciles of the planets 50
Chapter 7: On the detriments of the planets 55
Chapter 8: On the exaltations of the planets 56
Chapter 9: Why Aries is the exaltation of the Sun, and Libra his descension, and why the other signs are the exaltations of the planets 57
Chapter 10: On the fall or descension of the planets 58
Chapter 11: On the four triplicities of the seven planets 59
Chapter 12: On the movable, fixed, and common signs 60
Chapter 13: On the aspects of the planets 62
Chapter 14: On the bounds of the five planets besides the luminaries 64
Chapter 15: When the bound is preferred to the triplicity, and when the triplicity is preferred to the bound 67
Chapter 16: On the direction which comes to be through the Lords of the bounds 69
Chapter 17: On the faces of the signs 70
Chapter 18: In order to find out whose face any degree of any sign is 71
Chapter 19: On the strengths of every planet in any of its own dignities 72
Chapter 20: Which of the signs are called rational, and which having beautiful voices, and which domestic, and which having wings, and which four-footed 74

Chapter 21: Which part of the body each sign is said to have, and what signification in every limb, and which moral qualities of men, and what it signifies of seeds and regions, and the like 76
Chapter 22: What part of the body each planet signifies in every sign. 83
Chapter 23: On the masculine degrees and feminine degrees in each sign 85
Chapter 24: On the bright, dark, smoky, and empty degrees 86
Chapter 25: On the welled degrees 87
Chapter 26: On the degrees of *azemena* 88
Chapter 27: On the degrees increasing fortune 89
Chapter 28: On the degrees having power together and conforming in virtue 89
PART 3: On the Nature of the Accidental Circle 91
Chapter 1: On the division of the circle by houses 91
Chapter 2: On the division of the quarters of the circle 92
Chapter 3: Which half is called ascending or descending, and what part is called right or left 93
Chapter 4: On the angles, cadents, and succeedents 94
Chapter 5: On what is signified by the twelve houses 95
Chapter 6: On the significations of the twelve houses in the contrary direction of the aforesaid approach 114
Chapter 7: On the numbering of the houses and why they begin from the 1st and go toward the 4th, and from the 4th to the 7th, and from the 7th to the 10th, and from the 10th to the 1st 135
Chapter 8: Which houses are strong, which stronger, which weak, which weaker, and which middling 136
Chapter 9: That the planets go against the firmament, namely against the first motion 139
Chapter 10: On the colors which the houses signify 139
Chapter 11: In which houses the planets rejoice 140
Chapter 12: On the significations of the houses, or of the angles [and] the succeedents, and [the significations] of the Lords of the angles, succeedents, and cadents 141
Chapter 13: On the signification of the Lords of the angles, and concerning the angles, and first on the Lord of the first [angle] in the 1st 142
Chapter 14: On finding the significator of a quaesited matter 145
Chapter 15: On accidental powers 147
TREATISE 3: PLANETS 149
[PART 1] 149
Chapter 1: On Saturn–what he would signify 149
Chapter 2: On Jupiter–what he would signify 156
Chapter 3: On Mars–what he would signify 159
Chapter 4: On the Sun–what he would signify 164

- Chapter 5: On Venus–what she would signify 168
- Chapter 6: On Mercury–what he would signify 173
- Chapter 7: On the Moon–what she would signify 179
- Chapter 8: On the Head and Tail of the Dragon–what they would signify 187
- Chapter 9: What any one of the planets would do in the conception of children..................188
- Chapter 10: How the native's life would be disposed according to the years of nourishing of each planet..................190
- Chapter 11: Which of the days and which of the nights each planet would have, and why they are denominated from it, and on the unequal hours, and on the masculine and feminine hours..................191
- Chapter 12: On the shapes or figures which the signs give to a native 193
- Chapter 13: On the diverse accidents which happen to men..................195

PART 2: On the Particular Judgments of the Stars 198
- Chapter 1: On those things which happen to the planets in themselves..................198
- Chapter 2: When the planets are northern, and when southern..................201
- Chapter 3: On those things with happen with the planets to each other, namely to one of them from another..................202
- Chapter 4: On the *al-'ittisal* of the planets..................206
- Chapter 5: When the planets are said to be oriental, and when occidental 207
- Chapter 6: Of the two inferiors, when they are oriental and when occidental..................208
- Chapter 7: On the *dastūrīya* or *haym* of the planets..................210
- Chapter 8: On the three superiors, after they have appeared from under the rays of the Sun..................212
- Chapter 9: On the conjunction of the planets according to latitude ..213
- Chapter 10: On the voiding of the course of the planets 214
- Chapter 11: On the transfer of nature of the planets..................215
- Chapter 12: On the return of the light of the planets, and its cutting-off 218
- Chapter 13: On the prohibition of conjunction and why sometimes matters are not perfected 220
- Chapter 14: On the return of virtue, when a planet returns it to him who gave it to him..................227
- Chapter 15: On the restraining of the planets 230
- Chapter 16: On the contrariety of the planets..................232
- Chapter 17: On the frustration of the conjunction of the planets 234
- Chapter 18: On the cutting-off of the light of one planet by another 236

Chapter 19: In which places the planets become strong, and in which weak, and in which they become benefic, and in which malefic....239
Chapter 20: When, and in what places the planets become weak........242
Chapter 21: On the besieging of the planets and signs..........................244
Chapter 22: How one planet loves another, and how it is loved by another, and how they hate one another..245
Chapter 23: On their friendship..247
BIBLIOGRAPHY..248
INDEX..254

Book Abbreviations:

Abu 'Ali al-Khayyat:	*The Judgments of Nativities*	*JN*
Abū Ma'shar:	*Liber Introductorii Maioris ad Scientiam Iudiciorum Astrorum (Great Introduction to the Knowledge of the Judgments of the Stars)*	*Gr. Intr.*
	On Historical Astrology: the Book of Religions and Dynasties (On the Great Conjunctions)	*OGC*
	The Abbreviation of the Introduction to Astrology	*Abbr.*
	The Flowers of Abū Ma'shar	*Flowers*
Al-Biruni:	*The Book of Instruction in the Elements of the Art of Astrology*	*Instr.*
Māshā'allāh:	*De Receptione (On Reception)*	*OR*
	De Revolutionibus Annorum Mundi (On the Revolutions of the Years of the World)	*De Rev. Ann.*
Pseudo-Ptolemy:	*Centiloquium (Centiloquy)*	*Cent.*
Ptolemy	*Tetrabiblos*	*Tet.*
Sahl ibn Bishr:	*De Electionibus (On Elections)*	*On Elect.*
	De Quaestionibus (On Questions)	*On Quest.*
	Introductorium (Introduction)	*Introduct.*
'Umar al-Tabarī:	*Three Books of Nativities*	*TBN*
Vettius Valens:	*The Anthology*	*Anth.*

Table of Figures

Figure 1: Bonatti's Table of Bounds 66
Figure 2: Table of Faces 71
Figure 3: Masculine and Feminine Degrees 85
Figure 4: Bright, Dark, Smoky, and Empty Degrees 86
Figure 5: Welled Degrees 87
Figure 6: Degrees of *Azemena* 88
Figure 7: Degrees Increasing Fortune 89
Figure 8: Transfer of Nature (a) 216
Figure 9: Transfer of Nature (b) 217
Figure 10: Rendering of Light 218
Figure 11: Return and Cutting-Off of Light 219
Figure 12: Prohibition of Conjunction (a) 221
Figure 13: Prohibition of Conjunction (b) 222
Figure 14: Reception and Commission of Disposition (a) 224
Figure 15: Reception and Commission of Disposition (b) 226
Figure 16: Return of Virtue (a) 227
Figure 17: Return of Virtue (b) 229
Figure 18: Restraining 231
Figure 19: Contrariety 233
Figure 20: Frustration 235
Figure 21: Cutting-Off of Light (a) 237
Figure 22: Cutting-Off of Light (b) 238
Figure 23: Besieging by benefics 240

TREATISE 1:
DEFENSE OF ASTROLOGY

Chapter 1: On the usefulness of astronomy in general

The soul is the most noble thing which is found in man, for it gives being and perfection to the body, and its foods are most noble with respect to the body's foods, since [the soul] is most noble with respect to the [body]. And [the soul] rejoices in intellectual wealth, and [this wealth] depends on knowledge, that is to say philosophy; and the soul rejoices in this, and delights in it. And that in which it rejoices, is its food, wherefore since it is on the side of truth, it loves truth; nor can it apprehend so truly and so fully through any science as it does through astronomy.

And there is nothing (besides first philosophy) in which the soul gains so much wealth as in astronomy or astrology. For through it, we know and understand impassible and unalterable creatures, and those not changing into another essence, as are the supercelestial bodies. And through those creatures we can reach an understanding of the Creator, and know about Him however much more the human mind can attain to, and we can perceive Him to be impassible and unalterable. And because the aforesaid bodies are from what is perfect and most noble (which no one denies), their shapes are most noble and perfect–namely spherical–to which there is found neither beginning nor middle (the center being excluded) nor end. And thus their operations are most noble and most perfect [compared with] the rest of the operations of all professions which there are in this world, even if the profession of medical doctors is of the noble, or rather the more noble professions of the terrestrial world. But the profession of the stars and their works is most noble, and exceeds all other professions, and all other workings. For a cause is complete, and what is complete induces an effect. For the medical doctor gets involved with inferior and corruptible bodies, and those susceptible to alteration, and the like; but the astrologer gets involved with the operations of the supercelestial bodies, which are neither corrupted nor altered, for they *act in* the inferior corruptible bodies concerning which the medical doctor busies himself. Indeed in [the world] there is nothing corporeal which may act [but] does not suffer [change] nor will not suffer, up to that day which God wills (about which it has been said that neither angels nor the Son, but the Father alone, *etc.*)[1]

Wherefore all inferior bodies, namely those made of elements, consist of four elements, which are all corruptible; and that this is true, no one is in doubt. Indeed the celestial bodies consist of another essence (namely the quintessence[2]), which is different from those four elements, [and] which is incorruptible and impassible. Wherefore if [the celestial bodies] were of these four elements, they would have suffered, and alteration (namely increase and decrease) would have happened to them, just as happens to these corruptible inferior ones. And therefore it is said that the supercelestial bodies are of a fifth matter, or of a fifth essence. But those bodies are moved by a natural motion, as it seemed to certain people; and to certain people it seemed that they are moved by a voluntary motion, because they are movable but not changeable by an alterative motion; and they are bright and round and spherical, the which shape is the most noble one beyond the rest of the shapes.

And the changes and alterations and conversions [are] those which come to be by the stars' motions surrounding and moving and corrupting the elements (and because of them in [their] ends, as was said), and [their] whirling circular motion, which is not ended nor will it be ended, except as has been said.[3] Philosophically it is said that the terrestrial motion is joined to the celestial world; but this must be understood metaphorically, not unconditionally; and therefore changes and alterations and corruptions in this corruptible world come to be. Wherefore the solidity of the celestial world comes to the elements, and surrounds them (namely fire, and fire the air, and air the water and the earth which appears, and water the earth); and thence come to be the corruptions of the elements and of individuals of the elements.

Chapter 2: That the stars imprint in inferior bodies, and that the changes which come to be in this world come to be by means of their motions

Principles should not be proven, but supposed, wherefore all principles are reduced to one principle which is before all. For I do not believe there is any doubt but that the motion of the heaven surrounding the elements changes fire

---

[1] *Matt.* 24:36: "But about that day and hour no one knows, neither the angels of heaven, nor the Son, but only the Father."
[2] Lit., "the fifth essence."
[3] I.e., when God brings the world to an end.

and air; and they change the other elements (namely water and earth), together with ensouled and vegetative things, and the rest of what has being under the lunar circle (and they exist in them), and things susceptible of change or alteration. Because the Sun and air operate in all earthly individuals and parts of individuals, wherefore the alteration of earth does not happen except due to the change of the Sun—namely through the four signs, the four seasons of the year (which are spring, summer, autumn and winter), which appears manifestly in the fruits and foliage of trees, and even in animals (which are joined together in the rest of the seasons of the year, and are moved to the generating of the individuals of their own species, and particularly in spring more so than in the other seasons of the year); [and] it is made manifest in the fig tree and shrubbery of vegetative things (if indeed the fruit is present).

And we even see the earth heated (and chilled, dried, and moistened) by his daily whirling motion. And likewise we even see, in definite times of the year, an excess of the waters and other changes which come to be on account of the circular revolution of the acting heaven, and thence happen alterations to all things posited on the earth—and especially in the increase and decrease of the Moon's light, because she is more close to the earth than the rest of the stars, and her impressions are felt more. And likewise from the heat of the Sun, which is sensed above all the others; [and] even if perhaps the other planets sometimes increase his efficacy, sometimes they decrease it (insofar as it is natural to them), inasmuch as they are applied to him, or he to them. Indeed the impressions of the other stars are not so felt, but their effects appear in longer times. The effects of the Sun even appear manifestly in foliage and flowers and the fruits of trees and herbs, and even in those which are sown and which are planted, more openly so than in the others, because even though they operate, they cannot appear so openly to the common man; but they are known by the most skilled of the sciences. Indeed the other stars act with the planets on inferior things by means of motion and generation.

Chapter 3: How we arrive at the science of the judgments of the stars, and how it is that it can be excused

But concerning this knowledge it is certain that we are able to know not only the cognition of present things, the recalling to mind of past things, and the foresight of future things, namely of kinds and individuals (and even of the two parts of the world).[4] For through the subjects of the sciences are known their effects and their benefit, even if certain jealous people might say that astronomy is nothing. It is certain that it is one of the four mathematical sciences, namely the more noble one; and if it is more noble, it has more noble effects, and its benefit is greater (just as will be stated in its own place in what follows), wherefore the subjects of the other mathematical sciences are below the subject of astronomy. For the subject of arithmetic is number; of geometry, measure; of music, harmony (just as is stated elsewhere), which are more noble, but by reason of [their] demonstrations. Indeed the subject of astrology is the quality of the motion of the supercelestial bodies. The astrologer knows of what kind is every motion of every supercelestial body. If he knows the qualities of motions, he knows what kinds of impressions they imprint, and of what kind their significations are, and all things which come to be in earth according to the natural order, and come to be in the rest of the elements from the motions of the supercelestial bodies (which no one seems to doubt, unless perhaps he is silly or an idiot). And these things are known by the astrologer for the aforesaid reason. Therefore, all things which come to be in the present, and which have been hitherto, and which come to pass in the future, can be known by the astrologer, if he knows the qualities of the motions which there were, which there are, and which will be afterwards, in what times they will be, and what will fall together from them or because of them.

Chapter 4: Against those who say that the knowledge of the stars cannot be known by anyone

Those who say this knowledge is to be despised, have found some reasons (even if frivolous ones) to reject [it].

Of which the first is that the knowledge of the stars cannot be wholly known, saying that the empyrean heaven is entirely a star,[5] and that it influences and imprints just as the rest of the stars do (just as certain fools in tunics have [said]); and the astrologer does not make mention about that. Therefore it seems that the knowledge of the stars may not be known in full.

---

[4] I believe Bonatti means the part of the world in which the corruptible elements are, and the supercelestial world–since we can have this knowledge both of earthly events and of celestial mechanics.

[5] Not "full of stars," as Hand/Zoller say.

To whom it seems to me that it can be responded to briefly in one way, namely that they do not prove it to be so, and so their contradiction is null. But if we wish to confess plainly what is so, it seems that it can be responded to them in such a way, namely that even though their objections have an appearance, they do not have [genuine] existence. If the ninth heaven is entirely a star, as they say, there is no motion to it (as was said). Moreover, all its parts are equally powerful, nor can one part do more than another, nor less; and so it is necessary that it influence or imprint equally and everywhere with all of its parts, because its parts are all and individually coequal and equally powerful, nor do they differ in light nor number or some virtue, nor is it moved from place to place nor toward a place. Indeed the parts of the other heavens differ in light, number, and virtue, for the greater virtue of each is aggregated in different parts. For the splendor of light of each heaven of the seven planets is aggregated in one sensible body. Indeed the light or splendor of the eighth heaven is aggregated in different places or sensible bodies to different parts of it, for different operations deputed to it from the first cause; and so they can imprint many and diverse significations, just as the first Artisan constituted it for them from their formation. Indeed, in the impression of the ninth heaven, sameness is preserved; in the impression of the other heavens sameness is not preserved, but difference, just as I will tell you in its own place and time; and without them, generation and corruption would not come to be. And the impressions of the sensible heavens are sensed according to their difference. And if it were to receive the impressions or influence (either different or not different) from the ninth heaven, still they cannot influence or imprint in inferior things uniformly, but in diverse ways and differently; nor can the ninth heaven influence nor imprint in inferior things unless it is with the mediating sensible heavens, whose impressions are manifest. Indeed [the ninth heaven's impressions] are hidden, because they cannot be manifest, unless they are made diverse—like the wind or water, when it enters through tight and narrow passages, is more powerful, and its virtue appears more and is sensed more; and like water which runs through the channel of a mill operates more strongly and is more powerful than that which runs through the breadth or spaciousness of a riverbed. And just as the light or splendor of the Moon, when it enters through some narrow place, if it would find a horse having a suture on its back, and it should pierce the wound of the suture totally, the horse would die from it; indeed if the horse would stand fully in the splendor of the light of the Moon, even so that it as a whole would be looked at by the Moon, and be covered by the splendor of her light (both the place of the suture and the other parts of the horse), it would not kill it, nor would the horse be wounded by that—as the physicians testify.

Moreover, we can go against [the objectors] in this way: because there are none now who reprehend astronomy, except certain ones who call themselves theologians (if that is what they are), who say that astrologers did not know all of astronomy, and if they do not know it all, they cannot judge according to it nor predict anything about future things, since the stars are practically innumerable, and astrologers do not make mention [of this] except for 1,022 of them apart from the planets.[6]

To which it can be responded that the astrologer, even if he does not denominate all the stars (because it would be very prolix), still he uses all of them, because he uses the twelve signs under which approximately all stars are comprehended. And it can be said that even they do not know all of theology, but nevertheless they preach every day: for if *they* preach while knowing little theology, much more strongly can the astrologer judge while knowing much astronomy. For so little cannot be known of astronomy without it being much with respect to that which can be known about theology. For the first cause is greater with respect to the heaven, than the heaven is with respect to grains of mustard. And the astrologer knows more about the heaven than about a grain of mustard.[7] And they do not know about God with respect to Himself, as much as a grain of mustard is with respect to the heaven; therefore it remains that the astrologers know more about astronomy, than [theologians] do about theology; therefore [astrologers] can judge more strongly so than [theologians] can preach.

For the astrologers know as much about astronomy as the stars and sensible heavens can imprint and signify. But concerning the empyrean or imperceptible heaven, [there is] nothing for the astrologer, and nothing for judgments, nor for the motions of the stars, nor for those things which fall together from them. For just as that heaven is immovable and immutable, so it is not an agent; because the stars do not act in these inferior corruptible things because they are stars, but because they have motion, and because they are moved.

---

[6] This is the number of fixed stars catalogued by Ptolemy.
[7] Undoubtedly a reference to Matt. 13:31-32.

Chapter 5: Against those who said that the planets or other stars do not signify anything about generation, nor about corruption, nor about any of those things which come to be on this side of the globe of the Moon

Another pretext is that of certain people who said that the planets or other stars do not signify anything about generation nor about corruption, nor about any of these things which come to be on this side of the globe of the Moon. To whom it must be responded this way, that all the wise agree in this, that inferiors are ruled by superiors; not that the stars rule a man or a horse, or a chariot or ship (or other corruptible instruments) through the means by which they rule men, who are corruptible. For it does not suit an effect to rise to the dignity of its cause, but they rule them by moving and corrupting the elements and converting them, and from them generation and corruption come to be, and individuals are made out of the elements which are corrupted; until at last the individuals are corrupted and return into the elements, and so they are annihilated (which they themselves say).[8]

Chapter 6: Against those who said that the planets have signification only over something universal

Another pretext is that of those who say that the planets signify only over universal things, and not particular ones. To whom it must be responded in such a way: that every individual made of the elements consists of four elements, and the elements constitute it; nor can they constitute something else, unless they are corrupted by the planets; but this does not exclude the other stars moving themselves around with continual and whirling circular motion: because if the planets signify species universally (just as they said, and it was true), it is necessary that they would signify the individual constituting species, and not only individuals, but parts of individuals (like the hand, foot, head, and the like). And the planets, through the conversion of the elements and their change, and alteration, even make individuals grow, be increased, grow old, grow weak, and the like, on account of the corruption and conversion of the

---

[8] The idea here is that effects must be correlated suitably with their causes; but a mere individual man and his accidents are not conformable to something so universal as a star, nor does an individual star speak to *this* man. Rather, the stars act generally on the elements, and *this* man arises from *this* arrangement of the elements, which is under the influence of *this* or *these* stars. See the following paragraph, which is meant to emphasize this point.

elements; and again [they make them] be corrupted, and return into the elements.

Chapter 7: Against those who said that the stars signify only two things, namely the necessary and the impossible; but not the possible

Another pretext is that of those who said that the stars signify only two things, namely the necessary and the impossible, but not the possible; just as it is necessary for fire to be hot, and impossible for a horse to fly; not that it is possible that a man be moved or write.

To whom it must be responded in this way, namely that certain things are necessary, certain ones impossible. For some are necessary, like that the heaven be turned by its own nature; some impossible, like that fire be cold by its own nature; and some are possible, as that water be hot by accident and not by its own nature. And it is possible for a man to speak through his own nature, [or] that a man speak now, and that he has hitherto spoken, and that he will speak in the future. But even if he had spoken at two times, then and now, still it is not necessary that he will speak in the future.

For what is necessary or natural for the species is what belongs to every individual of that species, like flying, because in every individual of those species, this is found (namely the power of flying). Indeed what is possible for a species is possible for every individual of that species.

Whence it appears—because it is possible—that it is not necessary for a man to swim, nor is it impossible for a man to swim, whence we see certain man swimming, certain others not swimming. And it is possible for this man, when he is born, that he be a king; and it is possible for this same man that he not be king. If however he were not the king, it would be[9] impossible for him to be king. But between the necessary and the impossible, the middle is the possible; and between the necessary and the possible, the middle is judgment. Therefore the possible exists, and judgments of the stars are true and useful (and therefore natural), whence it is not a cause by accident but from what it natural to it. Whence judgments are not to be reputed as nothing, as the envious say; and so they spoke badly who said that the possible does not exist: because we see manifestly that the possible does exist, and so the works of the stars and judgments exist.

---

[9] Reading *fuerit* for *fuit*.

It is even necessary that if it rains there is some cloud; it is impossible that if there is no cloud that it rain perceptibly; but it is not necessary that when there is a cloud it should rain, nor is it impossible but that from any cloud it may rain; but it is possible that from this cloud there may be rain, and it is possible that from this cloud there may not be rain. Therefore the possible exists, and the judgments of the stars exist. Wherefore by the motions and dispositions of the supercelestial bodies, and the variation of the air, you can know from what cloud there should be rain, and from which one there should not be rain (just as will be stated in the Treatise on the mutation of the air).

Moreover, if someone has an edible thing in his mouth, it is possible that he may eat and swallow it; and it is possible that he may not eat it nor swallow it; and this possible thing holds of both, namely the necessary and the impossible, because if it is possible for him to eat, and if he were to eat it, the possible thing has been made necessary, because it has come into act, and possibility is taken away from him, and [the possibility] is effected, and comes under the definition of the necessary. Likewise if it is possible, after which it does not come into act, [it is] impossible, and it comes under the definition of the impossible, and possibility is taken away. And so the stars and the elements signify possible things, and not only the necessary and the impossible. For it behooves the astrologer to know the truth, and to predict future things.

Chapter 8: Against those who speak against the judgments of astronomy, and who condemn it, not knowing its dignity because it is not lucrative

Another pretext is that of those who say that the judgments of astronomy do not have value because they do not see monetary benefit (if it exists); and [because] *they* know how to figure out when and how [to make money], they say this knowledge is nothing.

To whom it seems to me it should be responded in this way, namely that they do not care about the wheat, but only the chaff—for it is so regarding knowledge with respect to money, as it is for wheat with respect to the chaff. For those who say the advantage of money is to be preferred to the knowledge of the judgments of the stars, seem to show that among them nothing is held so noble as monetary accumulation—which can easily be lost. And they say that he who abounds in riches lacks nothing (because it does not harm him if he is not wise), saying that wealth suffers stupidity, and that the fortunate fool is not in need of knowledge–not considering their error, and not understanding their false–or rather empty–proofs. For every thing which is subject to proof, is proven by something similar in all respects, just as knowledge by knowledge, and substance by substance; and I have most often seen that the vulgar man does not commend anything else but the accumulation of money; nor is this surprising, because they sometimes see certain people (both religious and others who believe) wise in astronomy and medicine and in other sciences, give heed regarding this–the opinions of whom, if they are considered well, seem to me able enough to be made void. Because knowledge, with respect to money, is most noble; for money, with respect to knowledge, is most base; for [money] can be given to the wise, the foolish, the honest, the base, the idle, the weak, and to him who is otherwise reputed to be nothing, and is practically nothing; nor will there be someone be so wealthy in money (if he were otherwise low-class or foolish), but that it may be said about him (and it is true), "he is nothing, but guards his money for others, or a stranger's money." Nor is money given to him on account of his strength, wherefore we see certain strong people lack money, and certain other strong ones abound in money; some weak people lack money, some weak people abound in money. Why this is so, will be stated below in the business of judgments, or perhaps in the Treatise on nativities.[10]

For there is nothing by itself that can make a man noble without the support of another, except for wisdom. Magnanimity cannot completely make a man noble without money, because the magnanimous man cannot perfectly show his magnanimity unless he [already] has what he would give to others. The moneyed man cannot show his riches without magnanimity and the will to do well, because his heart does not suffer to do well, and so his money is a buried treasure. But knowledge is something which alone can ennoble a man without the support of another. And so knowledge prevails over all other accidents.

And if no other cause may be praised, a man is praised on account of knowledge: because a man can be deprived of all other accidents apart from knowledge, and [knowledge] cannot be adopted by someone on account of strength, nor on account of weakness, nor on account of birth, nor on account of riches. For riches can be adapted on account of [knowledge], but the true sage does not care about temporal things, because [there is] nothing for him from them which can be taken away from him, besides the corruption of the

---

[10] This topic goes back to the principle of conventional goods and happiness, and Bonatti's statement in Ch. 1 about the soul's food. While money may be a conventional good, it does not feed the soul, nor can it create happiness (which pertains to the soul). And conventional goods like money pertain to *fortune*, as he says in Tr. 7.

subject. And this is the reason why the sage does not care about them, because he is not praised [by fools] on account of wisdom and on account of intellect and discernment and the understanding of things making man worthy with nobility. For a man is more worthy than the other animals, and this does not happen to him except on account of the wisdom and philosophy and understanding belonging to them (which are not understood by the other animals) and through the instrument of reason and the capability of being rational which are in a man; and this is wisdom, and the understanding of things; and this consists more in the understanding of what was, what is, and what will be.

And knowledge is such an accident that by how much more it is increased in a man, by that much more does it remove him from the other animals; and he is made more worthy and nobler than them on account of this (which is the soul of the same knowledge and discernment and the understanding of things which were, which are, and which yet will be). And by how much less there is of wisdom in him, by that much more is he removed from what is capable of reason, and [is] closer to the brutes. And this cannot happen to him (namely that he be more worthy and nobler than the other animals), except by wisdom and philosophy; and *that* cannot come to him, unless by literature; nor can it come to him on account of accumulated substance, but he can live in peace because of substance. But the point is not to live, but to live truly—whence Seneca, "Leisure without letters is death, and the tomb of the living man."[11] Whence, if a man is not wise, he is not more worthy than the other animals (as indeed [man] is); because all the animals participate with him in other things, except for in wisdom; because [of] those who live, all eat; some drink; and some eat and drink, and generate, are born, grow, are increased, are diminished, grow old, die–just like men. And so through wisdom and understanding and intellect, a man is made more worthy than the rest of the animals. And if that which makes a man worthy with nobility is wisdom, it is necessary that that wisdom which is more noble and more worthy and higher, makes a man more noble and more worthy and higher, and more intelligent. And this is the knowledge of future things, which cannot be known except through the knowledge of the stars: therefore the knowledge of the stars is more noble than the other sciences, apart from first philosophy; nor however can it[12] be known nor perfectly had, except through the science of the stars.[13]

---

[11] This is a famous line from Seneca's letter "On the natural fear of death."
[12] The knowledge of future things.
[13] Therefore the astrologer is the most wise and the most distinctly human of all.

Chapter 9: Against those who said that the knowledge of the stars is not useful, but rather harmful because it induces sorrow and distress to those who would have foreknowledge of future accidents, whence they are made sad for that reason before the impediment comes

Another pretext is that of those who say[14] that the judgments of the stars are not of value, nor is there usefulness in them, but rather harm; for even if this knowledge is true, and its judgments are true, still it is more likely harmful than useful. Because if some trouble which is supposed to happen to someone is seen ahead of time from afar, it will send fear and sorrow into him before the time of pain, up until when the evil happens to him; and nevertheless, afterwards, it is necessary for him to be made sad and to be pained and to lament; nor can the astrologer avert that trouble which is going to come according to the stars; and even if he were to avert it, he at least could not avert the anger and distress (which he to whom the evil will come [and] be made plain, will suffer), up to the hour of its coming.

To whom it can be responded in the familiar way, that clearly they do not know what it is to say what they are saying, wherefore it seems that they are ignorant of how great is the dignity, and how great is the usefulness, of this wisdom; because if they knew, they would not have said what they are saying. For if some evil (which is going to come, according to the stars) would threaten some man, and he knew the future evil beforehand, he will see how evil it is, and of what kind the evil was, and he will oppose himself to it. For Ptolemy says in the *Centiloquy*, "The best astrologer is able to avert many evils which are going to come according to the stars."[15] For future accidents are either universal or particular: universal like winter, summer, heat, cold, the distemper of the air (like rain, snow, hail), pestilences like mortality, famine, sterility; an abundance of things born of the earth, and the like. For of these universal things, certain ones are known only by the wise; certain ones are known not only by the wise, but even by the vulgar. The wise know them by their industry, namely through this science (namely that of the stars). For the laity, and others unskilled in this knowledge, know certain universal things are going to be, through long

---

[14] This argument goes back at least as far as the ancient Skeptic Sextus Empiricus (fl. 2nd and possibly 3rd Centuries AD).
[15] This seems to be a paraphrase of Aph. 5.

experiences which they have seen in their own times, and they heard from others older than they, who even saw them in *their* own times.

For in the climes in which the horizon is turned back to the north, they saw cold grow more strong when [the Sun] enters Gemini, and last until Virgo–even if [only] according to more and the less. At other times the weather would be dissimilar to this, whence in summer when they feel heat, they say in such time it will be cold, there will be snows, rains, winds, and the like: then they secure themselves with grain, wine, wood, clothing, and other necessities by which they can drive away contrary things in that time; and those who do not have homes apply themselves to building them so they are able to flee rain, snows, and other contrary things to come; which if they did not know beforehand, they would not be secured with the above-said necessities; and so it could be the reason for their ruin. Therefore it remains that the foreknowledge of future things has value.[16]

Likewise, they know by the above-stated experiences in which seasons they should sow, so that they may collect it in the future, whence they can lead their own lives according to the different kinds of different things; and they even plant trees in seasons in which they are used to seeing them live, according to the diverse kinds of plantings. For every kind of seed or planting is not sown or planted in all seasons of the year equally, nor in every region according to the season of that same year. For one plants one way in Spain, another in England, another in Lombardy, another in Romania,[17] another in Apulia, another in Asia, another in Ethiopia, another in the Alps, another on the plain, another in the winter, another in the summer; and other things are sown and planted in one season rather than in another, each of them in the season suitable for it, and in which future benefit is hoped for from it; and so according to diverse regions, and according to diverse situations of places; and those experienced in places know all of these things ahead of time, so that they are most rarely wrong: therefore the foreknowledge of future things is useful.

But some tunic-wearing people could rise up (one of which was that fool),[18] and say that these things do not come from the impressions of the planets– whence it cannot be disputed with them, because they do not consider that

---

[16] This response does not explain *how* astrology is compatible with free will, but is meant to say that if you condemn the astrologer, you might as well condemn the weatherman or people who buy heavier clothes in anticipation of winter. This response pertains to *universal* phenomena.

[17] Or perhaps Romagna, the Italian province in which Bonatti's hometown of Forlì now is.

[18] It is unclear which "fool" Bonatti means.

every region and every site of a region grows hot on account of the approach of the Sun, and is made cold on account of the removal of the Sun; and on account of his excessive approach a region withers, and on account of his excessive removal, it is made excessively cold; whence then they know any seed should not be sown, nor any planting should be planted, on account of the excess of heat or cold. And they do these things because they know beforehand these things are going to happen, on account of the long experiments which they saw, and which they practiced; which if they did not know, they would not know in what season they ought to do the above-said, and thus they would lose their investments and their labor.

Indeed other universal things which happen universally to the body of citizens of every clime, or every region–some of them can be avoided, some cannot be avoided. But their effects can be diminished or altered in such a way that they can be a benefit for those who knew them beforehand. They cannot all be known except by those skilled in this knowledge; but certain ones of them can be known by skilled doctors (whence Hippocrates in his aphorisms).[19] For those things which are known by the astrologers (nor can they be known ahead of time by the vulgar man), are many, such as are pestilences, famine, sterility, want, infirmity, mortality (both of rational [beings] and the brutes), rains, snow, hail, the usual cold or heat exceeding measure, and the like, of which he who knew ahead of time can beware: and so the foreknowledge of future things is useful, and not harmful. An unknown evil is not avoided, but a known one can be avoided, if it is known ahead of time, especially far ahead. For if someone knew ahead of time that the grain would be expensive, he could buy it for himself when it is cheap, and reserve it for the time being in which it was useful for him; the same goes for wine and oil, and the like.

If someone were to know ahead of time about a future mortality in some clime, or in some region, he could move and go away from that region, and go to another in which the plague will not threaten in that year. If he knew ahead of time about a future infirmity in some region, he could oppose himself to the reason threatening the infirmity, or go likewise to another region in order to live safely; and so the foreknowledge of that matter will be the reason for the health of the one seeing that future matter, and of his escaping from the future danger.

Likewise, if someone were to see a future rain ahead of time, he can flee to cover before the arrival of the rain, and to places in which the rain could not drench him. Likewise if someone is going to sail the sea, and he were to see a

---

[19] Bonatti brings up this point of Hippocrates again in the beginning of Tr. 6.

future wind or another tempest ahead of time, he could arrive at a port in which he would be safe before the advent of the tempest, lest he suffer shipwreck; or he would not enter the sea until the time of doubt passes. Likewise if a question about some infirm person were made, or if the astrologer knew the beginning of the infirmity, he could know ahead of time whether the infirm person ought to escape from the infirmity, or whether he should die from it. Which if he were to foresee that he is going to die, he could predict death for him, and the sick person (who perhaps did not believe himself to die from that illness), would take penance and confess his sins, and Jesus Christ our Lord will provide for him in the future life (even though [it is] an imperceptible one), and he could even devise a will and arrange his home, and put his affairs in order, and arrange things with his creditors and debtors. Which if he did not do it, there could be danger for those who remain after him and who are supposed to inherit his goods; and his goods could come to people to whom the infirm person did not want his goods to go; and those to whom he wanted that his goods should go, could be in need of them; and so he could be reproached and condemned after death. For sometimes a man esteems one of his heirs more so than another; sometimes a male more than a female, sometimes only his natural [heir] more than the lawful one. And [the situation is] likewise [for] one who was about to enter the sea, if the astrologer did not predict for him that a future tempest could be the reason for his danger. And so it is good and useful to know future things ahead of time, and bad and harmful to be ignorant. Therefore these are the reasons (and many other ones could be assigned) that knowing what is to be regarding matters is most useful.

Likewise there are certain future particular things which it can be very much useful to know ahead of time: like if someone's nativity is known, or his universal question is had (or even a particular one about some matter which he wished to know), you or some other astrologer could see what ought to happen to him from that matter. Whence if harm would threaten him, he could avoid it; and if it promised wealth for him, he could get it, and it would be useful for him. And if you were to see, in some year of his revolution, that some danger threatened him, he could avoid it: like if it was an infirmity, you could predict the cause of the illness for him, and he would oppose himself to it, and turn his nature to the contrary of the cause; and [you could predict] what kind of infirmity ought to come; whence if the infirmity did come (or it did not approach him), or if it did approach, it will harm less; which if he did not watch out for himself, such an illness could overcome him, so that it could be the reason for his ruin (or if the illness became chronic, and ultimately he could die from thence). If it is death, he could predict his death for him in that year, and he will put his affairs in order just as was said; nor could he be taken by sudden or unexpected death without putting his affairs (both spiritual and temporal) in order. If it is the infirmity or death of the brothers, or children, or the father, or the mother, any one of them could oppose himself [or herself] in his [or her] own being. If it is the ruin of animals, and he were to have both large and small animals, he could divide [or remove] them before the arrival of the plague, whence he would not suffer harm from thence; and understand these concerning the significations of every house.

Likewise, if someone even asks [of you], fearing lest his enemy inflict some injury on him, you could predict for him whether he is going to attack him, and then he could protect himself with friends and arms and the like, so that he could expel the enemy from himself; which if he did not look out for himself beforehand, he could be killed by him or be treated badly.

These (and many other particular causes can be assigned which can happen to men) are those which it is useful to know beforehand, and even harmful to none (as certain people wanted to say). Likewise skilled doctors, when they see the corruption of the air in one season of the year (by one change of it from one condition into another, by some noted winds or by much rain, or on any other occasion), they predict future diseases, like quartan fevers, acute ones, headaches, difficulties in hearing, inflammations of the eyes, and the like: whence men can prepare themselves for expelling those future harmful accidents with drugs, diet, and contrary causes of those from which the future harmful accidents are going to be. Which if they did not look out for themselves ahead of time, they could fall into illnesses and pestiferous diseases, and the like. Moreover, doctors (and even the vulgar man), on account of the fact that they saw in their times that the heat was growing stronger in summer, oppose themselves to the hot humors in the spring, and they draw them out with medicines purging them, lest the summer heat increase the keenness of the hot humors and be the reason for illnesses that exterminate. And so the foreknowledge of future accidents is most useful.[20]

Wherefore, just as a skilled doctor can preserve the bodies of men from the imminent diseases stated above, so even the astrologer can avert many horrible future things which are going to come according to what is signified by the

---

[20] Note the implicit distinction between events that seem unavoidable (like death) and those which are more avoidable (like attacks by enemies).

stars. Which if he did not know ahead of time, they would be the reason by which many harms would pursue men. And so it is manifestly obvious that the knowledge of future things is most useful, and in no way harmful. Whence those who wish to pretend they do not see truth, can know manifestly that just as the astrologer can foresee future accidents, so can he know how to say how their dangers could be avoided.

For indeed the foreknowledge of future things is useful in two ways. The first, because were a man to know ahead of time that some contrary thing ought to happen to him, he can properly diminish it or totally avoid it (or in part). Indeed [secondly,] if the accident were useful, he to whom it should come will rejoice and be happy from the hour in which he knew he was going to achieve a matter which he strives for, up to the time in which he achieved it; which if he had not known that he ought to achieve it, and it was a matter which he strove for, he would be saddened and distressed in it, and fatigued, and he would make his friends tired of it, and even spend of his own goods so that he could achieve it, until the time of the achievement would be completed for him.

But someone would object against this: "The foreknowledge of some matter induces grief or sorrow after he has achieved the matter, because he would no longer hope to achieve it." To whom it must be said that this is far from the path of truth. For if this were true (that after someone will have achieved what he desires, that once the desire is fulfilled, grief could overcome him), it would not be proper for someone to get involved with delightful things—because those things in which a man is delighted, do not always last. Nor however is a man saddened after their achievement, but rather his mind is at rest, because what he prepared for was achieved. For if it were so that after someone will have achieved what he desired, he would be saddened, he should not get involved in any delightful things. For a man would not be happy in the embraces of a beautiful woman, nor in dinner parties, nor in beautiful things, nor in beautiful clothing, nor in musical sounds, nor in dignities, nor in anything in which nature rejoices, because they do not always last in the same condition of being happy. For the completion of joy is when the mind is at rest, and is sated of that which he desires; before the achievement it is not joy, but the hope of coming to the fulfillment of the desired thing. For hope and joy differ, just as fear and sorrow do; wherefore hope and fear are of those which are potential, sorrow and joy of those which are in act.[21]

Chapter 10: Against those who said that the judgments of the stars are not of value, nor are elections of value, saying that it can be elected for the enemy just as for him for whom it is elected

Another pretext is namely that of those who say that the judgments of the stars are of no value, nor are elections (which astrologers make according to astronomy) of value. It is not surprising if they say this, because they do not see truth, and however much what they say seems like to truth (and this refutation seems practically to comprehend the others and prevail over all the above-stated ones), neither does it seem, nor even do they themselves believe, that it could be contradicted or resisted; but rather it seems that it is practically something impossible that it could be otherwise except that it be as they say it.

For they say, "You who elect for one army, and tell it, 'If you were to go at such an hour, with such a sign ascending, you will win.' If the adversary moves his own army at that same hour, under that same Ascendant, who will win?" You can say to him, "He who is stronger and has the greater host." And they will say, "each is equally strong as the other, and has a host equally as great as the other, and equally strong and equally proven knights and foot-soldiers. Who will win?" You will say "He who more wisely brought forth his army." They will say, "Each brings forth his own army equally wisely. Who will win?" You will say, "The leader of the army who was born at night." They will say, "Each general was born at night. Who will win?" You will say, "That army will win, who first began to do battle." And they will say, "both armies began to do battle at one and the same time. Who will win?" And you will say, "That which were to move from the east and was [facing] towards the west, or which moved itself from the north and went toward the south; and that one will succumb which moved itself from the west and went toward the east, or which moved itself from the south toward the north." And then they will say something practically impossible: "Each army moved itself from the east and went towards the west, or moved itself from the north and went toward the south. Who will win?" You tell them that they are fools, nor is it to be discussed with them. For it seems

---

[21] This is an interesting parallel, given that the 11th and the 8th are places of hope and fear, and they are *succeedent* signs, coming after the angular houses which *go towards* the 10th (achievement) and the 7th (enemies, opposition).

impossible that two contrary armies and enemies should move themselves from the same place at one and the same time without there being some easterliness or westerliness or northerliness or southerliness between them.

But were they (being such fools or critics) to say, "Let it be put that both armies move themselves from the east or from the west or from the south or north," this does not seem possible. And it must be said to them that they are positing something unseen and unheard of, that two armies ever held fast in one place when one began to go against the other, just as it is impossible that the sky should fall; but tell them it is so posited that the sky should fall–where will the stars remain? And if the sky were to fall, wouldn't the earth be submerged? Let it be put that a jackass may fly–the vulture will not lose his [power of] flight.

Still, lest they say you have failed in your response, you could respond in this way: that they do not have anything further to ask, and that you will cut off every path of asking and rebuking and reproaching. And you could respond to them in this way: that he in whose direction were the Part of Fortune, will win; that one will succumb who had his back toward the west or the parts more adjacent to it, and his face toward the east; or his back towards the south or the parts more adjacent to it, and his face toward the north; and he who had his back toward the east, or the parts more adjacent to it, and his face towards the west, or his back towards the north and his face towards the south or the parts more adjacent to him, will win. And thus are cut off and removed all paths of the reproachers and maledictors. Which if he were to say again, that the Part of Fortune will be from the side which had his back toward the south or toward the north, say that [it is] he from whose side the Part of Fortune were–and so will end their objections, which, even though they might seem to have an appearance, still do not have [genuine] existence.

Perhaps even certain fools not speaking rationally rose up, saying, "Why do you, who are an astrologer, [not] forego for yourself any evil thing to come, when you should be able to know all future things ahead of time which should happen to you?" To which we respond that such things number among all the judgments happening casually, in practically imperceptible times, like if a thorn is fixed in one's foot or that the foot is withdrawn so that a man falls, and the like–regarding casual things of which there is no art. Because judgment does not pertain except to those about which it can be deliberated before they happen; indeed those things concerning which a quick occurrence does not permit one to make a deliberation, are left to the industry or caution of the wise; for those things are not considered from the Art, nor from nature, which come about by accident (as they believe).[22]

Chapter 11: Against those who said generally that astrology was not anything; [and] to show that it is, and what it is

For I have said I was going to speak about the judgments of astronomy, and about those things which seem to pertain to judgments, and about certain things which I told you in the beginning of this work. It now[23] seems to me appropriate that I tell you what astronomy is, insofar as the sages of this science define it; and that it might be shown to those who said it is nothing, and so that they can see manifestly that it is something, and is a useful matter, and truthful, and natural, and good. For nothing of natural things is found which can lawfully be said to be evil or useless or lying, or false.

Astronomy is the rule[24] of the stars, as certain sages defined it. For it is a rule, rightly ordered, and manifestly declaring that which is according to the truth of its being. Not that truth is taken up because of the rule, but that because of that which is truth, the rule may be born.[25] But a lawyer, even if (not by altering the opinion) he says, "The rule is the matter which is," he speaks briefly; not that justice is taken up because of the rule, but that the law which is the rule, comes to be from [justice].

Indeed certain people not far from these sentiments, defined it thus: Astronomy is the knowledge through which understanding is given not only of present things, but even of past and future things. It is even defined in another way, according to two parts or species of it: briefly, the contemplative and the active (which are astrology and astronomy). In what these two parts differ, I will tell you:

Astrology, which is its contemplative part or species, is the knowledge of movable magnitude which searches for the courses of the stars and the figures

---

[22] In other words, astrology cannot predict things of a certain particularity, but only as understood under certain general kinds. It will not say whether I will sit in this or that chair, or how many hairs I have on my head. Likewise, matters which come under deliberation have to be understood under certain general categories, and assume a power of choice.
[23] Reading *nunc* for *non*.
[24] *Regula*, i.e., a governing standard (and something less than a "law")–not "rule" in the way that a king rules a nation. Bonatti might even mean that it is a way of life, as monks follow the Rule of their order.
[25] I.e., truth comes first, and our discipline-based understanding and investigation of it comes later and is dependent on it.

of the stars around each other and around the earth, with a definite account. And of this part (namely astrology), there are three parts:

> The first of which is of the numbers and figures of the celestial bodies; of their orders in the world, of quantities, situations, proportions, the quantities of their distances between themselves.

> The second is of the motions of the supercelestials: how many there are, and that all their motions are spherical; and which of them would share in all the stars, and which is nearer, and how many are the kinds of motion of each of them, and in what directions they are moved (which are six), namely forwards, backwards (and to these are subordinated direct motion and retrogradation); then they are upwards, downwards, to the right and to the left. There even seem to be another six, even though they do might not seem [to be] of a consideration of astrology: generation and corruption, increase and decrease, alteration and change according to place[26] (certain people said that alteration is not a motion); and concerning certain aspects and conjunctions, and when they come to be, and the like.

> Indeed the third [part] inquires about this: what is inhabited on the earth, and on that which is not inhabited according to the disposition of the seven climes, and about the difference of the day and night according to each region.

Chapter 12: What astronomy is, which is the active part

Indeed astronomy is its second part, namely the active one, even if sometimes (or rather, often) one is put in place of the other. Concerning which these things may be inquired, that is: [1] what astronomy is, [2] what are its kinds, [3] what is its office, [4] what is its end, [5] what are its instruments, [6] who is its artisan, [7] why would it be called by such a name, and [8] in what order should it be taught.

[1] The definition of which is such as was stated above. Indeed others defined it in another way, saying "astronomy is the science which describes the

---

[26] These six types of motion and change come from Aristotelian physics, but from what has been said so far, these changes are predicted by the astrologers as well–in fact, predicting them depends on a consideration of the more abstract physical motions just described.

knowledge of the course of the stars and their disposition, according to the opinion of those who practice it, with the previous accounting of the times."

Moreover, what each of those parts is, is understood with its definition or its quiddity.[27] For the genus is that according to which one responds to a question about a proposition made to oneself (insofar as it is proper), by judging according to the position of the planets and signs, and their nature. But there are more sciences of judging, insofar as questions are proposed according to them: like geomancy, which is practiced in earth, and in other additional ways suitable for it; hydromancy, in water; aeromancy, in the air; pyromancy, in fire; chiromancy, in the hand (as Aristotle testifies in the book on animals); spatulomancy, in the shoulder-bone of some animal. And even many other sciences of auguring, as is the voice of some animal, or the song of some bird, or wailing or chattering, or the encountering of some thing–and many others which could be numbered, about which nothing at present. But this, namely astronomy, with all of its parts and kinds, is more worthy than the rest, since it has them[28] from the disposition of the most noble supercelestial bodies–it declares that of those things which are in the earth, past, present, and future, in accordance as all the philosophers agreed in this. Whence al-Fārābī[29] [said] of the sciences, astronomy is the science of the signification of the stars, namely what the stars would signify about many present, past, and future things. Its matter or subject is magnitude itself, as was said.

[2] But the parts or species of this [second] part, are four: in the first it deals with the position and form of the world, and with the celestial circles; in the second, it deals with the courses or motions of the planets and the other stars; in the third, it deals with the rising and setting of the signs; in the fourth, it deals with the eclipses of the Sun and the Moon and the other planets.

In this, or indeed concerning, these parts, approximately the whole virtue of astronomy is consisted. Its species are generally two, namely number or computation, insofar as it has a dependency with the first mathematical science (this is with arithmetic, which is prior to all other theoretical sciences, because

---

[27] *Quidditate. Quidditas* (lit. "whatness") was a term famously employed by the medieval philosopher and contemporary of Bonatti, John Duns Scotus (1265-1308) to describe what something's essence as captured by a real definition–that is, an essential definition of something's being, rather than a heuristic statement of how a word is used or how something is only considered from a given perspective. This is why Bonatti says astronomy's parts can be fully understood by its definition alone.

[28] *Ipsa*. I believe Bonatti means the events of the past, present, and future.

[29] This is Bonatti's own paraphrase of al-Fārābī's statements about astronomy in *De Ortu Scientiarum*, I.3. See Bibliography.

all other mathematical sciences are in need of it; indeed it is in need of none of them). The second species of astronomy is judgment. Computation or numbering turns on definition or the understanding of tables. Indeed judgment turns on the understanding of times, places, signs, planets, positions, and their aspects, and on things like these, and what falls together with them.

[3] Its office is to contemplate the courses of the planets and the conjunctions of all the stars, aspects, angles, succeedents, and the signs cadent from the angles which already were angles; [and] their effects, with the previous accounting.

[4] Its end, or its usefulness, is the intention of judging about present, past, and future things, [and] to be able to know the truth through the inspection of the above-stated, and the inquiry discussed.

[5] The instruments of this science are many, namely the astrolabe, the quadrant, the *armilla suspensoria*,[30] and the other *armillae*, the planisphere, the curvisphere, the *statua plosica*,[31] and the like.

[6] The artisan of this science is said to be any astronomer who practices the art with the name of astronomy, and observes the law of the stars by means of the previous interpretation.

[7] Why is astronomy called by such a name? I tell you that this name is composed from "stars" [*astris*] and *nomos*,[32] which is a rule–thence "astronomy," that is, the rule of the stars, or practical astronomy, or the working of the stars. Indeed the difference between astrology and astronomy is this: because astrology is (according to the truth of the matter) for intellectual or theoretical knowledge; astronomy (according to how those using it opine) is for its effect, or practical knowledge.[33]

[8] In what order should this science be taught? Certain people say that it was supposed to be taught before the other mathematical ones, because it is more noble. Certain [others] said after arithmetic, because it is in need of number. Certain [others] said after arithmetic and geometry, because it is in need of number and measure.[34] But to me it seems that it ought to be taught after all the other mathematical ones, both after music and after arithmetic and geometry, because it is well in need of harmony itself, both in number and measure.

---

[30] An armillary sphere hung on a ring.
[31] Unknown.
[32] I have taken the step of correcting Bonatti's Greek, reading *nomos* for *norma*.
[33] This is the opposite of our usage of the terms today.
[34] Bonatti is getting this from al-Fārābī's *De Ortu Scientarum* I.3.

Chapter 13: That this science should not be rebuked, since the Holy Fathers used it

This art should not even be rebuked, but rather it is worthy to be commended, because the Holy Fathers from antiquity used it. Whence they who rebuke it do badly, and especially those who follow in the footsteps of Abraham or who followed Abraham;[35] for he instructed the Egyptians (and others of the time then wanting [to have] astronomy) how to use it exceptionally.[36] And Atalanta in particular, who prevailed in this science over all the sages who then existed, so that she was reputed to be practically God. And from there it is said that Atlas held up the sky, on account of the fact that he knew more about the supercelestial bodies than any who was found in that time. And even the Lord himself, when he said to the Apostles, "Let us go again to Judea,"[37] and they said "Now the Jews sought to stone you, and again you go there?" Who, responding, said, "Are there not twelve hours in the day?"–as if he said one hour is good, even if another is bad. Wherefore in a bad hour they had a bad will against him, for that hour had passed, and a good one had supervened, whence He, knowing this, knew that a bad will was gone from their hearts, [and] wished to elect for Himself that hour in which they would not harm him.

And through this it is clear that He Himself used an election, nor did He reproach astronomy as certain jealous people and detractors do today. Even though it has been shown manifestly above that much usefulness and many good things can follow from the science of the stars and its judgments, both in the foreknowledge of matters and in others, still there were certain silly fools, of which one was that hypocrite John of Vicenza[38] of the Order of Preachers,[39] who said that astrology was neither an art nor a science, but it was a certain application by some people applying something discovered. To which it seems to me to be responded to in this way: namely that there are fools, and they err, and they will perish in their foolishness and in their errors. For it is well known

---

[35] Bonatti must be referring to Jewish critics of astrology.
[36] According to certain Jewish legends, Abraham had been a star-worshipper or one wise in the stars.
[37] John 11:7*ff.*
[38] An early 13th Century Italian who was influential in the popular medieval "peace movements." See Introduction. Bonatti describes his unsavory side in Tr. 5 (the 141st Consideration), painting him a contemporary who pretended to be a miracle-worker. Here we see a mutual enmity–not only did Bonatti believe he was a sham, but John returned the sentiment by denying the validity of astrology.
[39] The Dominicans.

to all that astrology is a science, and one of the seven liberal arts. And even though it is responded briefly to them, still it does not seem to me that proof should be omitted that astronomy is an art and a theoretical science, with sufficient and manifest reasons, even if the order may seem to be distorted.[40]

Chapter 14: To show that astronomy is an art and one of the four mathematical ones, namely with the theoretical sciences

That astrology is a science, is proven by evident reason in this way. Astrology is a science of movable magnitude which, having been inspected by reason, defines the motion of the celestial bodies according to a three-fold course of time. Or, astrology is a science which seeks out the courses of the stars and the arrangements and figures of the stars with respect to themselves and with respect to the earth, with investigatory calculation. Therefore from the ground of the definition, astrology is a science. Moreover, astrology is said to be from *astron*,[41] which is a star, and *logos*, which is a statement or knowledge, or a calculation concerning the stars. Therefore by this etymology or interpretation of the name, astrology is a science. Again, it can be proven in another way, thus: everything which is such that it is from the true, first, prior things, *etc.*, is a science; but astrology has a substantial genus, in which it differs from other sciences, a peculiar property and accident: therefore it is a science.

Moreover, all that is a collection of precepts tending to one end, is an art or a science; [and] astrology is such; therefore it is an art or science, which St. Augustine proves manifestly enough, saying, "An art is a precept which gives a certain path, and a reason of acting or speaking."[42] For all precepts of astronomy then tend to one end, namely to knowing or considering past, present, and future things; and in these precepts the whole intention of astrology consists. Whence Seneca: "to recall the past, consider the present, foresee the future."[43]

---

[40] Or "reversed" (*praeposterus*). Hand/Zoller read "absurd." But I believe that this statement anticipates Bonatti's ongoing concern with explaining to the reader why he treats of astrological topics in the order that he does—most notably in the beginning of Tr. 9.
[41] Reading *astron* for *astros*.
[42] I am not sure where Bonatti is getting this quote.
[43] This is derived from Seneca's letter *On the Shortness of Life*, where he says that the philosopher alone "is exempt from the limitations of humanity; all ages are at his service as at a god's. Has time gone by? He holds it fast in recollection. Is time now present? He utilizes it. Is it still to come? He anticipates it. The amalgamation of all time into one makes his life long." See Seneca (1968), pp. 67-68.

For those things cannot rightly be paid attention to except by the astrologer, who considers all of these, and he alone can know them.

Moreover, if astrology (or astronomy) were not an art or science, [then] that renowned thing which is universally preached by all would be destroyed, namely that the liberal arts are seven. Therefore there would not be but six, or none—because by what reason astronomy would not exist, by that same reason the six would not exist, which would be inappropriate and very horrible. Again, since astronomy or astrology is said to be one-fourth of *quadrivial* knowledge, if it does not exist, the whole *quadrivium*[44] does not exist: because one integral part, or the integral whole, having been destroyed, the entirety is destroyed—which is most inappropriate. Again, if the *quadrivium* does not exist, mathematics does not exist; and if mathematics does not exist, theory does not exist, since mathematics (according to the Philosopher) is one-third of theory. Again, if theory does not exist, philosophy does not exist, which is a brazen, ill-tempered, and absurd thing to say. Therefore astronomy is of necessity a science, for he who destroys astronomy, destroys science, just as he who destroys first principles, destroys wisdom (according to Aristotle in the second [book] of the *Metaphysics*).[45] Against such people who wish to destroy the sciences, one cannot argue, because they are worse than beasts.[46]

Moreover, Aristotle, Ptolemy, Jafar, Aaydimon,[47] Abū Ma'shar, Māshā'allāh, Almetus, al-Farghānī, Thābit [ibn Qurra], Jirjis, 'Umar, Dorotheus, al-Kindī, Albenait, Astaphaz, al-Mansur, 'Ali, Abu 'Ali, and many other sages wrote on this science and taught that astrology is a science. It is not like to truth (if it were not a science) that so many and such great men called it such. Moreover, every thing which posits something through a cause or through an effect, posits knowledge, according to Aristotle in the *Posterior Analytics*.[48] The astrologer makes the eclipse plain through a cause, namely through interposition, and makes the same interposition plain through the eclipse, on account of which, by this and many other causes, it is proven that astrology is manifestly a science.

---

[44] *Quadruvialium*. In medieval higher education, the *quadrivium* was a set of four of the seven liberal arts: arithmetic, geometry, music, astronomy. The *trivium* consisted of grammar, logic, and rhetoric.
[45] *Met.* II.2, 994b15ff.
[46] This last batch of arguments is of course superficial, because it rests on the unproven assumption that there must be so many sciences of the sorts he mentions, or that astronomy really is integral to the whole *quadrivium*. The thrust of the passage has value mainly as a scare tactic, i.e., that much of traditional learning would be upset.
[47] Lat. *Ahaydimon*. Unknown.
[48] *Post. An.* II.8.

TREATISE 2:
SIGNS AND HOUSES

On the division of the orb of the signs,
and their nature, and how they are ordered and disposed,
and why there are exactly twelve (neither more, nor less),
and why they are denominated by their names,
and on what is connected with this

PART 1

I will therefore speak, following the footsteps of our venerable predecessors, on those things which will seem to be useful for this work, calling to mind their opinions—namely, [those of] Ptolemy, Hermes, Jafar, Thābit [ibn Qurra], al-Qabīsī, [Abu 'Alī] al-Khayyat, al-Kindī, al-Andarzagar, Māshā'allāh, ad-Dawla, Jirjis, Albenait, Aaydimon,[1] Arastellus,[2] (and of others who studied in this science), by adding those things which will seem useful to me, according to how God grants me grace in organizing [them] and restores to me my memory.

Chapter 1: On the division of the orb of the signs, and that the signs are only twelve, and that they are neither more nor less

You should know this, because the circle of the signs is divided into twelve equal divisions, of which each one is called a "sign"—of which the first is Aries, the second Taurus, the third Gemini, the fourth Cancer, the fifth Leo, the sixth Virgo, the seventh Libra, the eighth Scorpio, the ninth Sagittarius, the tenth Capricorn, the eleventh Aquarius, the twelfth Pisces.

But it might perhaps be asked, why the signs are only twelve? For many reasons could be assigned why the signs are twelve (neither more, nor less). Of which one (even though it is not very powerful) is that the number containing twelve [or the duodenary] is more perfect than practically all other number-

---

[1] Lat. *Aardimon.*
[2] Lat. *Arestali.*

unities not exceeding it;³ and the multiplications out of which [twelve] arises, are multiplied in its own parts.⁴ For it receives in itself more ordered divisions than any other number. For it arises by the multiplication of the ternary by the quaternary, and the quaternary by the ternary, and the binary by the senary,⁵ and the senary by the binary, and it is divided by these same portions in so many ways.

And there is another reason, no less powerful than the aforesaid one, according to what Arastellus⁶ and Abū Ma'shar⁷ and Aaydimon said (whom none of the philosophers dared contradict): namely that all elemental things⁸ are composed out of four elements—namely, out of fire, air, water, and earth—and those individual elemental things, and the parts of individuals, all consist of the aforesaid four elements. And [in addition], these three things (namely the beginning, middle, and end) are present in every individual, whence four, multiplied by three, make twelve.⁹

For the signs are not corrupted, but the elements are corrupted. And the elements are four, which are corrupted by the signs and the planets, by their whirling, restless circular motion. Wherefore the elements would not be otherwise corrupted (as much as they are in themselves), unless they are corrupted by the stars and their whirling circular motion.¹⁰ For the circular whirling of the stars around the elements, corrupts them, and they are corrupted with respect to one another; and the more noble ones (namely the active ones) corrupt the less noble ones (namely the passive ones); on account of which they are complected with one another, which is the reason for the generation of individuals of every species.

And the signs were divided according to the number of the four elements, because by the four elements (which are of four different natures or qualities) is perceived the number of the twelve signs. Because one of the elements is hot

---

³ That is, the numbers 2, 3, 4, 6, *etc.*, considered as distinct wholes in themselves, with their own particular properties.
⁴ This seems to mean that the number-unities described below are multiplied together in various ways, to yield 12.
⁵ I.e., consisting of six.
⁶ Unknown.
⁷ See *Gr. Intr.*, I.4.
⁸ *Elementata*, i.e., things created out of elements. I will translate this as "elemental things" or "elemental," with the understanding that composition is implied.
⁹ Hence the zodiac contains the principles of, and speaks to, the entire cycle of change of all the elements.
¹⁰ That is, the elements would already corrupt each other to a certain degree, even without the planets; but with the planets, corruption and change is increased.

and dry (namely fire); another is hot and moist (namely air); another cold and moist (namely water), another cold and dry (namely earth).

And even though the elements may be said to be complected, still to each one there is only one peculiar property. For the peculiar property of fire is heat; the peculiar property of air, is moisture; the peculiar property of water, is coldness; the peculiar property of earth, is dryness.[11]

Whence it was necessary that the signs be according to the differences imprinting on inferiors (namely according to heat and dryness, heat[12] and moisture, coldness and moisture, coldness and dryness), so that three of these would be called fiery (namely Aries, Leo, and Sagittarius), another three of these would be called earthy (namely Taurus, Virgo and Capricorn), another three of these would be called airy (namely Gemini, Libra and Aquarius), another three of these would be called watery (namely Cancer, Scorpio and Pisces).

And thus it was found that the signs were only twelve, neither more nor less. There could not be more, because each of them acts in the four elements generally, and each of them acts in the element deputed to it, according to the three beings [or conditions], namely the beginning, middle, and end. Whence, since, according to the being of the three, the signs act in every element, and the elements are only four, it was necessary that the signs be exactly twelve, neither more nor less. Wherefore Aries, Leo, and Sagittarius (as was said) are fiery; Taurus, Virgo, and Capricorn, are earthy; Gemini, Libra, and Aquarius, are airy; Cancer, Scorpio, and Pisces, are watery.

Chapter 2: In what way the signs act in the elements, and in which elements every sign acts

It was stated, in the preceding chapter, that the signs act in the elements. Now in this chapter it must be stated in what element every sign acts, and in what way. For Aries, Leo, and Sagittarius, since they are fiery, act in the fiery element, but in different ways.

---

[11] The "peculiar property" is what is sometimes called the "primitive quality." Here Bonatti (or his sources) seems to be combining the Stoic theory of the elements (by which each element has only one quality) with the Aristotelian theory (which gives two to each element). But to be faithful to the Stoics (and probably to the sources' meaning), air should be assigned the cold quality and water the moist quality, as opposed to what is stated here.

[12] Reading *caliditas* for *caliditatera*.

On Aries

Wherefore Aries acts in the fire element by imprinting temperate heat and dryness into it. But what comes to be out of that temperateness, is the beginning of natural motion by the individual of each species, namely for one animal doing it with another so that they might generate the individuals of the species out of the same individuals, so that they might be preserved by succession. Wherefore they are not preserved by individuals for a long time, because individuals are deficient in the drawing out of time, and so species are destroyed and lost unless they are preserved by succession. And so the beginning of natural motion is likewise, for making seeds germinate, and for making trees flower and emit foliage and produce fruit; and for making herbs and germinated seeds be born and increased and multiplied, and all invigorating things be increased, and to undertake growth. And this is the first being by which the fiery signs are said to act, and they even act in the fiery element.[13]

---

[13] In other words, the elements both act in a fiery way on all things, and they act in and through the fiery element itself.

On Leo

Leo acts in fire by bringing into it heat and dryness far from temperateness, so that out of that remoteness from temperateness the beginning of natural motion comes to be, to the impediment of fruit and the leaves of trees and herbs, and for making them decline on the side of destruction (wherefore they mature, the which maturation is in a certain sense a destruction); and so that there are few seeds which then germinate, and few animating things undertake increase or growth; and few animals lacking free will are moved to the increase of their species or to their preservation–rather, certain animals begin to be hidden, and seem almost to be destroyed. Since Leo makes his operation in the fire element, the falling of seeds and their devastation takes place; more fruits of trees mature and rot, and the like, from the impression of Leo into the fire element. And this is according to the being by which the fiery [signs] act in the fire element.

On Sagittarius

Indeed Sagittarius acts in the fire element by impressing into it heat and dryness far from all temperateness—rather he acts for the destruction of seeds and herbs and to the completion of the falling and destruction of the leaves of trees (the leaves of which fall in winter); and for the wounding of many animals, and for the concealing of many species of animals (and their destruction), nor do [such animals] dare to appear above the earth.[14] And this is the third being by which the fiery signs act in the fire element.

And these are the three beings through which the signs act in the elements. All things come to be according to this order, insofar as it is from the natural signification of the signs and planets; and for the reason that the superior bodies act in the elements, even if sometimes and somewhere [they do so] according to more, and sometimes and somewhere according to less; even though a natural consideration would seem to be otherwise than these are; still, if they are rightly considered, each are the same [as described here].

On the earthy signs, and first on Taurus

Indeed Taurus, Virgo, and Capricorn, which are the earthy signs, act in the earth element, but in different ways—namely, because Taurus acts in earth by imprinting temperate coldness and dryness in it (namely what impedes little or not at all), so that in that temperateness the generation of many sensible things comes to pass: namely species, and the increase of animating things, and the like.

---

[14] Bonatti seems to be talking about hibernation.

On Virgo

But Virgo acts in the earth element by imprinting less temperate coldness and dryness, and [a kind] more akin to destruction, so that from that action natural motion comes to be, as animating things suffer detriment and decrease; and herbs are retarded, and the leaves of trees fall and are lacking. But the coldness is not so far from moderation, [so] that even though certain things are wanting and are destroyed, certain others are generated, and certain seeds germinate, and certain herbs are newly born and grow, and the like.

On Capricorn

Capricorn, indeed, acts in the earth element by imprinting intemperate coldness and dryness into it, destroying and killing; nor are animals generated smoothly then (and if they are generated, they are most few, and they are often of the domesticated ones, on account of the domestication of their way of life), nor is nature moved that herbs might be born or trees grow foliage or flower (unless fortuitously), nor do seeds germinate, and the like.

On the airy signs, and first on Gemini

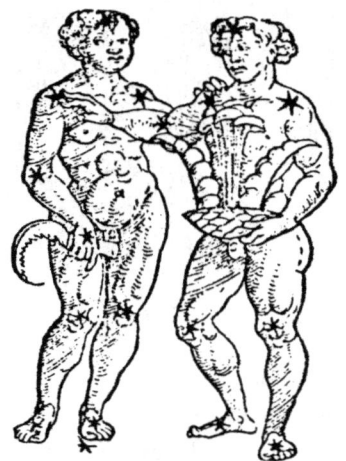

Indeed Gemini, Libra and Aquarius act in the air element, but in different ways. For Gemini acts in the air element by imprinting temperate heat and moisture into it, strengthening nature and every odor and every odiferous breeze, and strengthening natural heat and the temperateness of the air (in which the individuals of species rejoice), and making certain seeds germinate, and the like.

On Libra

Indeed Libra acts in the air element by bringing far-from-temperate heat and moisture into it, condensing and thickening it, and making it be commingled and harmful to the individual species, and to seeds and herbs and the foliage of trees and their fruits; and making it vaporous with dense and harmful vapors, and the like.

On Aquarius

Likewise, Aquarius acts in the air element by bringing intemperate and harmful and impeding heat and moisture into it, making it extinguished and destroying the individuals of species, and often those harmful things which animals and seeds and other invigorating things receive from the air; and those situations and that impression come to be because of the impressions which Aquarius makes in the air, and the like.

On the watery signs, and first on Cancer

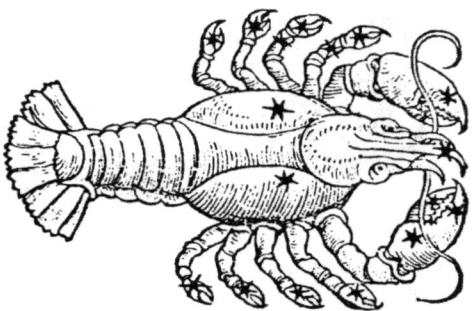

Indeed Cancer, Scorpio and Pisces, which are the watery signs, act in the water element, but in different ways—namely, because Cancer acts in water by imprinting temperate coldness and moisture into it, by which the movement of nature is for giving sweetness and nourishment by which animals are nourished and live, and all invigorating things together are nourished, and the like.

On Scorpio

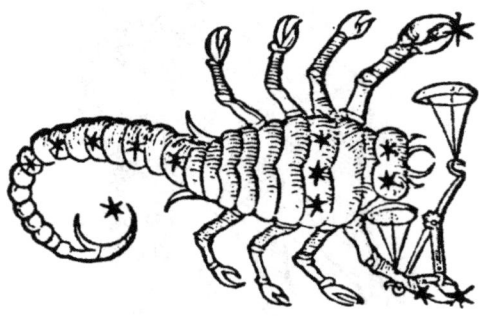

Scorpio acts in the water element by bringing far-from-temperate coldness and moisture into it, by which the movement of nature comes to be more toward corruption than toward nourishment or preservation, on account of the corruption and saltiness which the action of Scorpio brings into the water, barely adequate for providing nourishment, and to few things.[15]

On Pisces

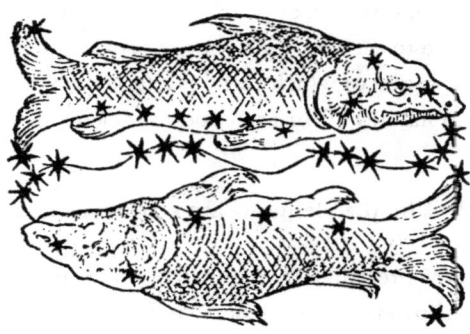

Pisces acts in the water element by bringing intemperate and harmful coldness into it, by which the movement of nature comes to be for killing and destroying animals and seeds, and practically all animating things as a whole, on account of the corruption and irritation [or bitterness] and foulness which the action of Pisces brings into water.

[Summary]

This is the reason why the signs are exactly twelve (neither more, nor less). Because the elements are only four, and the signs act in the elements according to three modes: according to the first being, nourishing and increasing; indeed according to the second being, not totally nourishing, nor totally destroying; according to the third being, destroying.

And these three beings contain in themselves the beginning, middle, and end. And every three signs acts in one of the four elements, but the three fiery ones act in fire according to the said three modes; the three airy ones act in the air according to the said three modes; the three watery ones act in water according to the said three modes; the three earthy ones act in earth according to the said three modes.

And therefore Ptolemy, Aaydimon, Astaphan, Arastellus, Abū Ma'shar, and the rest of the philosophers are agreed that the triplicities of the signs are four, because every three signs of that same nature act in the element deputed to that

---

[15] *Paucissimum et paucis rebus valens nutrimentum praestare.*

nature (namely the fiery ones in fire, the airy ones in air, the watery ones in water, the earthy ones in earth), and because of this, they could not be more nor less.

There is another reason why the signs are exactly twelve: namely because the zodiac consists of four quarters, of which two are northern, two southern; out of which one is given to the fiery signs, one to the airy ones, one to the watery ones, one to the airy ones; of which each [quarter] contains three signs according to the aforesaid natures of the aforesaid four elements.

Chapter 3: Why the elements are so disposed and ordered

It was stated in the preceding chapter in what element each sign acts, and by what mode. Now however it must be stated in this chapter, why the four elements were so disposed or ordered: namely fire above, bordering immediately on the Moon in the concavity of the globe; then air, then water, then earth.[16]

Chapter 4: To show that the elements are only four, neither more nor less

It was stated in the preceding chapter how the elements are ordered or disposed. Now it must be stated in this chapter that the elements are only four, neither more nor less, even though many of those things which have been said about them, and which are [now] said about them, do not seem to be in the consideration of the astrologer. But it cannot be but that mention be made of them, wherefore it behooves us to make mention about all of these, [since] they fall very often into our work.

For the elements could not be but four, neither more nor less, because each elemental body consists of four elements, and it has in itself four qualities (namely heat, dryness, coldness, and moisture); and these four things happen to it, namely generation, durability or conservation, corruption, and destruction–speaking thusly, it is generated most strongly by heat, it endures by dryness, it is corrupted by moisture, it is destroyed by coldness: understand these things soundly. These four beings abide in every, and about every, elemental thing. For it takes heat from fire, moisture from the air, coldness from the water, dryness

---

[16] Note that Bonatti never says *why* this is so. Like many of Bonatti's "arguments," this passage consists of descriptive assertions.

from the earth: whence, since the accidents of the elements are not found nor exist except by being four, and they are drawn from the elements, it is necessary that the elements be exactly four, neither more nor less.

Insofar as the elements are simple or pure in their own spheres, they have simple qualities ruling in them: fire, heat; air, moisture; water, coldness; earth, dryness. But insofar as they are connected and entangled, they have composite qualities with respect to each other, namely: fire, heat and dryness; air, heat and moisture; water, coldness and moisture; earth, coldness and dryness.

Chapter 5: Why the signs are so ordered or disposed

It was stated in the preceding why the signs are exactly twelve (neither more nor less), and why the elements are only four. Now however it remains to say in this chapter why the signs are so ordered or disposed.

The ordering or disposition of the signs begins from the fiery ones, as Aaydimon and Abū Ma'shar said.[17] And the fiery ones were put in the beginning, then the earthy ones, then the airy ones, then the watery ones. But you could ask, "why didn't the sages order the signs according to the order of the elements, by beginning from the fiery ones, then from the airy ones, then from the watery ones, then from the earthy ones, according to how the elements are successively posited in their own order?"[18] Indeed, the reasons which moved the sages to ordering [them] thusly, were many. Of which one was because the elements (as was said) receive corruption and alteration from the motions, and by the continual and restless revolution of the signs and the heavens; and because of that corruption and alteration, the four qualities which happen to elemental bodies come to be–namely generation, conservation, corruption and destruction.[19]

And because generation is more noble than the other qualities of elemental things, they began from the signs through which generation (or the natural motion toward generation) comes to be–and those are the fiery ones.

---

[17] *Gr. Intr.*, II.4.
[18] I.e., from just below the sphere of the Moon, down to the center of the earth.
[19] Whereas if the signs were ordered: fire, air, water, earth, the natural cycle of things would be said to end in preservation, which is contrary to fact.

And the quality which is noble next to generation, is durability or conservation; and it comes to be from the signs through which the motion of nature to conservation or durability comes to be (insofar as corruptible things receive durability)—and those are the earthy ones.

And the quality which is ignoble and after durability is corruption, and it comes to be from the signs through which nature is moved to corruption—and those are the airy ones.

And the more ignoble, or rather worse quality which is after corruption, is destruction; and it comes to be from the signs through which nature is moved to destruction—and those are the watery ones.

Another reason why it had to begin from the fiery signs and end with the watery signs is because heat and coldness are agents, but dryness and moisture are patients, and since heat is the stronger agent (which signifies generation), it deserved to be the preferred one of the agents. Likewise since dryness is a strong patient, it deserved to be put in the front of the patients. And because generation precedes durability, the signs signifying generation were put before the signs signifying durability. And because corruption precedes destruction, the signs signifying corruption were put before the signs signifying destruction. And thus, since generation is the beginning of every generable and end-able thing, the signs signifying destruction (namely the watery ones) were put last.[20]

Moreover, the fiery signs were put at the beginning, because heat rules in fire, by which bringing-to-life (which is the most noble thing) comes to be.

And the earthy signs were put immediately after the fiery ones, on account of the affinity which they have with fire, because of the dryness ruling with them.

And the watery ones were put last, as they are directly opposite the fiery ones in position of place, just as they are opposite them directly in nature.

---

[20] The principles are: active before passive, strong before weak, beginning (generation) before durability, corruption before destruction.

And the airy ones were put before the watery ones (immediately before them) on account of the affinity which they have with them because of moisture.

And thus both agents were put at the ends, and the patients between each.

These are the reasons which moved the sages of this profession to make this ordering of the signs in this way, namely by putting first the fiery ones, then the earthy ones, then the airy ones, then the watery ones. And of the fiery ones, by putting Aries first, and of the earthy ones by putting Taurus first, and of the airy ones by putting Gemini first, and of the watery ones by putting Cancer first, on account of the reasons assigned above.

Chapter 6: Why the denomination of the signs begins from Aries, and not from any other of the signs

It was stated in the preceding chapter why the signs were so ordered. Indeed in this one it must be stated why the denomination begins from Aries and not from any other of the signs, when the heaven is a spherical body, and everything spherical lacks a beginning (and what lacks a beginning lacks an end, and what lacks a beginning and end, lacks a middle center–this being excluded in bodily things).[21]

The reasons are many, of which one is that the denomination of the signs begins from Aries because the circle of the signs intersects the circle of the equator of the day in the beginning of Aries and in its opposite, not at a right angle but obliquely, so that six signs are northern and six southern, just as will be stated at length elsewhere. And the part which is northern is stronger than that which is southern, because when the Sun goes out of Pisces it enters Aries, and Aries is the first sign of the northern part; and the northern part is more noble and stronger than the southern part. And that this is true, is not in need of proof (even though this could be proven completely), because all proclaim it, and none says the contrary. And therefore the denomination of the signs begins

---

[21] Bonatti's argument (placed in the mouth of an objector) is this. The heavens differ from regular bodies in that normal bodies (like our own) have clear boundaries that can serve as beginnings, endings, and middle points. But the surface of a sphere lacks any obvious point to act as a beginning, since every point on the sphere bears the same relation to all others. Therefore there is no *prima facie* reason to treat Aries as the beginning of a circle drawn on the sphere, since any point would serve equally well as a beginning.

from Aries, because the stronger part of the zodiac begins from the beginning of Aries.

Another reason why the denomination of the signs begins from Aries[22]

Another reason is because, when the Sun enters Aries, the day then begins to be increased over the night. Whence, since increase is a noble thing, the sages of this Art were agreed that the denomination of the signs would have to begin from the sign in which the increase begins.

Another reason why the denomination of the signs begins from Aries[23]

Another reason is because, since the four qualities (which are hotness, and coldness, dryness, and moisture) are simple, and since they are simple they do not increase, nor do they diminish, [but] when they are put together (namely hotness and moisture, coldness and dryness, hotness and dryness, coldness and moisture), certain ones of them signify an effect and increase, others of them signify corruption and decrease. Whence it ought to have begun from Aries more so than from any other of the signs: because when the Sun enters Aries, then things begin to be effected and increased; and since effect and increase are noble things and friends of nature, and defect and decrease are ignoble things and enemies of nature, the denomination ought to have begun more deservedly from Aries, because then things grow tender–the which quality is likened to youth (which is the most powerful part of life): and so it is the most powerful part of time, when the aforesaid come to be. Because then the Sun recedes from the equator of the day, and approaches the northern regions, and heat acts on the moisture which had existed from the preceding winter season; and nature is moved then to generation and the increase of things, and herbs grow, and trees bear foliage, and flower, and produce fruits, and many seeds germinate (while this does not happen in the other seasons of the year, unless perhaps sometimes fortuitously). Therefore the denomination of the signs had to begin more deservedly from Aries than from any of the other signs.

---

[22] Not treated as its own heading in 1550.
[23] Not treated as its own heading in 1550.

Chapter 7: Why the signs were named by these names

It was stated above why the denomination of the signs has to begin from Aries. Now however it must be stated why the signs are denominated with these names.

The reasons are many, of which one is because in those places which are called signs, are stars so disposed and so organized, that if a line were drawn from one to another, such a figure would result from thence—just as is the sign denominated to them. And it is said that Ptolemy went toward the south so far, that he was below the equator, and stood there to a degree that he saw all of these things.

There is another reason why the signs are denominated by such names: namely, when the Sun enters Aries heat is increased, for the reason that the Sun begins to be elongated from the equinoctial line and approaches toward the zenith of the northern regions; and he is made strong in accordance with how the ram [Aries] is said to have powers with respect to the strong ones of the animals.

> Then heat is increased and made stronger, more so than it was when the Sun was in Aries; and this is likened to the nature of the bull [Taurus], because the bull is an animal stronger than the ram, and the declination of the Sun from the equator (and his approach to the zenith of the northern regions) becomes greater than when he was in Aries.

> Then the Sun enters Gemini, and this sign is called "the twins" because then heat is doubled and duplicated beyond what it had been at first. And this is the last point of his elongation from the equator of the day, and of his approach to the highest point over our heads.

> Then the Sun begins to return toward the equator of the day, and then it is said that he enters the crab [Cancer], because the crab is a backwards-moving animal: whence, just as the crab is said to go sometimes forwards and after that to return backwards, so when the Sun is elongated from the equinoctial line to his last elongation, he is returned from [the last elongation] toward [the equinoctial line]—then he is said to go backwards like a crab goes.

Then when the Sun goes out of Cancer, he enters Leo. And it is said that he is in the lion [Leo] because heat is increased and becomes stronger and sharper and harder on account of the depurified air, and he does not then take part in any moisture. Whence, because the lion is a hard [or inflexible] animal, strong and very rough, this sign was denominated from that animal.

Then heat is relaxed, nor does the increase of things happen, nor a generation which is ordained (apart from the generation of certain seeds). And this sign is called "virgin" [Virgo], because a virgin is a humble and sterile animal, wherefore all things tend toward decrease and virtual sterility.

Then the Sun enters the scales [Libra], because then the day is equated with the night, and heat is relaxed, and effected in equality between coldness and heat: because then cold begins somewhat to take on power, and all things are then in equality.

Then the Sun enters the scorpion [Scorpio], and cold is increased above heat, and now cold comes to be, now hot, and the air is made distemperate,[24] and rains come to be, and vicious illnesses are generated, and pestilential ones, and ones bringing death in the manner of poison, and the like. And therefore this sign is denominated from that poisonous animal, the scorpion.

Then cold is clearly increased over heat, and then the Sun is said to enter the archer [Sagittarius]: because then mutations of the air take place, and the air comes down on the side of coldness, and strong hoar-frosts come upon [things], and snows, and ice emitted from the air, like arrows wounding ensouled and invigorating things.

Then the cold is increased above heat, and the hot is practically put to rest, and the air comes down to a distemperate and melancholic coldness, and then many snows come to be, and the ultimate cold, and ice, and the

---

[24] I.e., its mixture is bad, as is hinted by its being inconsistently hot or cold.

like–whence since the goat [Capricorn][25] is a cold and dry animal, and melancholic, this sign was denominated from that animal, and the Sun is then in his final declination from the equator toward the south.

Then the Sun begins to turn back toward the equator, and then the cold begins to be diminished somewhat, and sometimes rains take place instead of snows, and the air is made more moist: whence that sign is denominated [Aquarius, the water-bearer] from such a disposition of the air then thriving.

Then the Sun enters Pisces. And that sign is denominated from the fish, (which is a watery animal), because then rains abound more so than in the other seasons of the year, unless perhaps by accident; and if there were snows or hoar-frosts or ice, they are converted more quickly into water than in the other winter times.

---

[25] Technically the *Capricornus* is not a standard goat, but a mythical goat-animal having some sea-creature features (which would not make it as dry). A goat in the normal sense is *caper*.

PART 2: On the Nature of the Essential Circle

Chapter 1: On the division of the orb of signs into twelve signs, and of every sign into thirty degrees, and of every degree into sixty minutes, and of every minute into sixty seconds

In those things which were stated before in this Treatise, many things were shown which seem to be (and are) useful for this work, and particularly on the number of the signs and their organization, and on their division.

In this chapter we must speak about the division of the orb of the signs, following the footsteps of our most reverend predecessor Ptolemy, and of those who must be honored, namely: Hermes, Abū Ma'shar, al-Andarzagar, ad-Dawla, [Abu 'Ali] al-Khayyat, Thābit [ibn Qurra], Astaphan, Arastellus, and other prudent men who studied in this science—and by adding those things which will seem to be useful, according to how God shows me the grace of organization, and restores to me my memory.

Indeed you ought to know that the circle of the signs (which is called the zodiac or zodial), is divided into twelve equal divisions, of which each one is called a "sign." And the signs (as was said above) are said to be in the likeness of certain animals which are formed according to their shapes, just as I told you. Therefore the first sign is called a Ram, the second a Bull, the third Twins, the fourth a Crab, the fifth a Lion, the sixth a Virgin, the seventh a Balance, the eighth a Scorpion, the ninth an Archer, the tenth a Capricornus, the eleventh a Water-Bearer, the twelfth Fishes.

And every one of these signs is divided into thirty equal parts, of which each one is called a "degree."[26] And every degree is divided into sixty equal parts, of which each one is called a "minute."[27] And every minute is divided into sixty equal parts, of which each one is called a "second."[28] And every second is divided into sixty equal parts, of which each one is called a "third."[29] And every third is divided into sixty equal parts, of which each one is called a "fourth,"[30] and so on up to the end of the numbers—but these will be dispensed with by you in your work, and especially in the equations of some number beyond these,

---

[26] *Gradus*, lit. "a step."
[27] *Minutum*, lit. "a little piece."
[28] *Secundum*, lit. "a second" division of a degree.
[29] *Tertium*, lit. "a third" division of a degree.
[30] *Quartum*, lit. "a fourth" division of a degree.

even though the Order of Preachers went down to the fifth and sixth (not in order to philosophize, but so that they would appear to be philosophizing).

Chapter 2: To show which signs are northern and which southern

It was stated above that the signs are twelve, and in how many parts each sign is divided. Now it must be stated which of them are northern, and how many; and which are southern. The northern ones are six, namely those which are from the beginning of Aries up to the end of Virgo (namely Aries, Taurus, Gemini, Cancer, Leo, Virgo). And they are called "northern" because they are of the northern direction from the equator of the day. The remaining six are those which are from the beginning of Libra up to the end of Pisces. And they are called "southern" because they are of the southern direction from the equator of the day.

Chapter 3: Which signs are of direct ascension, and which of crooked [ascension]

It was stated which signs are northern, and which southern. Now it must be stated which signs are of direct ascension, and which of crooked [ascension]. These six are of direct ascension, namely those which are from the beginning of Cancer up to the end of Sagittarius. And they are said to be of direct ascension, because they ascend directly and in a longer time than their opposites. Indeed the remaining six, namely those which are from the beginning of Capricorn up to the end of Gemini, are said to be of crooked ascension, because they do not ascend so directly as their above-said opposites ascend. And they are said to be ascending crookedly because they (namely Capricorn, Aquarius, Pisces, Aries, Taurus, Gemini) ascend crookedly and in a lesser time than do their above-said opposites, because each sign ought to ascend in two equal hours. Indeed the direct ones ascend in more than two hours, but the crooked ones in less than two hours.

Those which are obedient

Al-Qabīsī said[31] that those ascending crookedly obey those ascending directly. Namely, two signs which are of the same longitude from the beginning of

---

[31] Al-Qabīsī I.8.

Cancer: the one which ascends crookedly obeys the one which obeys directly—as Gemini [obeys] Cancer, because the end of Gemini is so far distant from the equator of the day as the beginning of Cancer is; and the end of Cancer, as much as the beginning of Gemini. And for the same reason Taurus is said to obey Leo; Aries, Virgo; Pisces, Libra; Aquarius, Scorpio; Capricorn, Sagittarius.

[Those which agree in journey][32]

And this same philosopher said[33] that the two signs which are of the same longitude from the beginning of Aries, are said to be "agreeing in journey," like Aries and Pisces: for the end of Aries is so much distant from the equator of the day as is the beginning of Pisces; Taurus, so much as Aquarius is; Gemini, so much as Capricorn is; Cancer, so much as Sagittarius is; Leo, so much as Scorpio is; Virgo, so much as Libra is.

[The greater or Solar half, and the lesser or Lunar half]

And[34] there is another method of dividing between the ascensions of the signs, according to two halves of the circle of the signs. And certain signs are said to be greater than certain ones opposite them—not that one sign is greater or longer than the other is in its circle, but because they have more time in ascending than their opposites do; and they set in a lesser [time]. And they begin from Leo (which is the domicile of the Sun), and it is called the greater half. And the half of the Sun is said [to be] from the beginning of Leo up to the end of Capricorn, because the Sun has such virtue in that whole half, as the other five planets do in their own bounds.[35]

Indeed the remaining half (namely that which is from the beginning of Aquarius up to the end of Cancer), is called the lesser half—not that it is lesser than the other, but that they ascend in a lesser time than their opposites do, and they set in a greater [time], according to the diversity of climes and regions.[36] And it is called the half of the Moon, because the Moon has such virtue in that

---

[32] Title not in original. I will occasionally add titles in brackets to clarify divisions in topics and the text.
[33] Al-Qabīsī I.9.
[34] Based on al-Qabīsī I.10.
[35] Unfortunately, the doctrine of the bounds is not conceptually developed enough (if it ever was developed very much) by the Medieval period, to tell exactly what al-Qabīsī meant by this.
[36] Climes (*climata*) are bands of geographical latitude, regions (*regiones*) areas of geographical longitude. See Tr. 8.

whole half as do the other five planets in their own bounds, on account of the many impressions and many effects which she has in us, more so than do the other planets. (And this was the reason why bounds were not assigned to the Sun or the Moon in the signs as they were assigned to the other five planets, as will be stated below when I speak about the bounds of the planets.)

[The hot half and the cold half]

And[37] that half of the circle which is from the beginning of Aries up to the end of Virgo, is called the "hot half." And the other half (namely that which is from the beginning of Libra up to the end of Pisces) is called the "cold half."

[The quarters of the circle of the signs]

And[38] that one-fourth of the circle which is from the beginning of Aries up to the end of Gemini is called the hot, moist, vernal, childish, sanguine quarter; and it signifies the childish age up to youth. And the next quarter which is from the beginning of Cancer up to the end of Virgo is called the hot, dry, summery, choleric, youthful quarter; and it signifies youth up to its completion (namely into the beginning of middle age). And the next quarter, which is from the beginning of Libra up to the end of Sagittarius, is called the cold, dry, autumnal, melancholic quarter, and it signifies middle age up to the beginning of old age. Indeed the remaining quarter, which is from the beginning of Capricorn up to the end of Pisces, is called the cold, moist, wintry, phlegmatic, senile, defective quarter; and it signifies old age and senility up to the end of natural life.

Chapter 4: On the order of the circle of the seven planets, and the disposition of those seven planets, and their courses, and in what times they perfect their courses

In this chapter I will speak to you according to what the philosophers said– and it is true–concerning the order of the circles of the seven planets, of which the first and higher and superior one, and the nearer one to the orb of the signs, is the circle of Saturn; then the second is the circle of Jupiter, the third is the circle of Mars, the fourth is the circle of the Sun, the fifth is the circle of Venus,

---

[37] Al-Qabīsī I.10.
[38] Al-Qabīsī I.11.

the sixth is the circle of Mercury, the seventh is the circle of the Moon (who is inferior and nearer to the earth than all the others).

But[39] of the seven planets, the higher and superior in course, and slower than all, is Saturn, who perfects his own course in approximately 30 years. Then Jupiter, who perfects his own course in approximately 12 years. Then Mars, who perfects his own course in approximately 2 years. Then the Sun, who perfects his own course in 1 year. Then Venus, who perfects her own course in 1 year, just like the Sun. Then Mercury, who likewise perfects his own course in 1 year. Then the Moon (who is faster and inferior and nearer to the earth than all the others), who perfects her own course in approximately 27 days and one-third of a day.

There are even two places in the circle of the signs to be understood apart from the planets, of which one is called the Head of the Dragon, and the other the Tail of the Dragon. And they are two opposite crossings which the circle of the Moon makes through the circle of the Sun, and they signify certain things which will be stated below when we treat of the Head and the Tail.

Chapter 5: What powers the planets have in the signs

Every[40] one of the planets has powers in the signs, of which some are by nature, some are by accident. By nature are these: domicile, exaltation, bound, triplicity, face. By accident are these: the joys of the planets, their appearing in the places and strong houses, and when they are received (namely when one receives another), just as [there are] other strengths[41] which will be stated in their own place and time.

Chapter 6: On the domiciles of the planets

The[42] signs, as was shown, are twelve; and they are assigned as domiciles to the seven planets. Wherefore Leo is the domicile of the Sun, just as the

---

[39] Al-Qabīsī I.12.
[40] Based in part on al-Qabīsī I.13.
[41] *Fortitudines.* I will always translate this word as "strength" or "strengths," instead of "fortitudes" (as became more popular after Lilly). Sometimes it seems to refer to the pointing system for measuring the strength of essential dignities, sometimes not, but I have not been able to detect a consistent, unambiguous, technical use of this term.
[42] This long section corresponds to a brief few sentences in al-Qabīsī I.14. Bonatti follows al-Qabīsī's order, but feels free to elaborate or draw on other sources.

philosophers testify; Cancer is the domicile of the Moon; Gemini and Virgo are the domiciles of Mercury; Taurus and Libra are the domiciles of Venus; Aries and Scorpio are the domiciles of Mars; Pisces and Sagittarius are the domiciles of Jupiter; Aquarius and Capricorn are the domiciles of Saturn.

But you could say, "Why were the domiciles of the planets so ordered, and why do the Sun and the Moon have only a single domicile apiece, while the other planets have two of them apiece, when the luminaries would seem more likely to have two than any of the others, on account of their own strengths and on account of the many causes[43] which they can be assigned, and especially when Abū Ma'shar says[44] that the Sun and the Moon are stronger and greater benefics than the rest of the benefics?"

To which it can be responded in this way: "Because among the ancients there was diversity in the ordering of the domiciles of the planets: for some began from the houses of the luminaries, some began from the domiciles of Saturn, some began from the domiciles of Mars, some began from the domiciles of Jupiter, some began from the domiciles of Mercury, some began from the domiciles of Venus; and each one assigned his own reason, according to how it seemed to him.[45] Nevertheless, I do not put much stock in their differences. For many reasons could be assigned, but I do not want to assign them, nor do I want to recite all the opinions of the ancients, because it would take a long time, nor would it be useful to you. But I will assign to you one [reason], and let only this suffice for you. One reason why Leo was assigned to the Sun as a domicile (and no other sign), is because the Sun is the greater luminary, and he is the diurnal luminary, and he is bright, and is judged hot and dry, and his heat is intense, and the virtue of his heat appears more strongly when he is in Leo than when he is in any other sign; and the nature of summer appears more strongly then, than in the other seasons. And the Sun is a masculine, diurnal planet, and he signifies heat and dryness by his own nature. And Leo is a masculine sign, fiery (namely hot and dry), and when the Sun is in it, then it is the culmination of summer and the full degree of the increase of heat. And no other sign is so close to the nature of the Sun as Leo is: because even though Aries and Sagittarius are fiery signs, still the strength of the Sun's heat is not so openly apparent (nor his light so clear, nor so fine) as it is in Leo. And Abū Ma'shar

---

[43] *Causae.* Bonatti means that they cause many things to happen on the earth.
[44] *Gr. Intr.*, IV.5.
[45] This statement seems so exaggerated and unlike anything I have read, that I am tempted to say Bonatti is making it up as a false concession to an opponent before he gives his real reason.

said[46] that the Sun and Leo agree in this, namely because the Sun is in the middle of the planets, and Leo is in the middle of the summer, wherefore then is the ultimate and stronger heat of summer, when the Sun is in Leo.

Why is Cancer the domicile of the Moon? Indeed, Cancer alone was assigned to the Moon (who is the nocturnal luminary) as her domicile, on account of the fact that Cancer is the first movable sign (from the beginning of the signs) which agrees with the Moon in femininity, mobility, coldness, and moisture. And it is more near to the domicile of the luminary from which the Moon receives the light, than any other movable or cold or moist sign that agrees with the nature of the Moon. And the Moon is even called the luminary of the Sun, because she receives light from him, and those two domiciles are brighter and more splendid, and agreeing more with the natures of the luminaries, than any of the other domiciles in all the climes and in all the regions in the world.

Why are Capricorn and Aquarius the domiciles of Saturn? Just as the Sun and Moon are brighter and more splendid and more luminous bodies than the rest of the supercelestial bodies, and their light is perceived more, and more manifestly, than the light of any of the others, and they are increasers of fortune, so the obscurity and darkness of Saturn is perceived beyond all the other obscurities and darknesses of the other supercelestial bodies; and he is worse than all the malefics, and is a destroyer. Whence, since light and splendor are direct contraries to obscurity and darkness (and *vice versa*), and the luminaries[47] signify splendor and light and clarity, and Saturn signifies obscurity and darkness, therefore his domiciles were directly opposite theirs in a direct line. And this was the reason why Capricorn and Aquarius were assigned to Saturn as his domiciles. And likewise, Capricorn and Aquarius are domiciles of darkness, so that when the Sun is in them, the air is more obscure and more removed from purity, and particularly when he is in Aquarius (because then it is the culmination and extreme of winter's cold).

Why are Sagittarius and Pisces the domiciles of Jupiter? Sagittarius and Pisces were assigned to Jupiter as his domiciles next to the domiciles of Saturn, because Jupiter succeeds Saturn immediately in the order of circles, and he is a strong benefic, so that he breaks the malice of Saturn. And these two signs aspect the domiciles of the luminaries by a trine aspect, which is an aspect of unbroken and complete friendship, just as the opposition is the aspect of ultimate enmity. And therefore, since he is a benefic beyond the rest of the

---

[46] *Gr. Intr.*, V.3.
[47] Reading *luminaria* for *luminaris*.

benefics (apart from the luminaries), it was necessary that his domiciles be arranged in such places that they would aspect the domiciles of the luminaries with an aspect of love[48] beyond the rest of the aspects. For Pisces aspects Cancer (which is the domicile of the nocturnal luminary) from a trine aspect, and it is of its triplicity (which even increases the goodness of an aspect). And Sagittarius likewise aspects Leo (which is the domicile of the diurnal luminary), from a trine aspect, and it is of its triplicity.

Why are Aries and Scorpio the domiciles of Mars? Aries and Scorpio were assigned to Mars as his domiciles next to the domiciles of Jupiter, because Mars immediately succeeds Jupiter in the order of the circles. And he is a malefic and unfortunate, but his misfortune and his evil are less than the misfortune and malice[49] of Saturn. And these two signs aspect the domiciles of the luminaries from a square aspect, which is an aspect of medium enmity. And therefore, since he is a malefic less so than Saturn (who signifies extreme evil), it was necessary that his domiciles be arranged in such places that they would aspect the domiciles of the luminaries with the aspect of medium enmity. For Aries aspects Cancer (which is the domicile of the nocturnal luminary) from a square aspect, nor is it of its triplicity, so that it even worsens the aspect. Likewise, Scorpio aspects Leo (which is the domicile of the diurnal luminary) from a square aspect.

Why are Taurus and Libra the domiciles of Venus? Taurus and Libra were assigned to Venus as her domiciles next to the domiciles of Mars, because she succeeds the Sun (to whom is assigned his own domicile) in the order of circles. And therefore the domiciles of Venus succeed the domiciles of Mars. And Venus is a good benefic, but she is not so perfect[50] a benefic that she breaks every malice of the malicious ones (which Venus cannot do). But even though she cannot break the malices of the others like Jupiter can, still she subtracts from them as she is able, and through herself she confers fortune and good. And her fortune and her goodness is below the fortune and goodness of Jupiter. And these two signs aspect the domiciles of the luminaries from a sextile aspect, which is an aspect of medium friendship. And therefore, because her good fortune is below Jupiter (who signifies complete and extreme goodness and

---

[48] Literally, "so that they would look at the domiciles of the luminaries with a look of delight." Remember, an "aspect" is a way of "looking."

[49] This parallel between *malum...malitia* shows that Bonatti does not want to take away the moral connotations from the word *malitia*. Sometimes I translate *malitia* as "badness," but I will tend to favor "malice."

[50] Reading *perfecta* for *praefecta*.

friendship), it was necessary that her domiciles be arranged in such places that they would aspect the domiciles of the luminaries by an aspect of medium friendship. For Taurus aspects Cancer (which is the domicile of the nocturnal luminary) by a sextile aspect, which is the aspect of medium friendship, even though it is not of its triplicity. Libra aspects Leo (which is the domicile of the diurnal luminary) from a sextile aspect.

Why are Gemini and Virgo the domiciles of Mercury? Gemini and Virgo were assigned to Mercury as his domiciles, next to the domicile of Venus, because he succeeds Venus in the order of circles, and he is commingled: but in his own nature he is more a benefic than a malefic; but he converts to the nature of him to whom he is conjoined. And this is the reason why he is called "commingled," namely that his domiciles do not aspect the domiciles of the luminaries by any aspect, because they are likewise bordering on them[51]–and because Mercury is not so elongated from the Sun that he himself could be in any aspect with him.

But you could say that Gemini aspects *Leo*, and Virgo *Cancer*.[52] Still, this does not have a role in this case; because according to this consideration, no sign is said to aspect the domicile of any luminary from any aspect such that the domicile of the other luminary falls within those boundaries. Whence Gemini is not said to aspect Leo, because Cancer (the domicile of the Moon) falls within those boundaries; nor is Virgo said to aspect Cancer, because Leo (the domicile of the Sun) falls within those boundaries. And understand thus with all the signs, because Aries does not aspect Leo by a trine aspect, on account of Cancer (the domicile of the Moon, which it does aspect by a square aspect), which falls within those boundaries. Scorpio does not aspect Cancer by a trine aspect, on account of Leo (the domicile of the Sun, which it does aspect by a square aspect), which falls between the other boundaries. Taurus does not aspect Leo by a square aspect, on account of Cancer (the domicile of the Moon, which it does aspect by a sextile aspect), which falls within those boundaries. Libra does not aspect Cancer by a square aspect, on account of Leo (the domicile of the Sun, which it does aspect by a sextile aspect), which falls within those boundaries.

You will consider all of these according to the consideration why the signs were assigned to the planets as domiciles. But it is otherwise with the planets appearing in those signs, as will be discussed fully in the chapter on the aspects

---

[51] Reading *eis* for *ei*.
[52] I.e., that these domiciles *do* aspect the luminaries' domiciles from the other side.

of the planets.[53] Many other reasons[54] and opinions of the philosophers could be assigned, but in order to avoid prolixity, let the above-stated reason suffice for you.

Chapter 7: On the detriments of the planets

The detriment[55] of any planet is said to be the seventh sign from its domicile, namely its opposite one (and it is even called its "fall"),[56] just as Libra is the opposite of Aries, and Aries of Libra; and Libra is the detriment of Mars, and Aries the detriment of Venus. And Taurus is the opposite of Scorpio, and is the detriment of Mars.[57]

And Sagittarius is the opposite of Gemini and is the detriment of Mercury. And Gemini is the opposite of Sagittarius and is the detriment of Jupiter.

Capricorn is the opposite of Cancer and is the detriment of the Moon. And Cancer is the opposite of Capricorn and is the detriment of Saturn.

Aquarius is the opposite of Leo, and is the detriment of the Sun. Leo is the opposite of Aquarius, and is the detriment of Saturn

Pisces is the opposite of Virgo, and is the detriment of Mercury. Virgo is the opposite of Pisces, and is the detriment of Jupiter.

And al-Qabīsī said[58] that if two signs were the domicile of one planet, they are said to be agreeing in the *zone* [of the zodiac],[59] that is, in the circle which is

---

[53] E.g., a *planet* in Scorpio can still aspect a *planet* in Cancer, even if the domiciles in themselves do not.
[54] Reading *multae aliae causae* for *multas alias causas*.
[55] *Detrimentum* comes from *detero*, to "wear out, diminish, weaken, impair." In political contexts it can mean defeat or overthrow. The connotation of detriment, then, is that a planet is weakened, worn out, and its power is overthrown when it is in such a sign.
[56] Bonatti often seems to treat "detriment" and "fall" as equivalent terms when speaking of sign-based debilities.
[57] Clearly there should be a sentence here that reads: "Scorpio is the opposite of Taurus, and is the detriment of Venus."
[58] Al-Qabīsī I.14.
[59] Lat. *almantica*, from the Ar. *al-mintaqah* (المنطقة), "zone, area, territory" (al-Qabīsī I.14). Burnett *et al.* translate this as the "belt." But Abū Ma'shar (*Gr. Intr.* VI.6) says this is called

broad in the middle and bound tight in the twisting[60]–namely in the zodiac, which appears in a handmade sphere:[61] because where the zodiac crosses through the equator, there the circle is said to be bound tight, and where it declines from it to the south or to the north, there it is said to be broad.

Indeed, Abū Ma'shar said[62] that two signs which are domiciles of one planet, are said to be agreeing in *journey*–like Aries and Scorpio, which are the domiciles of Mars; Taurus and Libra, which are the domiciles of Venus; Gemini and Virgo, which are the domiciles of Mercury; Sagittarius and Pisces, which are the domiciles of Jupiter; Capricorn and Aquarius, which are the domiciles of Saturn; Cancer and Leo, which are the domiciles of the luminaries.

On the joys of the planets according to Dorotheus

Dorotheus said[63] that Saturn rejoices in Aquarius, Jupiter rejoices in Sagittarius, Mars rejoices in Scorpio, Venus rejoices in Taurus, Mercury rejoices in Virgo.

Chapter 8: On the exaltations of the planets

Abū Ma'shar[64] and al-Qabīsī[65] said that the Sun is exalted in Aries, namely in its nineteenth degree. The Moon is exalted in Taurus, namely in its third degree. Saturn is exalted in Libra, namely in its twenty-first degree. Jupiter is exalted in Cancer, namely in its fifteenth degree. Mars is exalted in Capricorn, namely in its eighteenth degree. Venus is exalted in Pisces, namely in its twenty-seventh

---

"agreeing in the journey" (*at-tarīqah*, الطريقة)–see the next paragraph. There is some confusion here in the terminology which connects (a) having the same Lord or (b) having equal rising times, with (1) "agreeing in the belt [of the zodiac]" or (2) "agreeing in journey." Abū Ma'shar links (a2) and (b1), al-Qabīsī connects (a1), and al-Bīrūnī connects (b2). The confusion could simply be that a "zone" (*al-mintaqah*) is not that different from a "path" or "journey" (*at-tarīqah*), so that different astrologers wound up switching the terms. At any rate, signs ruled by the same domicile Lord are linked, and so are signs which have equal rising times (i.e., those which fall on opposite sides of the Aries-Libra axis: Aries and Pisces, Taurus and Aquarius, *etc.*).

[60] *Ligatura*, "ligature, band, twisting." Bonatti must be imagining the ecliptic as forming a knot or twisting sort of joining at the point where it crosses the celestial equator.

[61] According to Hand/Zoller (p. 33, n. 209), this is an armillary sphere, a brass instrument modeling the heavens.

[62] Abū Ma'shar, *Gr. Intr.* VI.6.

[63] Dorotheus, *Carmen* I.1; but clearly Bonatti is simply following al-Qabīsī's text (I.14).

[64] *Gr. Intr.*, V.5.

[65] Al-Qabīsī, I.15.

degree. Mercury is exalted in Virgo, namely in its fifteenth degree. The Head of the Dragon is exalted in Gemini, namely in its third degree. Its Tail is exalted in Sagittarius, namely in its third degree.

And Abū Ma'shar said[66] that the stated exaltations of the planets were in the above-said degrees, because they were in those degrees when they were formed.

Chapter 9: Why Aries is the exaltation of the Sun, and Libra his descension, and why the other signs are the exaltations of the planets

Abū Ma'shar said[67] that Ptolemy (the author of a book of judgments) said, that when the Sun enters Aries, he begins to ascend to the north, namely to the zenith above our heads, and then the day is increased in length over the night, and then his nature begins to be increased in heat, and especially when he descends to the nineteenth degree of Aries. And when he is in Libra, he begins to descend toward the south, by receding and elongating himself from the zenith above our heads; and day is decreased, and night is then increased over the day in its length, and then his nature begins to be diminished in heat, and his noble and useful operations are diminished, and especially when he descends to its nineteenth degree.

Moreover, Abū Ma'shar said[68] that he has found in the books of certain ancients that they made Taurus the exaltation of the Moon, because when the Sun is in Aries (which is his exaltation) and the Moon is in Taurus, then there will be an appearance of the Moon's light. And Taurus is even the first sign of the triplicity of the Moon, because [Taurus] follows the sign of the Sun's exaltation, and she is conjoined to the Sun in her own operations. And they made Scorpio her descension, because it is the opposite of her exaltation.

And they made Libra the exaltation of Saturn, and Aries his descension, on account of the fact that Saturn is opposite to the Sun in nature and operations, and therefore they were opposite their exaltations, just as they are opposite each other [by natural domicile] as was said above.

And they made Cancer the exaltation of Jupiter, because Jupiter by his own nature signifies northern winds, and when he is in Cancer, nourishing northern winds arise, and bestow growth on animating things, and they strengthen the

---

[66] *Gr. Intr.*, V.5.
[67] *Gr. Intr.*, V.6.
[68] *Gr. Intr.*, V.6.

nature of Jupiter. And they made Capricorn his descension, because it is opposite Jupiter's exaltation.

And they made Capricorn the exaltation of Mars, because Capricorn is southern [in declination], and is opposite the exaltation of Jupiter ([these planets] are inimical to each other); and because the nature of Mars is southern, burning up, and the heat of Mars is strengthened when he is in Capricorn. And they made Cancer his descension, because it is opposite his exaltation.

And they made Pisces the exaltation of Venus, because the nature of Pisces is moisture, agreeing with the nature of Venus; and then the moisture of the season begins to thrive, and the humidity of Venus is strengthened in it. And they made Virgo her descension, because it is opposite her exaltation.

And they made Virgo the exaltation of Mercury, because the dryness of the autumn season begins from it, and the nature of Mercury is drawn back to dryness (unless by accident). And if he were in Virgo, his dryness is strengthened. And they made Pisces his descension, because it is opposite his exaltation.

Indeed Gemini was made the exaltation of the Head of the Dragon, on account of the fact that Gemini is the first bicorporeal and common sign after Aries, and the Head is likewise bicorporeal, because it is composed of two natures (namely Jupiter's and Venus's, which are two benefics). Sagittarius was made the exaltation of the Tail of the Dragon, because Sagittarius is the opposite of Gemini, just as the Tail is opposite the Head.

Chapter 10: On the fall or descension of the planets

Abū Ma'shar[69] and al-Qabīsī[70] said that every seventh sign from the exaltation of any planet is said to be its descension or fall.

For the Sun falls in the nineteenth degree of Libra, just as he is exalted in the like degree of Aries.

The Moon falls or descends in Scorpio, just as she is exalted in Taurus, in a like degree.

Saturn falls or descends in Aries, just as he is exalted in Libra, in a like degree.

---

[69] *Gr. Intr.*, V.5.
[70] Al-Qabīsī, I.15.

Jupiter falls or descends in Capricorn, just as he is exalted in Cancer, in a like degree.

Mars falls or descends in Cancer, just as he is exalted in Capricorn, in a like degree.

Venus falls or descends in Virgo, just as she is exalted in Pisces, in a like degree.

Mercury falls or descends in Pisces, just as he is exalted in Virgo, in a like degree.

The Head of the Dragon falls in Sagittarius; the Tail in Gemini.

And there is a distinction between fall and descension, even though one is sometimes put down for the other: because "fall" is said peculiarly in regards to the domicile, descension is said in regards to the exaltation. Because a domicile is likened to one's own peculiar thing; indeed exaltation is likened to honors or dignities, both those coming to [one] and hereditary.

Chapter 11: On the four triplicities of the seven planets

The aforesaid philosophers said the triplicities are four; and they are distinguished so, namely because every three signs which agree in one nature and in one complexion, make one triplicity; and it is called a triplicity, like a "three-foldness."[71]

On the first triplicity

Therefore Aries, Leo, and Sagittarius make the first triplicity. For Aries is a fiery, hot, and dry sign; and so one sign is hot and dry. And likewise Leo is a hot and dry sign—and so two signs are hot and dry. And Sagittarius is a hot and dry sign—and so the hot and dry sign is tripled. And so the three signs become fitted [or agreeing] in one complexion. And this triplicity is said to be hot and dry, because each one of these signs is fiery, hot, dry, masculine, eastern, diurnal,

---

[71] *Trina plicitas*, from *tres* (three) and *plico* (to fold).

choleric, bitter in taste. And this triplicity is said to be eastern, the Lords of which triplicity are the Sun in the day, in the night Jupiter; whose participant in both day and night is Saturn.

On the second triplicity

Indeed Taurus, Virgo, and Capricorn make the second triplicity, because each one of these signs is earthy (namely cold and dry), feminine, nocturnal, melancholic, southern, sharp or acidic.[72] And this triplicity is said to be southern, the Lords of which triplicity are Venus in the day, in the night the Moon, whose participant in both day and night is Mars.

On the third triplicity

But Gemini, Libra, and Aquarius make the third triplicity, because each one of these signs is airy (namely hot and moist), masculine, diurnal, sanguine, western, sweet in taste. And this triplicity is said to be western, the Lords of whose triplicity are Saturn in the day, in the night Mercury, whose participant both in the day and night is Jupiter.

On the fourth triplicity

Also, Cancer, Scorpio, and Pisces make the fourth triplicity, because each one of these signs is watery (namely cold and moist), feminine, nocturnal, phlegmatic, salty in taste (and weak, according to certain people).[73] And this triplicity is said to be northern, the Lords of which triplicity are Venus in the day, and in the night Mars, whose participant both in the day and night is the Moon.

Chapter 12: On the movable, fixed, and common signs

Know that of the above-stated twelve signs, four are movable, namely: Aries, Cancer, Libra, Capricorn; and four are fixed, namely: Taurus, Leo, Scorpio, and Aquarius; the remaining four, namely Gemini, Virgo, Sagittarius and Pisces, are common.

---

[72] *Acre sive acetosum*. *Acer* means either sharp or pungent; *acetosus* has vinegary, i.e., acidic connotations.

[73] I.e., just as we say in English that something weak-tasting is "watered down."

But signs are called "movable," not because they are moved (unless like the other signs are), but they are called movable because when the Sun enters one of those signs, the disposition of the air changes then, nor does it persevere in that state in which it was.

But signs are called "fixed," because when the Sun enters one of those signs, then the air's disposition is fixed, and it perseveres and stays in that same state of fixedness and firmness (even if sometimes perhaps it is changed by accident, but it is not changed by nature).

Indeed, signs are called "common," because if the Sun were to enter one of those signs, the weather becomes common, nor is it truly called fixed, nor movable, but it participates with each, namely with the fixed and the movable. Whence part of the weather belongs to one, and part to the other.

For when the Sun enters Aries (which is a movable sign), then the weather (namely the disposition of the air) is changed, because then winter is turned into spring. And when he goes out of Aries and enters Taurus, then the weather is fixed, namely because then it perseveres in the state of spring. And when he goes out of Taurus and enters Gemini, then the weather of spring is changed, and is made partly vernal and partly summer-like. And when he goes out of Gemini and enters Cancer, then the weather is changed, and the weather is made summer-like. And when he goes out of Cancer and enters Leo, then the summer weather is fixed, and it perseveres in that same state. And when he goes out of Leo and enters Virgo, then the summer weather is changed, and is made partly summer-like and partly autumnal. And when he goes out of Virgo and enters Libra, then the weather is changed, and the weather is made autumnal. And when he goes out of Libra and enters Scorpio, then the autumnal weather is fixed and perseveres in the same state. And when he goes out of Scorpio and enters Sagittarius, then the weather becomes common, because it holds partly of the autumn and holds partly of the winter. And when he goes out of Sagittarius and enters Capricorn, then the weather is changed, and autumn is turned into winter. And when he goes out of Capricorn and enters Aquarius, then the winter weather is fixed, and perseveres in the same state. And when he goes out of Aquarius and enters Pisces, then the weather is made common, because it partly holds of the winter, and partly of the spring.

Chapter 13: On the aspects of the planets

Māshā'allāh[74] and al-Qabīsī[75] (and many other philosophers) said that the signs are said to look at each other by diverse aspects, namely by the sextile, square, trine, and opposition.

But the sextile aspect is that which has one-sixth of the heaven, namely 60° forwards or backwards.[76]

The square aspect is that which has one-fourth of the heaven, namely 90° forwards or backwards.

The trine aspect is said to be that which has one-third of the heaven, namely 120° forwards or backwards.

Indeed the aspect of the opposition is said to be that which has one-half of the heaven, namely 180°.

And it is said that the sextile aspect is a good aspect, and it is an aspect of medium (but not complete) friendship and agreement. And it is said to be an aspect of medium friendship, because it is drawn from Venus and from the luminaries, since the domiciles of Venus aspect the domiciles of the luminaries from a sextile aspect, as was said above. And therefore this aspect is said to be of medium friendship, because Venus is a semi-strong benefic, and not a perfect one.

And the square aspect is said to be moderately bad, and it is an aspect of medium enmity and disagreement,[77] but not of the complete [sort]. And it is

---

[74] Source unknown at this time.
[75] Al-Qabīsī, I.18.
[76] In this section, my word "forwards" (*ante*) means "in later degrees, forward in the order of signs"; my word "backwards" (*post*) means "in earlier degrees, backwards in the order of signs."
[77] *Discordia*, i.e., discord or a disagreement of hearts. Bonatti is explicitly opposing *discordia* to *concordia* (concord or agreement). I have retained "agreement" and "disagreement" instead of the more abstract "concord" and "discord" in order to help the reader recover some of the anthropomorphic imagery.

said to be an aspect of medium enmity, because it is drawn from Mars and from the luminaries, since the domiciles of Mars regard the domiciles of the luminaries from a square aspect, as was said above. And therefore this aspect is said to be of middle enmity, because Mars is a lesser malefic than Saturn is, just as Venus is a lesser benefic than Jupiter is.

But the trine aspect is said to be a good aspect, and it is an aspect of perfect friendship, and of perfect agreement, and complete goodness. And it is said to be an aspect of perfect friendship and agreement because it is drawn from Jupiter and from the luminaries, since the domiciles of Jupiter aspect the domiciles of the luminaries from a trine aspect. And therefore this aspect is said to be of perfect friendship, because Jupiter is a strong and perfect benefic beyond all the other benefics, [and] from whom no goodness is missing.

But the aspect of the opposition is said to be an evil aspect, and it is an aspect of extreme enmity, and extreme malice, and extreme disagreement. And such an aspect is said to be of extreme enmity, because it is drawn from Saturn and from the luminaries, since the domiciles of Saturn aspect the domiciles of the luminaries from the opposition. And therefore this aspect is said to be of extreme enmity, because Saturn is the greater malefic, and stronger beyond all the other malefics.

For example, of all the aforesaid aspects, let it be put that some planet is in the first degree of Aries. Then he aspects one who would be in the first degree of Gemini ahead of him, and the aspect is said to be an anterior sextile or "from the face." And he aspects one who would be in the first degree of Aquarius behind him, and that aspect is said to be posterior sextile, or "from the back." And such an aspect is said to be a hexagonal radiation, because it shines or aspects from a one-sixth portion of the heaven.

And he aspects one who would be in the first degree of Cancer ahead of him, and the aspect is said to be an anterior square or "from the face." And he aspects one who would be in the first degree of Capricorn behind him, and that aspect is said to be a square aspect "from the back," or posterior. And such an aspect is said to be a tetragonal radiation, because it shines or aspects from a one-fourth portion of the heaven.

And he aspects one who would be in the first degree of Leo ahead of him, and this aspect is said to be an anterior trine or "from the face." And he likewise aspects one who would be in the first degree of Sagittarius behind him, and that is said to be a posterior trine aspect or "from the back." And such as aspect is said to be a trigonal radiation, because it shines or aspects from a one-third portion of heaven.

And he aspects one who would be in the first degree of Libra, and this aspect is said to be the aspect of the opposition. (But certain people said that the opposition is not an aspect; I however do not assent to them.)

Whence if some planet were in these signs aspecting each other thus, [the former] is said to aspect another who is in the other, above-said signs, and [the latter] aspects [the former] with a like aspect.

And a planet who is in Taurus aspects him who is ahead of him in Cancer, and him who is behind him in Pisces, by a sextile aspect. And he aspects him who is ahead of him in Leo, and him who is behind him in Aquarius, by a square aspect. And he aspects him who is in Virgo ahead of him, and him who is behind him in Capricorn, by a trine aspect. And he aspects him who is in Scorpio by the opposition. And understand thusly about all the signs.

And just as the first degree of one sign aspects the first degree of another sign, so the second degree aspects the second degree, and the third the third, and the fourth the fourth. And understand thusly about all degrees.

Chapter 14: On the bounds of the five planets besides the luminaries

Five planets (namely Saturn, Jupiter, Mars, Venus, and Mercury) have distinguished and delimited bounds in every sign, according to how I will tell you below. They are called "bounds" or "ends" because when a planet is in those degrees, it is said to have a certain power which is called a "strength." And the philosophers found by long experience, that at such a time that a planet is in those degrees which are assigned to him as his bound in every sign, that it more strongly imprints in inferior things, than when it is in the other degrees of that same sign. And therefore they are called "bounds" because just as bounds are fixed by fields, they impose an end [limit], and they divide field from field; so those degrees assigned to a planet as its bound, impose an end on its virtue, and they divide the virtue of one planet from the virtue of the next.

And there was diversity among the ancients in the division of the bounds, because Ptolemy assigned two kinds of bounds according two opinions, namely that of the Egyptians and of the Chaldeans. And afterwards, he set down his own opinion, and followed the sayings of certain ancient people which he found in a certain very old book (as he reported it), and he approved of their sayings.

But Abū Ma'shar listed[78] five opinions of the bounds of the ancients, namely of the Egyptians, and Ptolemy, and the Chaldeans, and of a certain philosopher who was called Asthoatol,[79] and the Indians—the opinions of whom would take a long time to put down here. Wherefore I will dismiss them, and put down for you only the reasons which Ptolemy reported he had found in the said old book. For he, not wanting to boast, did not attribute the invention of those bounds to himself, but only to those whom he believed had written the book.[80] And he and Abū Ma'shar said[81] that the degrees of the bounds written below (which are noted in the present table) were so divided, and so attributed to the five planets, that by them the knowledge of the greater[82] years of every one of the five planets is given to us, concerning which, having been collected together as one, yielded 57 for Saturn, 79 for Jupiter, 66 for Mars, 82 for Venus, 76 for Mercury—the which having been collected together, they make 360°. And this was the reason why the greater years of the planets were to many, neither more nor less, because how many degrees each one of the five planets had as its bounds, so many are its greater years to be found. And this is a table showing the bounds themselves:[83]

---

[78] *Gr. Intr.*, V.8-13.
[79] The Latin edition of the *Gr. Intr.* by John of Seville reads *Asthoatnol*. This may be the (pseudo-) Aristotle who is quoted numerous times in the *Book of the Nine Judges* (1509, see Bibliography).
[80] And yet Ptolemy's miraculous "discovery" of the bounds he happened to believe were the best, does not seem to be an accident.
[81] Source unknown at this time.
[82] Reading *maximorum* for *malorum*.
[83] There are several errors in this table, undoubtedly due to distortions in how Ptolemy's table was passed down. In the following footnotes I give the corrected values based on Robert Schmidt's translation of Ptolemy.

♈	♃ – 6	♀ – 8	☿ – 7	♂ – 5	♄ – 4
♉	♀ – 8	☿ – 7	♃ – 7	♄ – 2[84]	♂ – 6[85]
♊	☿ – 7	♃ – 6	♀ – 7	♂ – 6	♄ – 4
♋	♂ – 6	♃ – 7	☿ – 7	♀ – 7	♄ – 3
♌	♄ – 6	☿ – 7	♂ – 5[86]	♀ – 6	♃ – 6[87]
♍	☿ – 7	♀ – 6	♃ – 5	♄ – 6	♂ – 6
♎	♄ – 6	♀ – 5	☿ – 5[88]	♃ – 8[89]	♂ – 6
♏	♂ – 6	♀ – 7[90]	♃ – 8[91]	☿ – 6	♄ – 3
♐	♃ – 8	♀ – 6	☿ – 5	♄ – 6	♂ – 5
♑	♀ – 6	☿ – 6	♃ – 7	♄ – 6	♂ – 5
♒	♄ – 6	☿ – 6	♀ – 8	♃ – 5	♂ – 5
♓	♀ – 8	♃ – 6	☿ – 6	♂ – 5[92]	♄ – 5[93]

Figure 1: Bonatti's Table of Bounds

And someone could ask why the philosophers so ordered the bounds of the planets. To which it can be responded thusly, that the reason for it was already assigned above; but yet another [reason] can be assigned, even though it is more lengthy. For the philosophers considered first the Lords of the exaltations, second the Lords of the triplicities, third the Lords of the domiciles. And if one of them had two of those dignities (whether it were a benefic or malefic), they put him in the beginning, and gave him the first bound. And if a malefic did not have two of those dignities so disposed, they put him in the last bound of the sign, and then they preferred the Lord of the exaltation, and gave him the first bound. Then they gave the second bound to the Lord of the triplicity; they gave the third to the Lord of the domicile; and thus everywhere they preferred him who had two dignities to him who had only one, with the exception of Cancer and Leo, because they are the domiciles of the luminaries (to which are not assigned distinct bounds by the signs as with the other planets)–and they are the

---

[84] This should be 4.
[85] This should be 4.
[86] This should be 6.
[87] This should be 5, and ruled by Mars.
[88] This should be 8.
[89] This should be 5.
[90] This should be 8.
[91] This should be 7.
[92] This should be 6.
[93] This should be 4.

domiciles opposite the domiciles of Saturn, who is a malefic. And because Cancer is opposite the exaltation of Mars, therefore its first bound was assigned to Mars, and the first bound of Leo was assigned to Saturn; and therefore these two [malefics] are preferred in those signs, because in all the other signs they are usually placed at their end (except for in Leo, where Jupiter is placed after [the others]).

And the aforesaid bounds are so divided, because since Jupiter or Venus did not have two of the said powers in the same sign, nor in the second nor in the third nor in the fourth, they gave seven degrees to [each] as its bound; five to Saturn, and five to Mars; to Mercury, because he is commingled, six degrees are assigned to him for his bound. And likewise, when some [planet] has two of the aforesaid powers in some sign, one is added to him, just as Venus even has domicile and triplicity in Taurus, and therefore they assigned eight degrees to her as her bound in the beginning of Taurus, and that degree is subtracted from the bound of Saturn. And another degree is even taken likewise from the bound of a planet having only one dignity or none, and especially from Saturn and Jupiter, on account of the slowness of their motions (as Ptolemy said), and out of such a bound a strength can be taken up, because it is said that if a planet is in its own bound, it is like a man living among his own parents, and among the peoples who relate to and who love him, whether they are kindred or related by birth or marriage.

Chapter 15: When the bound is preferred to the triplicity, and when the triplicity is preferred to the bound

There were certain philosophers who preferred the Lords of the bounds to the Lords of the triplicities (and to the triplicities themselves). And there were certain others who preferred the Lords of the triplicities and the triplicities themselves[94] to the Lords of the bounds and the bounds themselves. And every one of them had a reason why he did this: for the bounds and the Lords of the bounds are preferred in directing, and indeed the triplicities and the Lords of the triplicities are preferred in nourishing. What direction is and what nourishing is, will be handled below; but here I will attach something here about them.[95]

---

[94] Reading *ipsas* for *ipsorum*.
[95] Here Bonatti is using "direction" (*directio*) in two ways. The first has to do with assigning triplicity rulers for thirds of life; the second has to do with what we would normally call "primary direction," which is what Bonatti calls "direction" proper in Tr. 9.

For someone could say that nourishing and direction are the same, but it is not so: because direction comes to be through all the Lords of the triplicity of the Ascendant. For a Lord of the triplicity of the Ascendant or question generally disposes the life of the native or querent, according to three divisions from the beginning of the native's life up until the end of his natural life. For the first Lord of the triplicity of the Ascendant of the nativity disposes the first one-third of the native's life, the second disposes the second one-third of the native's life, the third disposes the last one-third of the native's life, up to the end of life. For I said "natural life," because death often takes [one] ahead of time, so that the native does not reach to the end of the natural [life]; or rather, he dies accidentally before he ought to die naturally–sometimes by iron, fire, a fall, [falling] ruins, drowning, sometimes being hanged, sometimes suffocation, sometimes by some acute, or very acute, or really very acute illness (which sometimes happens on account of a disorderly diet, and on account of a disorderly manner of living), and by many other ways. And according to the being [or condition] of the Lord of each one-third is judged the native's or querent's condition in that one-third of his life.

For example, someone was born [and] made a universal question[96] about his condition (or about his fortune) in his own life or in that year, with Taurus ascending–the Lords of whose triplicity are Venus, the Moon, and Mars. And Venus (who is the first Lady of this triplicity) will dispose the first one-third of his life; and the Moon (who is the second Lady of the same triplicity) will dispose the second one-third of his life; and Mars (who is the third Lord of its triplicity) will dispose the last one-third of his life. Whence if Venus were well disposed, it will be well for this in the first one-third of his life (namely in adolescence, practically up to the thirtieth year). And if Venus were badly disposed, it will be ill for him at that same age. And if the Moon were well disposed, it will be well for him in his youth (namely in the second one-third of his life, from virtually the thirtieth year up to the sixtieth); and if she were badly disposed, it will be ill for him at that same age. And if Mars were well disposed, it will be well for him in the last one-third of his life, namely in old age; and if he were badly disposed, it will be ill for him at that same age. And if one of the

---

[96] See Tr. 6. A general or universal question is asked when the querent wants a more general, evaluative answer about matters. For example, if I ask what my professional life will be like in some year, or whether I will experience an improvement, that is a general question. But if I ask whether I will get a *particular* promotion, or whether *this* person can help me, that is a "particular" question. As we will see by the time spans Bonatti lists, the question posed here is extremely general (and for that reason the answer will only be very general).

aforesaid significators were disposed in a middling way, it will be middling for him (namely for the native) in the age deputed to that significator (and understand thus about all of the triplicities and their Lords).

But if someone will say, "this plays a role in nativities and not in questions, since it is given in the nativity what should happen to a native," the response is that nativities are not always had,[97] but questions are–whence it is necessary for us to take barley for grain; and a question after the nativity is like an appeal after a sentence.[98]

Chapter 16: On the direction which comes to be through the Lords of the bounds

But direction comes to be through the Lords of the bounds in this way: for let it be put that the first degree of Gemini is ascending, which is the bound of Mercury up to the seventh degree of the same sign. Then Mercury will dispose the life of the native or querent for so many years as there are degrees of that same bound. And from the seventh degree of that same sign, up to its thirteenth degree is the bound of Jupiter: and then Jupiter will dispose the life of the native or querent for so many years as there are degrees of that same bound. And from the thirteenth up to the twentieth is the bound of Venus: and then Venus will dispose the life of the native or querent for so many years as there are degrees of that same bound. And from the twentieth up to the twenty-sixth is the bound of Mars: and then Mars will dispose the life of the native for so many years as there are degrees of that same bound. And from the twenty-sixth up to the end of the same sign is the bound of Saturn: and then Saturn will dispose the life of the native for so many years as there are degrees of that same bound. And understand thus with respect to all the signs and all the Lords of the bounds. And I will tell you at greater length and better (for greater understanding) when the direction of the degrees through the right circle and through the oblique circle are treated in the ninth[99] Treatise.

---

[97] That is, a native does not always know his birth time–or even the correct day. This is still true today in many countries.
[98] See Bonatti's other use of this analogy in Tr. 9, Part 1, Ch. 2.
[99] Lat. *Quarto*, "four." Evidently Bonatti's original plan for the book changed later on.

Chapter 17: On the faces of the signs

But the faces of the signs are distinguished thus: because every sign is divided into three equal parts, of which each one is called a "face," and each of them consists of 10°. The first of them begins from the start of Aries, and lasts up to the tenth full degree of the same, and it belongs to Mars. And the second begins from the start of the eleventh degree of the same Aries, and lasts until the twentieth full degree of it, and that second face belongs to the Sun. Indeed the third face begins from the start of the twenty-first degree of the same Aries, and lasts up to the end of the same, and the third face belongs to Venus. Likewise, the first face of Taurus begins from the start of the first degree of the same Taurus, and lasts up to the end of its tenth degree, and it belongs to Mercury. The second one begins from the beginning of its eleventh degree, and it lasts up to the end of the twentieth full degree of the same, and it belongs to the Moon. The third begins from the beginning of its twenty-first degree, and lasts up to its end, and it belongs to Saturn.

The first face of Cancer belongs to Venus, the second to Mercury, the third to the Moon. The first face of Leo belongs to Saturn, the second to Jupiter, the third to Mars. The first face of Virgo belongs to the Sun, the second to Venus, the third to Mercury. The first face of Libra belongs to the Moon, the second to Saturn, the third to Jupiter. The first face of Scorpio belongs to Mars, the second to the Sun, the third to Venus. The first face of Sagittarius belongs to Mercury, the second to the Moon, the third to Saturn. The first face of Capricorn belongs to Jupiter, the second to Mars, the third to the Sun. The first face of Aquarius belongs to Venus, the second to Mercury, the third to the Moon. The first face of Pisces belongs to Saturn, the second to Jupiter, the third to Mars.

And in order that each face of any sign, [and] whose planet it is, might be more easily and manifestly laid bare to you, I put for you here a table made of the faces of the signs.

♈	♂ – 10°	☉ – 10°	♀ – 10°
♉	☿ – 10°	☽ – 10°	♄ – 10°
♊	♃ – 10°	♂ – 10°	☉ – 10°
♋	♀ – 10°	☿ – 10°	☽ – 10°
♌	♄ – 10°	♃ – 10°	♂ – 10°
♍	☉ – 10°	♀ – 10°	☿ – 10°
♎	☽ – 10°	♄ – 10°	♃ – 10°
♏	♂ – 10°	☉ – 10°	♀ – 10°
♐	☿ – 10°	☽ – 10°	♄ – 10°
♑	♃ – 10°	♂ – 10°	☉ – 10°
♒	♀ – 10°	☿ – 10°	☽ – 10°
♓	♄ – 10°	♃ – 10°	♂ – 10°

Figure 2: Table of Faces

Chapter 18: In order to find out whose face any degree of any sign is

If at some time there were some degree of some sign in some question or in some matter (which came into your hands), and you wished to know, of the face, whose planet that degree was, take all the complete signs which there are from the beginning of Aries, up to the sign in which is that degree which you wished to know whose face it is, and triple those complete signs, and divide the sum which results by 7; and what remains to you below 7, will be the number of the faces already passed. Therefore, begin to project according to that number from Mars (who is the first planet to which a face is assigned), and add from above the faces already passed of that sign in which is the degree which you wished to know whose planet it is, and give to each planet one of those faces which remained to you in the number under 7 (namely the first to Mars, the second to the Sun, the third to Venus, the fourth to Mercury, the fifth the Moon, the sixth to Saturn, the seventh Jupiter), and see where the number is finished–and on whatever planet that face were to fall, it will be [that planet's].

For example, let it be put that the eleventh degree of Leo occurred to you, and you want to know whose face it is. Count the complete signs which there are prior to Leo (after the beginning of Aries), which are four: namely Aries, Taurus, Gemini, Cancer. Therefore, triple the 4, and you will have 12. Now divide 12 by 7, and in this way 5 will remain to you; you must add on top of 5, 2: namely the first and the second face of Leo, because the eleventh degree of

Leo is the second face of it (the first on account of the 10 complete degrees which have transpired of Leo, which make one face, and the second because you have one degree of the second face, namely the eleventh degree of Leo, which touches the second face). Thus from the 5 (which remain below 7), and from these two superadded ones, afterwards 7 are made. Therefore, begin to project from Mars and give one to Mars, one to the Sun, one to Venus, one to Mercury, one to the Moon, one to Saturn, and thus the number (namely the seventh) will fall upon the seventh planet from Mars, which is Jupiter. And therefore Jupiter is necessarily the Lord of the second face of Leo.

And understand thus concerning all the signs and all the faces–like if it is some degree of Virgo, and let it be put that the degree is from its twentieth degree up to the thirtieth, and you want to know whose face it is: count the complete signs which there are before Virgo (which are 5). Therefore triple them, and you will have 15. Now divide the 15 by 7, and 1 will remain to you. Add 3 on top of that (because the degree falls in the third face of Virgo), and they become 4. Therefore begin to count from Mars, and give to him one of those 4, one to the Sun, one to Venus; then one will remain, namely the fourth of those 4, which is given to Mercury–since that face (namely the third [face] of Virgo) will necessarily belong to Mercury, who is the fourth planet from Mars. And it will be so regarding all the faces.

Chapter 19: On the strengths of every planet in any of its own dignities

Since it was stated above concerning the powers of each planet in each of the signs, now it seems fitting to treat of their strengths in them.

Al-Qabīsī said[100] that the Lord of the domicile has five strengths, the Lord of the exaltation has four strengths, the Lord of the triplicity has three strengths, the Lord of the bound has two strengths, the Lord of the face has one strength. And according to this method, you can know the strengths of the planets in the signs–whence, whichever one were to have more strengths in some sign, he is said to be stronger in that place, and more powerful, and of greater authority.

Whence Māshā'allāh[101] preferred the Lord of the bound to the Lord of the triplicity, and al-Andarzagar preferred the Lord of the triplicity to the Lord of the bound–whence they seem to be contrary, but it is not so: because Māshā'allāh spoke and turned his intention concerning direction, and al-

---

[100] Al-Qabīsī, I.77.
[101] Source unknown.

Andarzagar was speaking and was turning his intention concerning nourishment; and thus both spoke well and the statement of each is well preserved. What direction and nourishment are, seems to me to have been well laid out for you above. And he gave[102] such an analogy of this matter:

> Wherefore when a planet is in its own domicile, it is like a man who is in his own home, for he is however much stronger in his own home by law, than in another one, and often [stronger] in fact than another who otherwise would be stronger than him—whence Trutanus, "every vassal stands [as] a rooster before his own gate."[103]

> And while it is in its own exaltation, it is like a man who is in his own kingdom and in his own glory, like a kingdom, civil authority,[104] a dukedom, and as are other lay dignities which can forsake him before his own matters do.

> And while it is in its own bound, it is like a man who is among his own kinsmen[105] and blood-relatives and those related by birth, and by kindred, and kin by marriage, and those who relate to him by kinship.

> And while it is in its own triplicity, it is like a man who is among his allies and his people, and underofficials and followers,[106] who obey him and follow him, who are not related to him out of kinship.

> And when it is in its own face, it is like a man who is among unknown people, as sometimes happens to foreigners, and the like, though he lives among them because of an art and profession or service, or because of some other craftsman's or lay art.[107]

---

[102] Bonatti is undoubtedly referring to al-Qabīsī (I.23), but al-Qabīsī's own examples derive from al-Kindī's *Forty Chapters*, I.69.
[103] Unknown. I note that *Trutanus* means "vagabond."
[104] *Potestaria*. A kind of medieval magistracy.
[105] This could mean "relatives," but in feudal times ones neighbors usually were related to one in some way.
[106] In feudal times, lords and leaders often had military vassals housed with them, or had other vassals who were pledged to defend his interests and fight when he bade them to.
[107] In other words, he has no special status (nor do the people around him), but he is valued by them as having practical advantages. Thus a planet in such a position would have some practical advantage but will not be especially noteworthy or aided—and when it signifies the native or querent, it would probably indicate work to be involved in accomplishing a goal.

Chapter 20: Which of the signs are called rational, and which having beautiful voices, and which domestic, and which having wings, and which four-footed

Al-Qabīsī said,[108] that of the signs four whole ones are called rational, namely Gemini, Virgo, Libra, Aquarius–and the first half of Sagittarius–whose images are shaped in the images of humans. And they are said to have beautiful voices, and they are said to thrive when they are in the east, because their virtue will appear somewhat better, and will be [more] strong, when they are in the eastern quarter, than when in one of the other quarters.

And three of them are said to have wings, namely Gemini, Virgo, and Pisces.

And four complete ones of them are said to be complete quadrupeds, namely Aries, Taurus, Leo, and Capricorn–and the last half of Sagittarius.

And three of them are said to be domestic, because they are shaped in the images of domestic animals: namely Aries, Taurus, and Capricorn. And the [first] two, namely Aries and Taurus, are said to thrive in the south, because their virtue appears somewhat more and more fitly so in the southern quarter, than when in one of the other quarters.

And two of them are said to thrive in the north, namely Virgo and Aquarius. Indeed, certain people said that Virgo thrives in the east and in the north.

Indeed Capricorn thrives in the south and in the north. Aries and Taurus thrive in the south (as al-Qabīsī says).[109] Virgo, Capricorn, and Aquarius are said to thrive when they are in the north.

And of the signs, certain ones are called defective[110] and crooked, as are Aries, Taurus, Cancer, Scorpio, and Capricorn.

And certain ones of them are said to be having many offspring, namely Cancer, Scorpio, and Pisces. Whence if there came to be a question about children, and the Ascendant,[111] or the Lord of the Ascendant, or the house of children, or the Lord of the house of children, or the Moon, were in one of those signs, it is said to signify many children, unless something else impedes (as will be stated in the chapter on children).[112] And these three are said to thrive in the west.

---

[108] Al-Qabīsī, I.24.
[109] Al-Qabīsī, I.24.
[110] *Vitiosa.* This could also mean "wicked" or "depraved."
[111] Omitting an extra *fuerit*, as below with the half-voiced signs.
[112] See Treatises 6, 7, and 9, in the sections on the 5th House.

And three of them are said to be sterile: namely Gemini, Leo, and Virgo. Whence if a question arose about children, and some one of the aforesaid significators were found in one of the aforesaid signs, it signifies sterility, unless something else assists (as will be stated below in the chapter on children).

And six of them are said to be having few children, namely Aries, Taurus, Libra, Sagittarius, Capricorn, and Aquarius. Whence if a question arose about children, and some one of the aforesaid significators were found in any one of these six signs, it signifies a scarcity of children.

And four of them are said to be very defective, namely Aries, Taurus, Leo, and Capricorn.

And of the signs, certain ones are said to be having half a voice, as are whose which are shaped in the image of animals bleating, lowing, and roaring: as are Aries, Taurus, Leo, and Capricorn, and the last half of Sagittarius. Whence if the Ascendant or the Lord of the Ascendant or the Moon were in one of these signs in someone's nativity, the native will be of little discourse unless something else assists, as will be stated in the Treatise on nativities.[113]

And certain ones of them are said to be lacking in voice, namely those which are shaped in the images of animals lacking in voice, as are Cancer, Scorpio, and Pisces. Whence if the Ascendant or the Lord of the Ascendant or the Moon were in those signs, it signifies that the native will lack a voice unless something else assists (as I will tell you in the said Treatise on nativities, if God wills).

And two of them are said to be dark, namely Libra and Capricorn. Whence if the Ascendant or the Lord of the Ascendant or the Moon were impeded in one of these signs in someone's nativity, it signifies that the native will have a dull[114] or dark face.

And there is even a certain place in the signs which is said to be burnt [combust], namely the *via combusta*,[115] which is from the middle of Libra up to the middle of Scorpio.

But you could ask what usefulness there is in this thing which al-Qabīsī said—that the signs are said to thrive in the east or south, west or north; and that certain ones are said to be rational, certain ones four-footed, certain ones domestic, certain ones having a beautiful voice, certain ones half a voice, certain

---

[113] Bonatti does not in fact discuss this in Tr. 9, another sign that Tr. 2 was written before it. But see below, he begins to discuss this very topic.
[114] *Obtusae. Obtusus* has connotations of stupidity, so just as we say that someone speaks or looks brightly (suggesting intelligence and engagement), so Bonatti must mean that such a native will be unengaged and seemingly unintelligent in speech and appearance.
[115] The combust way or "burnt path/way."

ones lacking in voice. To which it must be responded that the philosopher's intention in this was namely that when someone is born, and his significator[116] or the Moon were in those signs, that the native's nature and being will be according to the being of the significator or the Moon in that sign–like if the significator, the Moon, and the Ascendant were [all] in one of the signs shaped in the images of humans, that the native will be more rational, and speak more and better than he who is born with his significators appearing in other signs. And if someone is born with the significator and the Moon and the Ascendant appearing in one of the signs shaped in the image of the lowing or bleating or roaring animals, then the native will speak less and will know less how to organize his words. And if someone is born with the significator and the Moon and the Ascendant appearing in signs which are lacking in voice and roaring and lowing and bleating, then the native will be a stutterer and speak little. And if the significator of the nativity or the Moon (namely only one [of them]) were impeded, the native will speak less according to the quantity of the impediment. And if both were impeded, the native will speak less again, and worse, so that he would hardly utter a word unless with labor and fatigue. Indeed if the significator of the nativity and the Moon were impeded in one of the signs lacking a voice, then the native will be mute–and more strongly so, if that sign were ascending.

And the signs are said to thrive in the quarters (as was said) because their virtue appears more then, when they are in those quarters–not that they had different significations in one quarter than in another, but it is with them in the same manner as it is for a tree which is in winter the same as it is in summer and spring, but in the beginning of spring it begins to bloom, when its leaves and flowers are expanded, but it remains the same tree which it was before. And Leo, which thrives in all quarters, is likened to trees thriving in all seasons of the year, like olive, pine, scarlet oak,[117] juniper, *etc.*

Chapter 21: Which part of the body each sign is said to have, and what signification in every limb, and which moral qualities of men, and what it signifies of seeds and regions, and the like

The body of a man is divided into twelve parts, in the likeness of the twelve signs; and each sign is said to have one of those parts.

---

[116] This must mean the Lord of the Ascendant, based on Bonatti's previous comments.
[117] Reading the singular as *ilex*, also known as black, red, and Spanish oak.

On Aries

For Aries has, of the body of man, the head and the whole face: whence it is said,[118] "And because the power of the ram is on the top of his head,"[119] therefore not undeservedly does it possess the head. Of regions,[120] Babylonia and Babel and Persia and Azerbaijan,[121] and Palestine. And Aries is said to have the head because the virtue or power of the ram thrives more in the head than in any other part of it. And Aries is said to have the aforesaid regions because those things which are signified by Aries appear more in those regions than in others.

On Taurus

Taurus has, of the body of man, the neck up to the beginning of the shoulders: whence it is said, "From there the bull has the neck for a like reason, whence [his] place is said to be following him [Aries]." And it has virtue in trees which are planted. And Taurus is said to have the neck, because [the bull's] power thrives more in the neck than in another part of it. And of regions it has as-Sawad,[122] Mahan [or Hamadan][123] and the land of the Kurds.[124] And Taurus is said to have those regions because his significations appear more in those regions than in others.

On Gemini

Gemini has, of the body of man, the shoulders, from the beginning [of them] onwards, and the arms and the hands: whence it is said, "From the shoulders it

---

[118] I am not sure where Bonatti is getting his astrological poetry, but I will translate as best I can.

[119] This phrase, undoubtedly from a poem (along with all of those following) seems to play on the words *vervex* (ram) and *vertex* (top).

[120] In what follows, Bonatti is using al-Qabīsī's chorography almost exclusively; but I do not understand why the Latin transliterations of the Arabic are not more accurate. Note also that few of the places have anything to do with Europe, as was to be expected from Arab and Persian sources. I take my chorography (so far as it seems best to match) from Burnett's translation of al-Qabīsī.

[121] Lat. *Adrabigen*.

[122] Lat. *Alzemiet*.

[123] Lat. *Almechin*.

[124] Lat. *Aricorad*.

presses forward; it possesses both twins [or what is doubled]"¹²⁵–from there, because from the shoulders a man is doubled. And it signifies the generosity and goodness of the soul of the native, if it were the Ascendant of someone's nativity. And of regions it is said to have Gurgan,¹²⁶ Greater Armenia, Azerbaijan, and Egypt. And it is said to have the shoulders and arms and hands, because a man is doubled from the shoulders onwards toward the hands. And it is said to have these regions because its significations appear more in those regions than in others.

On Cancer

Cancer has, of the part of the body of man, the chest up to near the diaphragm, and the adjacent things in those parts, and the lungs (and al-Qabīsī said¹²⁷ that it likewise has the spleen): whence it is said, "Therefore the Crab is called a celestial sign, because with [its] great chest it has the hollows of the chest."¹²⁸ And of regions it has Lesser Armenia, and it has the eastern part of Khorasan,¹²⁹ and China,¹³⁰ and it has a portion in Balkh¹³¹ and Azerbaijan. And it has virtue in tall trees which lose leaves in autumn, as do the poplar and the like. And it is said to have those regions because its significations appear more in those regions than in others.

On Leo

Leo has, of the body of man, the stomach and the heart and the lower part of the chest, where spiritedness¹³² thrives, and the diaphragm and the sides of the spine. And it signifies a hot, cunning man, and one who is much distressed and saddened; and likewise the spine of the back and *ilia*:¹³³ whence it is said, "From there Leo equally rules the lower part of the chest, below which the spirited part

---

¹²⁵ Hand/Zoller (p. 50) reads: "From the shoulders it strives to possess both of things brought in twos" (p. 50).
¹²⁶ Lat. *Iurgen*.
¹²⁷ Al-Qabīsī, I.28.
¹²⁸ Hand/Zoller (p. 50) reads: "Whence it has been called Cancer, and the celestial sign is so-called because like a great breast it possesses the hollows of the breast" (p. 50).
¹²⁹ Lat. *Huracen*. Burnett spells this: Hurasan.
¹³⁰ Lat. *Acin*.
¹³¹ Lat. *Baurath*. Burnett spells this "Balh."
¹³² *Animositas*, also "vehemence, wrath, boldness." In Plato, the emotional or "spirited" part of the soul was the seat of violent emotions like these.
¹³³ The lower part of the belly from the ribs to the pubes.

thrives."[134] And it has virtue in noble trees, like the silver-fir, the fir tree, and other trees which make many leaves without fruit and keep them in winter. And of regions it is said to have the land of the Turks[135] up to the end of the inhabited areas, and it has Mauritania and all its limits. And it is said to have those regions because its significations appear more in those regions than in others.

On Virgo

Virgo has, of the body of man, the belly and navel and the parts adjacent to the navel, and the intestines: whence it is said, "The navel has the boundaries [of] virginity, because the sign of Virgo cherishes it."[136] And it signifies the generosity and good will of him whose Ascendant it was at the hour of the nativity. And it signifies all seeds which are sown. And of regions it has Garamaqa,[137] and Syria[138] and the regions which are next to the Euphrates, and the Arabian peninsula,[139] and Persia.[140] And it is said to have those regions because its significations appear more in those regions than in the others (except that the signification which it has over seeds is generally for the whole earth).

On Libra

Libra has, of the body of man, the loins and the haunches, and the lower part of the belly up to the upper parts of the thigh, and it has the lower part of them, and it even has the buttocks. And it is said to have the haunches because a man begins to be practically balanced [or poised] there, because the haunches are made in a certain way in the manner of a balance-scale: whence it is said, "From

---

[134] Hand/Zoller (p. 51) reads: "Leo equally rules the lower part of the breast below which the spirit flourishes."
[135] Lat. *Achuthu*.
[136] Hand/Zoller (p. 51) reads: "The umbilicus has the borders of virginity." I have included the following clause in the quote, else the line from the poem would not refer explicity to Virgo as it has with the other signs.
[137] Lat. *Algeranica*.
[138] Lat. *Asten*.
[139] Al-Qabīsī's Arabic (which we should prefer here) is *al-Gazira* or "the island," a colloquial term for the Arabian peninsula (Burnett keeps the Arabic spelling). Modern readers may recognize the word as the name of the Arab television station *Al-Jazeera*. But John of Seville evidently believed the "island" or peninsula was Spain, hence he says *insulam quae Hispania* ("the island, which is Spain"). Bonatti follows him by saying *Hispaniam magnam*, "Great Spain."
[140] Lat. *Ferim*.

here[141] the balanced man begins thus to be forked [in two], and Libra draws the symbol of its name from that."[142] And Libra has all trees which Leo has, and on top of them those which grow quickly and quickly bear fruit, as do the peach and the almond and the like. And it even signifies the generosity and goodness of the mind, like Virgo. And of regions it has Apulia, Rome, and the lands of the Romans and their limits up to Ifriqiya[143] and Egypt,[144] and up to Ethiopia and Barqa,[145] as al-Qabīsī says.[146] And it has Kirman[147] and Sigistan,[148] and Kabul,[149] and Tabaristan,[150] Balkh,[151] and Herat.[152] And it is said to have those regions because its significations appear more in those regions than in others.

On Scorpio

Scorpio signifies, in the body of man, the private parts, and the whole thigh, and the bladder: whence it is said, "Scorpio, raised up from its stinging tail, rules the individual members of the penis and of Venus."[153] And it signifies generosity and goodness of soul, as do Virgo and Libra. And it signifies the trees which Cancer signifies, namely poplars and those which are of great height, which lose leaves in the autumn. And of regions, it has the Hejaz,[154] and the land of the Arabs, and their limits up to Yemen.[155] And it has a participation in Sind.[156] And

---

[141] Reading *hinc* for *huic*.
[142] Hand/Zoller (reading *huic*) reads "Level to this a man thus begins to be forked, and from this the Scales assume the omen of the name" (p. 51).
[143] Lat. *Aspicam*. The Arabic concept of Ifriqiya (Lat. *Africa*) covered portions of western Libya, Tunisia, and eastern Algeria. It was so-called because portions of this coincided with the ancient Roman province of "Africa" (which was not considered a continent in ancient times).
[144] Lat. *Azait*.
[145] Lat. *Barchan*.
[146] Al-Qabīsī, I.31.
[147] Lat. *Carmem*.
[148] Lat. *Segesten*.
[149] Lat. *Chebil*.
[150] Lat. *Cubrasten*.
[151] Lat. *Bacharch*.
[152] Lat. *Haugnoth*.
[153] Hand/Zoller (p. 51) read: "The Scorpion, pricking itself with its tail raised above itself, rules the pubic hair and each of the members of Venus." I say "penis," because the pubic hair (also *pecten*) has no limbs; and *pecten* signifies certain long instruments and long veins in wood—it must be a metaphor, so that the phrase refers to male and female genitals, respectively.
[154] Lat. *Helohiget*.
[155] Lat. *Argemon*.
[156] Lat. *Aceuith*, like *Acuich* below.

it is said to have these regions because its significations appear more in those regions than in others.

On Sagittarius

Sagittarius has, of the body of man, the hips: whence it is said, "Venus and the arrow equally are shot from the bow; and from the thighs the mighty horse delivers [or guides] what is loosed."[157] And it signifies an ingenious and clever man, and one who knows how to do many things and how take affairs concerning which he gets involved to the end which he wills; and who knows how to seduce men and lead them to those things which he wants (whether he wants to do good things or bad); and men rely on [or confide in] him, and he sometimes deceives them (even if not always under a pretext such that he would pretend to do well and is [really] a seducer—nor is it believed that he is one), but rather he is believed to be lawful; nor however is he totally faithful, nor totally unfaithful. And of regions it has Ethiopia, Mahruban,[158] and India. And it is said to have those regions because its significations appear more in those regions than in others.

On Capricorn

Capricorn has, of the body of man, the knees: whence it is said, "The goat grazing on the bank kneels on its knees." And it signifies a man who knows how to lead a good life, and one easy to anger, and who knows well how to provide and to look after his own business affairs, and even those of others. And he will know well how to counsel those seeking advice from him; and a clever man in good things and bad, if he wished; and likewise a man who is often and easily saddened. And of regions and lands it signifies the western part of Ethiopia up to Yemen[159] (where two seas are joined), and up to *Iacinthum*[160] and Lower India. And it is said to have those regions because its significations appear more in those regions than in others.

---

[157] Uncertain translation of second phrase. Hand/Zoller (p. 52) leave this phrase outside of the quote: "'Both Venus and an arrow are shot from the bow.' It is powerful in the thighs and the horse governs the flux [of blood]."
[158] Lat. *Maharobean*. This must be a mistake because al-Qabīsī attributes Mahruban to Capricorn below. Mahruban was a port city in Persia (modern Iran) located near the city of Daylam, off the coast of the Persian Gulf.
[159] Lat. *Ysmon*.
[160] Unknown. Could this be Sind? I think the location is right, but Bonatti's name is not like his other spellings of Sind.

On Aquarius

Aquarius has, of the body of man, the legs from the knees up to the ankles of the feet, so that it has the whole ankle: whence it is said, "And it denotes the legs, making the long shape of vessels; a man like a pourer of water in the cold."[161] And of regions it signifies *Azenguch*[162] and part of the black land of *Ceclem*,[163] and Kufa,[164] and those parts touching on it, and all of *Elfigem*;[165] and part of west Egypt, and the western part of Sind.[166] And it is said to have those regions because its significations appear more in those regions than in others.

On Pisces

Pisces has, of the body of man, the feet: whence it is said, "And Fortune makes the feet like fishes, and put together as though with spiny bones."[167] And it signifies a clever man, mixed up and not lasting long in his own proposal. And sometimes it signifies a very colored man, and sometimes it signifies a man of commingled colors. And of regions, it has Tabaristan[168] and the northern part of Gurgan.[169] And it has signification over the lands of the Romans[170] up to Syria.[171] And over Italy likewise it has a signification, and especially over *Romaniola*[172] and up to Marche[173] up to Venice. And it even has a participation in Egypt and Alexandria and the sea of *Aluven*.[174]

---

[161] Hand/Zoller, leaving the second phrase out of the quote, read: "'The legs fashioning the long form of the vessels.' It denotes a man like one who pours water from the coldness" (p. 52).
[162] Unknown.
[163] Unknown.
[164] Lat. *Alkulfa*.
[165] Unknown.
[166] Lat. *Acuich*.
[167] Hand/Zoller (leaving the second phrase out of the quote) read: "'They have been put together as if out of spiny bones.' Fortune makes the feet for Pisces" (p. 52).
[168] Lat. *Thabracen*.
[169] Lat. *Iurgen*.
[170] I.e., of the Byzantines.
[171] Lat. *Adessen*.
[172] Perhaps a portion of the modern Italian province of Emilia-Romagna.
[173] Lat. *Marchia*. Marche is a province on the eastern edge of Italy.
[174] Unknown.

Chapter 22: What part of the body each planet signifies in every sign

It was spoken above on the twelve signs and what part of the body each of them signifies; now however we must discuss what part of the body each planet signifies in every sign.[175] And we must begin from the Saturn (the first planet) and from Aries (the first sign). Whence if a question were put to you about some infirmity or about some pain which someone suffers, see then in what sign the significator of the querent (namely of the infirm person) is, and which it is:

> Which if it were Saturn and he were in Aries, it signifies an illness or pain in the chest: because Saturn, when he is in Aries, signifies the chest in the body of man; Jupiter the belly; Mars the head; the Sun the thighs; Venus the feet; Mercury the legs; the Moon the knees. And understand thus with regard to all the signs.[176]

> In Taurus: Saturn the belly; Jupiter the back; Mars the neck; the Sun the knees; Venus the head; Mercury the feet; the Moon the legs.

> In Gemini: Saturn the belly; Jupiter the private parts and those which follow them;[177] Mars the chest; the Sun the legs and ankles of the feet; Venus the neck; Mercury the head; the Moon the thighs.

> In Cancer: Saturn the male genitals and what follows them; Jupiter the thighs; Mars the chest; the Sun the feet; Venus the shoulders and arms and hands; Mercury the eyes; the Moon the head.

> In Leo: Saturn the private parts and what follows them; Jupiter the thighs and knees; Mars the belly; the Sun the head; Venus the heart; Mercury the shoulders and throat; the Moon the neck.

---

[175] The list follows al-Qabīsī, I.37-48.
[176] The rationale behind these attributions is that when a planet is in its own domicile, it signifies the head; in the following sign, the neck; and so on. Thus Mars, which rules Aries, will signify the infirm person's head if he is the significator of the infirm person and happens to be in Aries at the time the chart is cast.
[177] By "those which follow them," understand the "area around" them or what "spreads out from" them.

In Virgo: Saturn the feet; Jupiter the knees; Mars the belly; the Sun the neck; Venus the navel and the parts adjacent to it; Mercury the heart; the Moon the shoulders.

In Libra: Saturn the knees and what follows them; Jupiter the eyes and what is spread around them; Mars the private parts and what follows them; the Sun the shoulders; Venus the head; Mercury the private parts; the Moon the heart.

In Scorpio: Saturn the ankles of the feet and what follows them; Jupiter the feet; Mars the head, arms and thighs; the Sun the heart; Venus the private parts and what follows them; Mercury the back; the Moon the belly.

In Sagittarius: Saturn the feet; Jupiter the legs and head; Mars the feet and hands; the Sun the belly; Venus the thighs and arms; Mercury the private parts and heart; the Moon the back.

In Capricorn: Saturn the head and feet; Jupiter the knees and eyes; Mars the legs and shoulders; the Sun the back; Venus the thighs and heart; Mercury the private parts and what follows them; the Moon the thighs and what follows the private parts.

In Aquarius: Saturn the head and neck; Jupiter the shoulders and chest and feet; Mars the ankles and heart; the Sun the private parts and what follows them; Venus the knees and what follows them; Mercury the thighs and heart; the Moon the private parts.

In Pisces: Saturn the neck, shoulders and arms; Jupiter the head and heart; Mars the belly and the ankles of the feet; the Sun the thighs and what follows them; Venus the neck and back; Mercury the legs and private parts; the Moon the thighs.

Chapter 23: On the masculine degrees and feminine degrees in each sign

Abū Ma'shar[178] and al-Qabīsī[179] said that in every sign there are certain degrees, of which certain ones are called masculine, and certain ones which are called feminine. For the first eight degrees of Aries are called masculine, and its next five degrees are called feminine, then six masculine ones, then seven feminine ones, and then four masculine ones up to the end of the sign. And the first five degrees of Taurus are feminine, then six masculine ones, then six feminine ones, then four masculine ones, then three feminine ones, then six masculine ones.

And lest this work be excessively prolonged, and to avoid its prolixity, I will describe all of them to you in the table noted below, composed according to the said philosophers:

♈	8–M	5–F	6–M	7–F	4–M		
♉	5–F	6–M	6–F	4–M	3–F	6–M	
♊	5–F	11–M	6–F	4–M	4–F		
♋	2–M	6–F	2–M	2–F	11–M	4–F	3–M
♌	5–M	3–F	7–M	8–F	7–M		
♍	8–F	4–M	8–F	10–M			
♎	5–M	10–F	5–M	7–F	3–M		
♏	4–M	10–F	3–M	8–F	5–M		
♐	2–M	3–F	7–M	12–F	6–M		
♑	11–M	8–F	11–M				
♒	5–M	10–F	6–M	4–F	2–M	3–F	
♓	10–M	10–F	3–M	5–F	2–M		

Figure 3: Masculine and Feminine Degrees

You could perhaps ask why these degrees are called masculine, and why they are called feminine. The reason why the philosophers named them so, is this: because if there is a question about some matter in which it would be necessary for you to discern sex–as sometimes happens when it is asked about a woman having [a child] in her uterus, whether she bears a male or female one; or about a thief, whether it is male or female, and the like, and were the significator of the quaesited matter, or the Moon, found in one of those degrees which are called

---

[178] *Gr. Intr.*, V.19.
[179] Al-Qabīsī, I.49.

masculine, it attests to masculinity; and if it were found in one of those which are called feminine, it attests to femininity–and especially if the other signs of masculinity or femininity concur, as will be stated below in the Treatise on judgments, in the chapter on children and in the chapter on thievery.[180]

Chapter 24: On the bright, dark, smoky, and empty degrees

Abū Ma'shar[181] and al-Qabīsī [182]said that there are certain degrees in the signs, of which certain ones are called bright, certain ones dark, certain ones smoky, certain ones empty.

Whence the first three degrees of Aries are called dark; then five degrees of the same sign are called bright; then eight dark; then four bright; then four dark; the five bright; then one dark. The first three degrees of Taurus are dark; four bright; four empty; three bright; five empty; eight bright; three dark. And in order that I may explain myself more quickly, I will give you a table of these degrees made according to the same philosophers:

♈	3–D	5–B	8–D	4–B	4–D	5–B	1–D
♉	3–D	4–B	4–E	3–B	5–E	8–B	3–D
♊	4–B	3–D	5–B	4–E	6–B	5–D	3–E
♋	12–B	2–D	4–E	2–S	8–B	2–E	
♌	10–D	10–S	5–E	5–B			
♍	5–D	3–B	2–E	6–B	6–S	5–E	3–D
♎	5–B	5–D	8–B	3–D	6–B	3–E	
♏	3–D	5–B	6–E	6–B	2–S	5–E	3–D
♐	9–B	3–D	7–B	4–S	7–B		
♑	7–D	3–B	5–S	4–B	3–D	3–E	5–D
♒	4–S	5–B	4–D	8–B	4–E	5–B	
♓	6–D	6–B	6–D	4–B	3–E	3–B	2–D

Figure 4: Bright, Dark, Smoky, and Empty Degrees

For the above-stated degrees are called [this] for this reason: because if it appeared, by the Lord of the Ascendant of someone's nativity (or through the Lord of some nativity,[183] or through the Moon), that the native (or him about

---

[180] See Tr. 6, the sections on the 5th and 7th Houses.
[181] *Gr. Intr.*, V.20.
[182] Al-Qabīsī, I.50.
[183] It is not clear to me how Bonatti distinguishes the "Lord of the nativity" from the "Lord of the Ascendant" of the nativity. See especially Tr. 9.

whom the question [was]), ought to be of a bright color and a beautiful face; and if they were in one of the bright degrees, that he will then be clear and very handsome. Indeed if it were in the dark ones, he will be less handsome. And if it were in the smoky ones, he will be in between each, that is, he will be neither beautiful nor exceedingly ugly. And if the aforesaid significator or the Moon were in the dark degrees, and if the native were supposed to be ugly, he will be uglier and more filthy. And if it were in the bright ones, he will be less ugly and less filthy than he was supposed to be according to the nature of the Lord of the Ascendant. And if it were in empty degrees, whether he is handsome or ugly he will be of little sense and a small intellect–smaller than it would appear. And by however much more you were to inquire into his sense, or his intellect, by that much more will it displease you, and he will seem to you less strong with respect to other men, and he will said to be empty[-headed] by all.

Chapter 25: On the welled degrees

And the same philosophers said[184] that in the signs there are certain degrees which are called "welled,"[185] concerning which they likewise made a table noted below:[186]

♈	6th	9th	11th	17th	23rd	29th
♉	5th	13th	18th	24th	25th	
♊	2nd	12th	17th	26th	30th	
♋	12th	17th	23rd	26th	30th	
♌	6th	13th	15th	22nd	23rd	28th
♍	8th	13th	16th	21st	25th	
♎	1st	7th	20th	30th		
♏	9th	10th	22nd	23rd	27th	
♐	7th	12th	15th	24th	27th	30th
♑	2nd	7th	17th	22nd	24th	28th
♒	1st	12th	17th	23rd	29th	
♓	4th	9th	24th	27th	28th	

Figure 5: Welled Degrees

---

[184] Al-Qabīsī, I.51; *Gr. Intr.* V.21.
[185] *Puteales.* In English these are usually called the "pitted" degrees; but a *puteus/puteum* is a well or excavation, and Bonatti explicitly uses the proper word for "pit" (*foveum*) later in his description as an example, not as a definitional description of these degrees.
[186] I have based this table on al-Qabīsī, as Bonatti's 1550 table departs from al-Qabīsī and is littered with hand-written corrections.

But the degrees are called "welled" because if the significator of someone's nativity, or the significatrix (which is the Moon, which has participation in every matter) were in one of those degrees, it is said that it is in a well, namely in a certain weakness, just as is one who wants to go to some place, and is in some great pit (or in some valley or a cavern made in the manner of a well), wherefore he cannot do so freely, nor so quickly as he wishes; nor so quickly as one can go who is in a flat place outside the well; for he who is outside a well is not impeded without [nevertheless] being able to go more quickly than someone who is in the well. And so the native or querent is impeded in perfecting his business if his significator of the Moon is in some welled degree, nor can he lead it quickly to effect; and he will perfect it with great burden and with a greater complication than another who is not impeded by that impediment.

Chapter 26: On the degrees of *azemena*[187]

Ptolemy and al-Qabīsī[188] and others said that there are certain degrees in certain signs which are said to be of the *azemena*, that is, of a weakness. But *azemena* is a certain inseparable illness of the body, which often is acquired in the maternal uterus: however long the native were to live, he will always have it with him. And it is an illness inseparable from the native's body, like natural blindness, natural deafness, lameness, natural hunchbackness, and the like—concerning which degrees the table written below was made:[189]

♉	6th, 7th, 8th, 10th
♋	9th, 10th, 11th, 12th, 13th, 14th, 15th
♌	18th, 27th, 28th
♏	19th, 29th
♐	1st, 7th, 8th, 18th, 19th
♑	26th, 27th, 29th
♒	10th, 18th, 19th

Figure 6: Degrees of *Azemena*

---

[187] So far as I know, no one has been able to tell what disease *azemena* was.
[188] Al-Qabīsī, I.52.
[189] Again, I base the table on al-Qabīsī.

Chapter 27: On the degrees increasing fortune

The same philosophers said[190] that in the signs there are certain degrees which are called "degrees increasing fortune,"[191] concerning all of which the table noted below is made:[192]

♈	19th
♉	3rd, 15th, 27th
♊	11th
♋	1st, 2nd, 3rd, 14th, 15th
♌	3rd, 5th, 7th, 17th
♍	3rd, 12th, 20th
♎	3rd, 5th, 21st
♏	7th, 12th, 20th
♐	13th, 20th
♑	12th, 13th, 14th, 20th
♒	7th, 17th, 20th
♓	13th, 20th

Figure 7: Degrees Increasing Fortune

Chapter 28: On the degrees having power together and conforming in virtue

Al-Qabīsī said[193] that two degrees which are of one length from the beginning of the movable signs are said to be "having power together"—that is, they are said to be of one strength, and they are said to be participants and strengthened in virtue:[194] as are the twentieth degree of Capricorn (so that the twentieth is included)[195] and the tenth of Sagittarius (so that the tenth is included), and the twentieth degree of Cancer with the tenth degree of Gemini. For so much separates the tenth degree of Sagittarius from the beginning of Capricorn, as it

---

[190] Al-Qabīsī, I.53.
[191] I note that the exaltation degrees for the Sun, Moon, Saturn, and Jupiter are on the list; otherwise I do not know why these degrees were chosen. Perhaps at one time there were benefic fixed stars in them.
[192] I follow Burnett's table in al-Qabīsī, which is constructed from two lists given by Abū Ma'shar.
[193] Al-Qabīsī, I.54.
[194] This seems to be a version of the ancient *antiscia*, but the *antiscia* were reckoned only from the Capricorn-Cancer axis—not from every movable sign.
[195] Reading *includatur* for *excludatur*.

does the twentieth degree of Capricorn; and so much separates the twentieth degree of Gemini from the beginning of Cancer, as it does the tenth degree of Cancer from the beginning of Cancer. For between the included tenth degree of Sagittarius and its end, are 20°, and between the beginning of Capricorn and the included twentieth degree, are 20°. Likewise, the tenth degree of Gemini is distanced from the beginning of Cancer (or from the end of the sign of Gemini, which touches the beginning of Cancer) as much as the twentieth degree of Cancer is distanced from the beginning of Cancer.

And so much distances the twentieth degree of Aries from the beginning of Aries, as the tenth degree of Pisces is distant from the end of Pisces (which touches the beginning of Aries). And so much distances the twentieth degree of Libra from the beginning of Libra, as the tenth degree of Virgo is distanced from the end of Virgo (which touches the beginning of Libra). And the twenty-first degree of Libra is distanced so far from the beginning of Libra as is the ninth [degree] of Virgo; and the twenty-second of Libra is distanced so much from it, as is the eighth of Virgo; and the twenty-third of Libra, as much as the seventh of Virgo; and the twenty-fourth of Libra, as much as the sixth of Virgo; and the twenty-fifth of Libra, as much as the fifth of Virgo; and the twenty-sixth of Libra, as much as the fourth of Virgo; and the twenty-seventh of Libra, as much as the third of Virgo; and the twenty-eighth of Libra, as much as the second of Virgo; and the twenty-ninth of Libra, as much as the first of Virgo.

And understand thus about all other degrees, both of Capricorn and Sagittarius, both of Aries and Pisces, both of Cancer and Gemini. Nor do I distinguish them for you otherwise, because it would be long and tedious to put down and to distinguish all other degrees as we have listed the degrees of Libra and Virgo (which should suffice well enough for you as an example of any of the other degrees). And therefore they are called "having power together," because each one of them has strength in matters which it signifies, as much as its correlated one does—like the first of Aries and the last of Pisces, the second of Aries and the twenty-ninth of Pisces, the third of Aries and the twenty-eighth of Pisces, the fourth of Aries and the twenty-seventh of Pisces. And understand thus about the rest.

PART 3: On the Nature of the Accidental Circle

Chapter 1: On the division of the circle by houses

A division happens to the circle of signs, by which it is divided into four equal parts, inasmuch as two great circles divide it: of which one is called the horizon or circle of the hemisphere, and the other is called the circle of the meridian or the Midheaven.[196] And each of these quarters is divided into three unequal parts–and so the whole circle is divided into twelve unequal parts. And this [inequality] happens on account of the refraction of the horizons in the climes, and on account of the diversity of the regions, just as Thābit [ibn Qurra] has shown well in his introduction to the celestial sphere, in the treatise on how the circles in the sphere are to be imagined.[197] (And you will even find this in the book *A Catalogue on the Equations of the Stars*.)[198] And this division always begins from the ascending sign.

And each of these divisions is called a "house" or "cusp"[199] or "tower," and not simply a "sign." And the first of these houses is the ascending sign, namely that which is in Aries.[200] And Ptolemy said that the 5° which have crossed over the line dividing one of the houses from the next, is reckoned as, and is said to belong to, the house which is given to that line. Like if the fifth degree of some sign ascends, then those five degrees which have already crossed the line of the Ascendant are reckoned as, and are said to belong to, the 1st house–and likewise the twenty-five degrees which remain under the line. And understand [this] is supposed to happen with the rest of the houses. For always, the 5° which have crossed the line of a house are reckoned to be in that house–and the twenty-five which have not yet come to it (namely with the stipulation that each house has 30°).[201] Then follows the 2nd house; then the 3rd house; then the 4th, then the 5th,

---

[196] Lat. *Medii coeli*, lit. "of the middle of the heaven."
[197] Thābit ibn Qurra, *De Imaginatione Sphaerae et Circulorum Eius*. See Bibliography.
[198] At present I am unsure what book this refers to.
[199] Lat. *cuspis*, the "point" of something sharp.
[200] This is the sort of sentence that sums up the difficult historical and linguistic perplexity over whole-sign and quadrant houses: first Bonatti says the house *is* the sign itself, and then he said it is *in* Aries.
[201] Of course, as Bonatti has already stated, quadrant house systems do not yield houses of equal size.

then the 6th, then the 7th, then the 8th, then the 9th, then the 10th, then the 11th, then the 12th (which is the last of all the houses).

Chapter 2: On the division of the quarters of the circle

And al-Qabīsī[202] and 'Alī[203] said that the quarter part of the circle which is between the Ascendant and the Midheaven (which are the 12th, 11th, and 10th houses), is called the eastern, masculine, advancing, sanguine, vernal, puerile quarter, and it signifies the beginning of the native's life up to the end of adolescence–which is from the beginning or from the day of the nativity up to the twenty-first complete year.

Indeed the quarter which is from the Midheaven up to the western line (which are the 9th, 8th, and 7th houses), is called the southern, receding, summery, choleric, youthful quarter; and it signifies middle [age], namely youth taken all together, and it is called the advancement of youth. And it is called this quarter with respect to the other quarters, just as youth is with respect to the other ages–which is from the beginning of the twenty-second year up to the forty-first.

Indeed the third quarter, namely that which is from the 7th house up to the 4th (which are the 6th, 5th, and 4th houses), which is below the earth, is called the western, masculine, advancing quarter; and it is called the autumnal, melancholic, senile quarter. And it is called this quarter with respect to the other quarters, just as old age is with respect to the other ages of the native, which is from the forty-first year onwards up to the sixtieth. And certain people said that it signifies old age up to the end of life, which does not seem right to me; but they considered that men often pass away around the sixtieth year, or they go little beyond that.

Indeed the last quarter, namely that which is from the 4th house up to the Ascendant (which is the 3rd, 2nd, and 1st houses), is called the northern, feminine, receding, phlegmatic, vernal, defective quarter, and it is called decrepit. And it is called this quarter with respect to the other quarters, just as the decrepit is with respect to the other ages of the native, which is from the end of old age, namely from the sixtieth year, up to the ninetieth, and even up to the end of life if someone were to live to be more than 90 (which happens to few,

---

[202] Al-Qabīsī, I.56.
[203] Probably 'Alī ibn Ridwān, also known as Haly Abenrudian, who wrote an influential commentary on the *Tetrabiblos* and pseudo-Ptolemy's *Centiloquy*.

even though some sometimes say they are 100 years old and beyond, and they are perhaps 90 years or a little more); because the common life common of men contains three reigns of Saturn, which are 90 years.[204] And this quarter even signifies what would happen to a man after his own death: that is, what would happen with his goods and his inheritance, what would be said about him (namely whether he would be praised or blamed), and whether his corpse will be buried or cremated, or buried honorifically or shamefully, or [whether] his blood-relatives would weep over him and be pained at his death, or they would laugh and rejoice over it.

Chapter 3: Which half is called ascending or descending, and what part is called right or left

Indeed two of the aforesaid quarters (namely that which is from the line of the Midheaven up to the Ascendant, and from thence up to the line of the 4th house), are called the "ascending half." Indeed the remaining two quarters (namely that which is from the line of the 4th house up to the 7th, and from thence up to the line of the Midheaven) are called the "descending half."

And that part of heaven which is above the earth is called the "right of the heaven"; it is nobler and stronger. And that which is below the earth is called the "left of the heaven," and is weaker and less noble; and this inasmuch as the circle of the horizon of every region divides the heaven into two halves.[205]

And that part of the heaven which is from the Ascendant up to the 7th house [below the earth], is called the "right of the Ascendant," because the part which is from the Ascendant up to the seventh house above the earth is called the "left of the Ascendant."[206]

And that which is from the Ascendant, crossing through the north to the 7th house (inasmuch as the horizon divides what is above the earth from the heaven, from that which is below the earth), is called "right of the east." And that which is from the Ascendant, crossing through the meridian up to the 7th house is called the "left of the east."

---

[204] Reading *anni* for *gradus* ("degrees"). See a further discussion of this in Tr. 5 (136th Consideration).
[205] The reason for this terminology seems to be that, when facing the east, the planets will rise and pass to the south on one's right; likewise they will pass to one's left after setting and going under the earth.
[206] This perspective is gotten if we now turn and face west, with the Ascendant behind us.

And in this, the right of heaven and the right of the Ascendant and the right of rising [or right of the east] differ.

Chapter 4: On the angles, cadents, and succeedents

But out of all the above-stated halves and quarters, twelve houses come to be, of which four are called "angles": namely, the 1st and 4th and 7th and 10th. And these four houses are the stronger and firmer parts of the heaven; and they even differ in strength among themselves. For the 1st is stronger than the 10th (except in the dignities which pertain to secular glory, like kingdoms, dukedoms, positions of civil authority, and the like, because the 10th is preferred to all others in those), and the 10th is stronger than the 7th, and the 7th is stronger than the 4th.

Indeed the 2nd house, and the 5th and 8th and 11th, are called the "succeedents"[207] of the angles, because they are immediately next to the angles and are less strong than the angles by half (except that the 11th is very strong in matters which pertain to fortune, and concerning which hope is had, because it is a house of fortune and trust and hope, as is said in the Treatise on the houses).[208]

Indeed the 3rd house, and the 6th and 9th and 12th, are called the "cadents"[209] from the angles. And they are very weak houses, and do not promise good nor firmness nor durability nor prolongation of any matter, except that the 9th house is preferred in religions, and is more agreeable in them than all the other houses (and in those things which pertain to clerical dignities, like bishoprics, abbacies, priories, and the like).

Whence if a planet were the significator of some matter, and it were in an angle, it promises good, and is said to be successful. But if it were in one succeeding the angle, it is less successful than in the angle. Indeed, in one cadent from the angle, the planet is said to fail and be weak and useless—with the exception of what I told you about the 9th and the 11th. And every one of the aforesaid houses has its own peculiar signification in matters and in the conditions of men, as I am going to narrate to you in what follows.

---

[207] I.e., "those following."
[208] This is an indication that Bonatti had not yet determined that the material on the houses would be part of the current Treatise.
[209] I.e., "those falling."

Chapter 5: On what is signified by the twelve houses

On the first house

The 1st house, whose beginning is out of the direction of the east, is called the Ascendant. And this house (as ad-Dawla, Sahl, and al-Qabīsī, and all other sages said),[210] signifies the life and body of any native, or even of a querent; and it signifies the beginning of any work, and has a signification over every election, and over every beginning; and it signifies the beginning of the life of every nativity–and therefore the 1st house is called the beginning of all the houses.

And there is a certain likeness between the 1st house and those being born or asking questions. For just as this house ascends from that direction of the heaven which is hidden from our sight under the horizon, toward the upper part which we see above the earth, and comes from hidden things toward the light, and from the hidden parts to the manifest ones, so he who is born goes out of the darkness and distresses of his mother's belly, and arrives to the light of this world, and the breadth of the air. And he who asks [a question], makes plain his own intention and the secrets of his heart; and those things which were first hidden, afterwards shine through and lie exposed.

And ad-Dawla and al-Andarzagar said, in nativities, that the first Lord of the triplicity of the 1st house signifies the life and nature of the native or querent, and his enjoyments, and in what things he delights, and what he loves or hates, and what happens to him (whether good or bad) in the beginning of life, namely in the first one-third of it. And the second Lord of its triplicity signifies life and robustness, or virtue and strength, and what happens to him in the second one-third (namely that of his life). And the third Lord of its triplicity signifies that which the first and second ones do, and it signifies the end of life and whatever happens to him in the last one-third of his life. Whence, if someone's nativity is shown to you, or a universal question about fortune (or about the condition of someone generally) came to you, then look at the Lords of the triplicity of the 1st house (namely the first one, the second one, and the third one), and see what kind of condition each of them has; and according to what you see concerning their condition, judge according to that. For if the first Lord were to signify good, judge that good will happen to the native or querent in the first part of his

---

[210] In this section I will give citations only for unusual or one-time references. Otherwise, Bonatti's material comes from Sahl (*Introduct.*) and al-Qabīsī (I.57*ff.*). References to al-Andarzagar all seem to come from al-Qabīsī's text, whereas the sources for ad-Dawla are unknown.

life. And if the second Lord of the same triplicity were to signify good, good will happen to him in the second one-third of his life. And if the third Lord of the same triplicity were to signify good, good will happen to him in the last one-third of his life. You should say the same about evil, because whichever of the said significators were to signify evil, it will happen in that one-third of life which it signified, just as was said about nourishment.

On the other things signified by the 1st house: the 1st house signifies the substance or *census*[211] of hidden enemies, because it is the 2nd from the 12th. For hidden enemies are all those who pretend to be friends, and smile, and seem to be happy around other men, and say they love them, and openly announce good things to them, but envy them, and are pained about others' prosperity, and rejoice in their adversities, and strive to harm them secretly in all the ways in which they can.

And this house signifies the brothers of friends, because it is the 3rd from the 11th; and the parents of kings, because it is the 4th from the 10th; and the children of the religious, because it is the 5th from the 9th; and the infirmities of the household intimates of [the native's] partners,[212] and of public enemies, and of wives not staying with husbands, because it is the 6th from the 8th; and the wives of these people, because it is the 7th from the 7th; and the death of slaves, because it is the 8th from the 6th; and the religion of children and their long journeys, because it is the 9th from the 5th; and the magistracies or dignities of the father, because it is the 10th from the 4th; and the friends of brothers (and their good fortune), because it is the 11th from the 3rd; and the hidden enemies of household intimates, and their larger animals, because it is the 12th from the 2nd.

---

[211] In ancient and medieval usage, the *census* was a system of assessing land and counting people for the purposes of determining taxes and the levying of men for military purposes. Since modern census systems do not coincide exactly with the medieval type, I have allowed the Latin term to remain. Bonatti's text uses the term in five principal ways (see especially Tr. 8): (a) the "taking" or "taking away" of it, and its opposite, "rendering" or "turning over." This refers to the rendering of assets. (b) Being misleading in the *census*, which must refer to fraud in reporting the *census*. (c) Being the custodian of the *census*, referring to the office in charge of it. (d) There being "much" *census* or it being "multiplied," referring to the assets or property yielded by collecting it. (e) It being "broken" or "ruptured," probably referring to the treasury being bankrupt or otherwise in trouble.

[212] The 8th signifies household intimates by drawing on the ancient classification of slaves as movable assets. By the feudal period slavery was rare to non-existent in Christian Europe, but the earliest forms of vassals were military allies housed in the lord's household—we shall see that Bonatti classifies "allies" as 2nd house attributions. Therefore he might have added that the 1st house signifies the infirmities of his enemies' allies, as well.

On the second house

The 2nd house, as al-Qabīsī said, signifies substance and acquisition and assistants, and it signifies the end of youth. And ad-Dawla said that it signifies the aggregation of substance or possessions and of *denarii* or *bezants*,[213] and receiving and donations. And Sahl said that the 2nd house signifies substance and allies and letters,[214] and it does not aspect the Ascendant.

And al-Andarzagar said, concerning the Lords of the triplicity of the 2nd house (namely the first, second, and third), see which of them is stronger by condition and place, and you will rightly make that one the author of substance and the significator of the native's or querent's acquisition: which if it were in the Midheaven, he will find it from the king; if however it were in the domicile of one of the luminaries, he will find it because of religion; and understand thus about the rest of the houses. Likewise, the first Lord of the triplicity of the 2nd house gives substance in the beginning of life, namely in its first one-third; the second one in the middle of life, namely in its second one-third; indeed the third one gives it in the last part of the native's life. But this thing which al-Andarzagar said about the aforesaid significators, must be understood [to mean] that the said significator of substance will signify it at whatever age.

If it were in the 1st, the native will find substance or money because of his own body, namely from the labor of his own hands, and his own industry and concern.

If however it were in the 2nd, he will find it because of his own substance, like from the fruits of his own possessions and his own goods, and even from mercantile dealings and other mechanical and craftsman-like arts which work with movable wealth,[215] like a shoeshop[216] or furrier,[217] and the like; or because of some one of those things which are signified by the 2nd house.

If it were in the 3rd, he will find it because of brothers and sisters, or neighbors who are not related to him by [family-]relation or marriage-

---

[213] An ancient Roman currency and that of its Byzantine heirs, respectively.
[214] This latter point is a mistake–of course Sahl attributes letters to the 3rd house.
[215] *Capitali*.
[216] *Calzolaria*, following Hand/Zoller (p. 65).
[217] *Pelliparia*, following Hand/Zoller (p. 65).

relation, or because of short journeys, [or] of those lesser than him in riches and power and age (namely of those who hold him as someone greater, as will be said in the chapter on the 3rd house).

And if it were in the 4th, he will find it because of fathers and grandfathers[218] or other blood-relatives of his older ancestors and those more ancient than him, or fathers-in-law; or perhaps he will find a hidden or buried treasure, or because of some one of those things which are signified by the 4th house.

And if it were in the 5th, he will acquire it because of children, and journeys of moderate length (which are from two days up to the fifth), or because of edibles that are sold in taverns or similar places, or because of a game, or some one of those things which are signified by the 5th house.

If it were in the 6th, he will acquire it because of male or female slaves, or dogs or birds (just as hunters do sometimes) or other small animals which are not ridden, like sheep and the like; or because of one of those things which are signified by the 6th house.

If it were in the 7th, he will find it because of wives or partners or enemies, or some one of those things which are signified by the 7th house.

If it were in the 8th, he will find it because of death, or because of the goods which are inherited from the dead, or because of the goods of wives or partners or enemies, or some one of those things which are signified by the 8th house.

If it were in the 9th, he will find it because of long journeys (just as sailors and merchants often make, who set out for along time to make money), and even because of bishoprics or abbacies, or other religious things and the like; or some one of those things which are signified by the 9th house.

And if it were in the 10th, he will acquire it because of a kingdom and profession, as was said, or by means of a lay dignity (as are positions of civil authority, and the like).

---

[218] Reading *avorum* for *avarorum*.

And if it were in the 11th, he will acquire it because of friends or because of the king's soldiers, or because of the king's substance, or because of unexpected good fortune, or even because of some matter concerning which the native has hope, or some one of those things which are signified by the 11th house.

And if it were in the 12th, he will find it because of hidden enemies or because of prison or the incarcerated, as the guards of the incarcerated and the like sometimes do; or because of cows or camels or horses, or one of those things which are signified by the 12th house.

And the 2nd house even has other significations apart from the signification of the native's substance: because it signifies the brothers of the hidden enemies, since it is the 3rd from the 12th; and it signifies the fathers and grandfathers of friends, *et cetera*, because it is the 4th from the 11th; and it signifies the children of kings, and [kings'] journeys of moderate length, because it is the 5th from the 10th; and it signifies the infirmities of religious men, because it is the 6th from the 9th; and it signifies the wives and partners and enemies of the household intimates of enemies and partners, because it is the 7th from the 8th; and it signifies the death of wives and partners and enemies, [and of] those absent, because it is the 8th from the 7th. And it signifies the religion [and] long journeys of slaves, because it is the 9th from the 6th. And it signifies the professions of children, because it is the 10th from the 5th; and it signifies the friends and good fortune of fathers, *et cetera*, because it is the 11th from the 4th. And it signifies the hidden enemies of the brothers, and their large animals, because it is the 12th from the 3rd.

On the third house

Al-Qabīsī said the 3rd house signifies brothers and sisters, and close friendships and loves, faith and religion, and commands [or contracts][219] and legates,[220] changes [of place] and short journeys, and it signifies the condition of

---

[219] *Mandata*. Al-Qabīsī (I.59) reads "messages," but *mandatum* in Latin has two related meanings. On the one hand it indicates commands or orders from a ruler; but it can also mean a commission involving mutual obligations, hence "contracts."

[220] Here we see the link with the previous word. A *legatus* is an ambassador or messenger or deputy to whom some message or commission is entrusted. The 3rd must signify this because it is the 6th from the 10th–servants of the king.

life before death. And ad-Dawla said that it signifies male and female kindred, and their being [or condition], and changes from dwelling to dwelling, and patience [or endurance] and the like. And Sahl said that it signifies contention in sects, letters and dreams. And it signifies all sects and all heretics. And al-Andarzagar said that the first Lord of the triplicity of the house of brothers signifies younger brothers; indeed the second signifies middle brothers; the third signifies older brothers; and he said that their dignity and their condition will be according to the places[221] of those significators. And it seems the same to me, that it signifies all the above-said, and that it signifies all blood-relatives and relations who are younger than the native or querent, and neighbors, and even fellow-citizens (both masters and slaves, mothers and women, rich and poor), just as I stated above.

It signifies blood-relatives and relations who hold him as their elder, and who revere him and obey him; and those who are lesser than him in riches and power and wisdom; and who consult him in their affairs and their necessities; and who often want to handle their own affairs based on his advice and help. Whence, if a question arose about some one of the above-said, you always ought to give the 3rd house to him, and the 1st to the querent.

> Like if someone asks about blood-relatives or about one of the above-said, with Aries ascending (or any other sign), the 1st is given to the querent, the 3rd is given to him about whom it is asked; and according to how you were to see it regarding the Lord of the 3rd house, judge according to that—whether the Lord of the 3rd house signifies good or evil.

> And if someone is born, and you wished to know what good fortune he is going to have from the brothers or from some one of the above-said, see how the Lord of the first behaves with the Lord of the third, and how they aspect each other. Because if they were to aspect each other with an aspect of love, and they received each other, there will be love and good between them; indeed if they were to aspect each other with an aspect of enmity, he will not rejoice because of them, nor with them, nor will there be good from them, nor to them from him.

> Moreover, it is necessary for you to look to the Lords of the triplicity of the 3rd house. Indeed if the first one were to aspect the Lord of the As-

---

[221] *Loca.*

cendant with a good aspect (namely a trine or sextile), or it were to receive him, it will be good for him because of the brothers (who are signified by that planet), and understand thus about the other houses.

And if the Lord of the first were to aspect with any one of them by a bad aspect, it will be bad for him with them and because of those brothers who are signified by that planet. And if the Lord of the first did not aspect with some one of them, [then] with all and because of all the brothers it will be for him like with strangers. (What I told you about the Lord of the first, may you understand the same about the Moon.) Were the condition even of any one of these significators better, it will be better for those brothers who are signified by that planet, both in their own good fortune and in other things. And whichever one's condition were worse, it will be worse for [that brother's] condition.

Moreover, you ought to know that the 3rd house is always the Ascendant of the brothers and younger blood-relatives, neighbors, and other persons who are signified by it;[222] and the 1st is always the querent's, unless in excepted cases which you will find in places deputed to him. So, let it be put that someone asks about the affairs of his own brother or sister, and the Ascendant was Leo, and Libra was the 3rd house. Thus the 1st is the Ascendant of him who asks, and the 3rd belongs to him for whom it is asked; whence you should not judge according to the Lord of the Ascendant, but according to the Lord of the third; and you will judge regarding the affairs of the querent's brothers according to what you were to see regarding the being [or condition] of the Lord of the third. Moreover, if the first Lord of the triplicity of the 3rd house were well with the Lord of the Ascendant, it will be well for the native or querent with brothers and neighbors and younger relations, and other things which are signified by the 3rd house in the first one-third of his life (and for them from him). And if with the second one, it well be well for him because of them, and for them because of him, in the second one-third of his life. And if with the third one, it will be well for him because of them and for them because of him in the last one-third of his life—and *vice versa* if they bore themselves badly toward one another.

And the 3rd house has these other significations: because it signifies the substance of household intimates, since it is the 2nd from the 2nd; and the fathers of hidden enemies, and their homes, *et cetera*, because it is the 4th from the 12th;

---

[222] *Ipsum*, suggesting the sign.

and it signifies the children of friends, because it is the 5th from the 11th; and the infirmities of kings, because it is the 6th from the 10th; and religious men's enemies, and their partners and girlfriends, because it is the 7th from the 9th; and the death of those absent,[223] and of the household intimates of their enemies, and of [the enemies'] assistants, because it is the 8th from the 8th; and the religion of wives, because it is the 9th from the 7th; and the professions of slaves, because it is the 10th from the 6th; and the friends of children and their fortune, because it is the 11th from the 5th; and the hidden enemies of fathers (and their greater animals), because it is the 12th from the 4th.

On the fourth house

Al-Qabīsī said the 4th house signifies fathers, houses, lands, grandfathers, and all ancient people of the direct line of ancestors (older males and fathers-in-law[224]), and all inheritances apart from those which are inherited from the dead (which will be discussed in the 8th house). And it signifies all immovable things which are in the ground or above ground: like buildings, towers, roofed dwellings, cities, castles, and the like. And it signifies hidden treasures, and whatever is buried or underground. And ad-Dawla said that it signifies secret things and things secreted away, and prisons, and the incarcerated, and things hidden or put in the ground, and whatever happens to a dead person in his interment, and after his interment, and whether he will be buried or burned, or his corpse will be abandoned so that no one cares about him (as sometimes happens with those hanged or beheaded, or otherwise killed). And al-Mansur said that it signifies the end of matters.[225]

And al-Andarzagar said the first Lord of the triplicity of the house of fathers signifies fathers; the second one, cities and lands; the third, the end of matters and prisons. Whence it must be considered in someone's nativity or in some question which is made to you about some one of the aforesaid, because you ought to look to the 4th house if you wish to know those things (which are signified by the 4th house or by its triplicity Lords) which should happen to the native or querent from them. And see which of them is of a better condition, and judge according to what you were to see concerning them. For if the first

---

[223] Above, Bonatti implied that absent people were signified by the 7th; but it may depend on what kind of absent person is meant: see Tr. 6.

[224] Reading *soceros* for *sorores*.

[225] This may refer to the *Chapters of al-Mansur*, but I can only find a similar statement in Proposition 89, where the fourth angle signifies "death and tombs."

Lord of the triplicity of the 4th house were of good condition, and he were to aspect the Lord of the Ascendant of the nativity with a good aspect (namely a trine or sextile), or he him, it will be well for the native or the querent from the father, and for the father from him (and the grandfather, and the great-grandfather, and the father-in-law, and all older parents, even though the father-in-law is signified by the 4th house by accident). And if even the second one were of good condition, it will be well for him because of homes and lands, and inheritances which he will inherit from the above-said persons. And if the third one were of good condition, it will be well for him from prisons and the incarcerated (just as sometimes happens for the guards of captives, and the like), and from the end of matters (just as sometimes happens to someone in finishing some lawsuit, or some war, or by mediating something publicly sold between some people, as often happens to sellers of horses, or of other things whose sellers are in need of mediators, and the like). And if the aforesaid significators were made unfortunate, or [were] of bad condition, it will be ill for him because of the aforesaid significations. And consider in what part of life this will happen to him: because the first Lord of this triplicity signifies that this would happen to the native in the first one-third of his life, and the second in the second, and the third in the third, as was said in the other houses.

And the 4th house even signifies the substance of brothers, because it is the 2nd from the 3rd; and the household intimates and assistants of the brothers, because it is the 2nd from the 3rd; and the children of hidden enemies, because it is the 5th from the 12th; and the infirmities of friends and of the household intimates of the king, because it is the 6th from the 11th; and the enemies of kings, because it is the 7th from the 10th; and the death of the religious, because it is the 8th from the 9th; and the religion of those absent, because it is the 9th from the 8th; and the professions of enemies and partners, and their mothers, because it is the 10th from the 7th; and the friends of slaves, and their fortune, because it is the 11th from the 6th; and it signifies the hidden enemies of children and [the children's] larger animals, because it is the 12th from the 5th.

On the fifth house

Al-Qabīsī said the 5th house signifies children, delights, legates, donations, and what is said about a man after his death. And he said in addition that it signifies joy and clothing. And Vettius [Valens] said[226] that it signifies papers,

---

[226] Uncertain of source; perhaps this is drawn from a compilation based on Valens.

books, heralds, and novelties.[227] And [Abu 'Ali] al-Khayyat said[228] that it signifies everything in which trust is had: honor, seeking [or petitions], a woman, friendship, and the condition of the citizens, and the fruits of inheritance. And al-Andarzagar said the first Lord of the triplicity of the 5th signifies children and their life; indeed the second Lord signifies delights; the third, legates. Whence we must look at the Lord of someone's nativity, or of his question, and see how it behaves with the first Lord of the triplicity of the 5th house (which is called the house of children): because if it were to behave well with it, it will be well for him because of children, and for them because of him, in the first one-third of his life; if with the second one, in the second; if with the third one, in the third. But the life of children is taken more from the first Lord of that triplicity, than from the second or third.

Now look at the Lord of the 5th house, to see how he behaves with the Lord of the first house: for if the Lord of the 5th house were joined with the Lord of the first by means of a praiseworthy aspect (namely by a trine or sextile), or it were in the first, or the Lord of the first were in the fifth, he will have children, and especially if Jupiter were then in the 5th or he were joined to the Lord of the fifth (or to the Lord of the first), by means of a good aspect, or he were in the third or the eighth or in the eleventh with the Lord of the first or with the Lord of the fifth, or with the Moon: the children will live, and it will be well for them.[229] Indeed if it were Mars instead of Jupiter, the native will have children, just as we will see in the chapter on children; and their death, just as will be stated more broadly in [the Treatise on] judgments and on nativities, in the chapter on children.[230]

Moreover, we must look to all Lords of the triplicity of the house of children, and see which of them better aspects the Lord of the first or the Lord of the fifth, or the 5th house [domicile?] itself. Because if the first one were to aspect better, he will have children in the first one-third of his life; if the second, in the second. And if one of [the Lords of the triplicity] were the Lord of the first, or the Lord of the [fifth] (as sometimes happens), it signifies children in its own one-third of the native's life.

And the 5th house even has these other significations: because it signifies the goods of fathers and of other older relatives, since it is the 2nd from the 4th

---

[227] *Novellas.*
[228] Not in *JN*, but perhaps attributed to him or in an unknown book.
[229] Bonatti's sudden list of conditions has made him forget to explain where the conditions for having children cease, and those for the children living, begin.
[230] See Tr. 9, Part 3, 5th House.

(whence if its Lord were joined to the Lord of the first or to the Lord of the second, and it were received by one of them, the native or querent will attain their goods as a whole or to a great degree; and if the Lord of the second were joined to the Lord of the fifth, and the Lord of the fifth were to receive him, the parents will attain his goods).[231] And it signifies the brothers of brothers (if he had brothers from another father, or from another mother), because it is the 3rd from the 3rd; and the infirmities of hidden enemies, because it is the 6th from the 12th; and the enemies of friends, because it is the 7th from the 11th; and the death of kings and of those who are signified by the 10th, because it is the 8th from the 10th; and the long journeys of religious men, because it is the 9th from the 9th; and the professions or dignities of absent people, because it is the 10th from the 8th; and the friends of the native's or querent's enemies and his partners, because it is the 11th from the 7th; and the hidden enemies of slaves, because it is the 12th from the 6th.

On the sixth house

They said the 6th house is that of infirmities and male and female slaves. And it is said this house is that of illnesses, on account of the fact that it is outside the house of games and delights (which is the 5th), and goes toward the 7th, which is the house of public enemies. And al-Qabīsī said that it signifies whatever is going to be before old age, and it signifies the end of life. And ad-Dawla said that it signifies servants and beasts which are not ridden. And the 6th house signifies vassals and justices,[232] and it signifies change from place to place. And Sahl said the 6th house is cadent from the Ascendant, nor does it aspect it; and it is a malign place. And al-Andarzagar said the first Lord of the triplicity of the 6th house signifies infirmities and convalescences from them (and from evils). The second one signifies domestics and slaves. The third signifies what he will find because of them, and their usefulness and works; and it is a significator of beasts and cattle,[233] and all quadrupeds, and their strength, and their multi-

---

[231] See Tr. 9, Part III, 2nd House.
[232] In feudal Europe, the "justice" of a lord referred to the overall power which he had over his vassals, which tended to fetter most of the vassals' personal and social status–thus its relation to 6th house personages.
[233] *Pecorum*. Specifically, cattle–or sheep–considered as a mass (in a herd or flock). Note that none of these animals are ridden, and this category includes both "large" and "small" animals. See Bonatti's comment on this below.

tude and scarcity, and of their staying[234] his possession or their going out of it; of prison also, and confinement.

Whence it must be seen how the Lord of someone's nativity or question[235] behaves with the Lord of the 6th house, namely whether it is joined to it by a trine or sextile aspect, or by body, with [either] mutual or perfect reception.[236] Because if it were so, the native or querent will have good fortune in all (or because of all), those things which are signified by the 6th house. Indeed if they were to aspect each other from the said aspects without reception, there will not be great good fortune for him from them, even though there is some kind [of good fortune] for him because of them. Indeed if they were to aspect each other from the square aspect, or from the opposition, without reception, it will be ill for him in all and because of all, the above-said (indeed, if with reception, it will be less bad for him because of them). Indeed if the Lord of the first were to receive the Lord of the sixth, and the Lord of the sixth did not receive him, it will be better for the slaves and domestics because of him, then for him because of them: for they will be unfaithful and fraudulent. Indeed if the Lord of the sixth were to receive the Lord of the first, and the Lord of the first did not receive the Lord of the sixth, it will be better for him because of them than for them because of him, for he will not love them, nor do well for them, not even for those doing well to him and those standing faithfully by him, and for those well handling all of his business matters.

And look at the Lords of its triplicity: because if the first one were of better condition, the above-stated good things will happen to him in the first one-third of his life; if the second, in the second; if the third, in the third or last. And *vice versa* for bad [conditions].

And slaves differ in condition from domestics. For slaves are under him according to slavery; domestics, without slavery (and they belong to him in the family). And even though al-Andarzagar said that this house signifies quadrupeds, this was not his intention, unless [he meant it] concerning quadrupeds which are not ridden, like sheep, goats, pigs, dogs, and the like. And under the 6th house are comprehended chickens, geese, ducks, hawks, bees, and the like.

Moreover, this house has certain other significations: because it signifies the substance of children, since it is the 2nd from the 5th; and the brothers of fathers, because it is the 3rd from the 4th; and the fathers of brothers who are from

---

[234] Reading *morae* for *more*.
[235] In both of these cases, he means the Lord of the Ascendant.
[236] Bonatti defines "perfect reception" as reception by domicile or exaltation.

another father, because it is the 4th from the 3rd; and the children of household intimates, because it is the 5th from the 2nd; and the enemies of hidden enemies, because it is the 7th from the 12th; and the death of friends, because it is the 8th from the 11th; and the religion of mothers, and the long journeys of kings, because it is the 9th from the 10th; and the professions and lay dignities of the religious (for sometimes it happens that they receive positions of civil authority, and lay dignities of this kind), because it is the 10th from the 9th; and the friends of those who are absent, and of the household intimates of enemies and partners, because it is the 11th from the 8th; and the hidden enemies of wives, partners, and enemies, because it is the 12th from the 7th.

On the seventh house

Al-Qalandar said the 7th house is the house of women, and it signifies weddings and contentions. And al-Battani said[237] it signifies participation and opposition and every opposite thing. And ad-Dawla said that it signifies wives and war and hostile things. And al-Qabīsī said that it signifies the middle of the end of life, toward old age. And Ven[238] said that it signifies thieves and very pleasing things, and partners, and it is a house of buying and selling; and it signifies marriages and matters of marriage, and a fugitive and robber, cutters of roads[239] and a lost thing. And Sahl said that it signifies battles because it is the western angle,[240] and the 7th is opposed to the Ascendant; and it signifies contrarieties which come to be between people, and [between] the querent and the quaesited.

And according to certain people, it signifies medium-long journeys just like the 1st signifies the shortest journeys (which are from one district into another of the same land, or from the city to the fields [or gardens], or to cloisters[241] or pleasure-gardens bordering on–or practically so–the city). And [it signifies] the pure and simplest culture of the deity, and all houses of philosophers, and the foreknowledge of things, and the science of the stars, and the diviner, and letters, and legates, and dreams, faith, divine wisdom, and health and religion, and rumors, and every preceding matter (and [every] one passed over). And it

---

[237] Lat. *Albategni*. At present I do not know the source of this quote.
[238] Probably derived ultimately from Vettius Valens, but his *Anth.* II.10 does not give this list.
[239] I.e., highway robbers.
[240] Sahl does not say "because" (*Introduct.*, §2.7). This may be a pun by Bonatti, since "western" (*occidentalis*) also means "killing" (from *occido*), the implication being that just as the sun sets (*occidit*) in the west, and is killed, so the 7th signifies killing in general.
[241] *Clausuras*; perhaps simply, "enclosed places."

signifies a man overthrown by his burdens or his own work; and the foreknowledge of future things, and the matters of the future world, and thieves, and those like thieves, and pilgrimages or exiles, and the loss of things, and their purposes.[242]

And this sign is the enemy of the Ascendant. And al-Andarzagar said that the first Lord of the triplicity of the 7th signifies women, the second contentions, the third comminglings.[243]

And it even has these other significations: because it signifies the substance of slaves, since it is the 2nd from the 6th; and the brothers of children from another father, because it is the 3rd from the 5th; and the fathers of fathers (by living fathers), because it is the 4th from the 4th; and the children of brothers, because it is the 5th from the 3rd; and the infirmities of household intimates, because it is the 6th from the 2nd; and the death of hidden enemies, because it is the 8th from the 12th (and it could be said that it signifies the death of larger animals); and it signifies the religion of friends and their long journeys, because it is the 9th from the 11th (and it could be said that it signifies the professions of kings, even though it would seem not wholly fitting), because it is the 10th from the 10th; and it signifies the friends of the religious, and their good fortune, because it is the 11th from the 9th; and the hidden enemies of those absent, and of the household intimates of enemies, because it is the 12th from the 8th.

On the eighth house

Ad-Dawla said the 8th house is the house of fear, and it is called the house of death on account of the fact that it belongs to the assistants of public enemies, and it follows the 7th (which is the opposition of the Ascendant). And Abu 'Ali said[244] that it signifies labor, sorrow, wars and those who despise, and the bellicose, and the clients of adversaries. And [Abu 'Ali] al-Khayyat said[245] that it signifies something deposited for safekeeping, and estate management,[246] and cunning, and skills. And Sahl said the 8th house succeeds to the western angle, and signifies killing and lethal poisons, and whatever is inherited from the dead,

---

[242] This list is contradictory and many elements unrelated; but I believe we can reconcile the problem if we remember that the 7th is also a kind of all-purpose house for horary questions.
[243] This probably means "partnerships," both because it is the 7th house, and because *commixtio* is a common word both for association with people and with aspects between planets (as one may see throughout the book).
[244] Again, not listed explicitly in *JN*, but perhaps from another work of his.
[245] See above note.
[246] I.e., since one is handling another's possessions.

and all that perishes, and labor and sorrow and the allies of enemies or adversaries. And al-Qabīsī said that it signifies *al-mawārīth*,[247] that is, all that is inherited from the dead (namely both of those not related and of those conjoined [to one]) which the heirs should possess after their death; and it signifies the end[248] of the years of life after old age. And al-Andarzagar said the first Lord of the triplicity of the house of death signifies death, the second one ancient [or old] matters, the third inheritance,[249] and whatever his partners signify. And I agree to what the above-mentioned sages said, and I say that the 8th house signifies women's dowries, [and] the goods or *census* of enemies and partners. Certain people said that it signifies interest [on loans].

And it even has other significations: because it signifies the brothers of slaves since it is the 3rd from the 6th; and the infirmities of brothers, because it is the 6th from the 3rd; and the enemies and wives and partners of household intimates, because it is the 7th from the 2nd; and the religion and long journeys of hidden enemies, because it is the 9th from the 12th; and the professions and dignities of friends, because it is the 10th from the 11th; and the friends of kings, because it is the 11th from the 10th; and the hidden enemies of the religious, because it is the 12th from the 9th.

On the ninth house

And ['Umar] al-Tabarī said[250] the 9th house is that of faith and religion, and a long journey. And ad-Dawla said that it signifies vision and wisdom and the culture of the deity, and all houses of religion, and the foreknowledge of things. And al-Qabīsī said that it signifies wisdom, philosophy, writing [or scripture], books, letters, legates, the narration of future things, dreams, and it signifies the middle of life.[251] And Sahl said the 9th house is cadent from the angle of the 10th house. And I say that it signifies reputation according to how it and its Lord are disposed. For if the Lord of the 9th house were of good condition, and well disposed, and there were benefics in it (namely like Jupiter or Venus or the Head of the Dragon), and they were free, nor impeded, it signifies the reputation of the native and his great honor. If however there were malefics in it (namely Saturn or Mars or the Tail of the Dragon), it signifies his infamy; and by

---

[247] Lat. *Almuerith*. The Arabic is المواريث, "the inheritance."
[248] Reading *finem* for *fine*. Al-Qabīsī says "the last of the years."
[249] Lat. *Almaverith*. See above.
[250] Bonatti must be extrapolating from *TBN*, pp. 76 and 86.
[251] Al-Qabīsī says: "the beginning of the middle of life."

how much more the malefic were impeded, by that much more will the native's infamy be increased.

Al-Andarzagar said that the first Lord of the triplicity of the 9th house signifies pilgrimage and what will happen to the native or the querent on long journeys; the second signifies faith and religion, and their state and manner; the third signifies wisdom and dreams, the knowledge of the stars and their truth, and auguries and practice in them.

And the 9th house even has these other significations: namely the substance of household intimates, enemies, and partners, and wives, and of those who are absent, and their assistants, because it is the 2nd from the 8th; and the brothers of enemies, *et cetera*, because it is the 3rd from the 7th; and the fathers of slaves, because it is the 4th from the 6th; and the children of children, because it is the 5th from the 5th; and the infirmities of the fathers, because it is the 6th from the 4th; and the wives and partners and enemies of brothers, because it is the 7th from the 3rd; and the death of household intimates, because it is the 8th from the 2nd; and it signifies the dignities of hidden enemies, because it is the 10th from the 12th; and the friends of friends, because it is the 11th from the 11th; and the hidden enemies of kings, because it is the 12th from the 10th (and this is the reason why prelates and other religious men are always turned secretly against kings).

On the tenth house

Albuaz and other ancients said the 10th house is a royal house and signifies empire and kingdom, and professions and dignities and offices, and every art which someone practices whence he is called a "master." And he whom God willed to be a Master,[252] said that it signifies mothers, grandmothers, and all such old female ancestors, and mothers-in-law. And ad-Dawla said, wherefore it signifies divine things and honors and positions of civil authority and the like. And al-Kindī[253] said that it signifies the king, glory, and the reputation of [one's] worth. And al-Battani said that it signifies judges judging a case, and overseers of works. And a certain one of the ancients said that it signifies the stolen substance of thievery. And al-Qabīsī said it signifies the half of the years of life. And al-Andarzagar said the first Lord of the triplicity of the royal house signifies power[254] and exaltation, and the loftiness of the seat [of power], and the highest

---

[252] Māshā'allāh. This phrase comes from Sahl, *Introduct.* §5.3.
[253] Source uncertain.
[254] *Opes.* Or, political resources.

dwelling; the second one signifies the voice of command, and boldness of the same. The third one signifies its stability and durability.

Moreover, the 10th house has these other significations: because it signifies the substance of the religious, since it is the 2nd from the 9th; and the brothers of the household intimates of enemies, because it is the 3rd from the 8th; and the fathers of enemies and partners and wives, because it is the 4th from the 7th; and the children of slaves, because it is the 5th from the 6th; and the infirmities of the children, because it is the 6th from the 5th; and the enemies and wives and partners of fathers, because it is the 7th from the 4th; and the death of brothers, because it is the 8th from the 3rd; and the religion of household intimates and those who are absent, and their long journeys, because it is the 9th from the 2nd;[255] and the friends of hidden enemies, because it is the 11th from the 12th; and the hidden enemies of friends, because it is the 12th from the 11th.

On the eleventh house

The 11th house is the house of fortune, trust, and hope. And Sahl said that it succeeds to the angle of the Midheaven, and it signifies the substance of the king, and his renderings or tributes, and his soldiers and footmen or allies, and the man who succeeds the king, or the first prince after him;[256] and it signifies praises and children. And al-Qabīsī said that it signifies ministers, and it signifies the end of the years of the middle of life, and from the middle onwards.

And al-Andarzagar said, because the first Lord of the triplicity of the house of trust signifies trust; the second, friends; the third signifies usefulness, or their benefit.

And the 11th house has these other significations: because it signifies the substance of the king, since it is the 2nd from the 10th; and the brothers of the religious, because it is the 3rd from the 9th; and the fathers of the household intimates of enemies, because it is the 4th from the 8th; and the children of enemies and partners, because it is the 5th from the 7th; and the impediments

---

[255] It is not clear why the 10th would signify the religion of those absent (who are signified by the 8th house), unless perhaps it is because it is the 3rd from the 8th. But in that case, this statement should have been put earlier in the paragraph.

[256] These attributions go back to early feudal times. Feudal lords kept military companions in their own households, who were expected to fight for the lord as his companion and ally. The chief "princes" were the most powerful feudal lords, not necessary the children of the lord himself. Thus the 11th, by being the 2nd from the 10th, signifies all of these kinds of allies who are kept close to the king. In the later feudal period, fewer vassals were kept in the household as more were enfoeffed with tracts of land: astrologically, they became 6th house figures with respect to the lord, because they still owed allegiance and service and loyalty to him..

and infirmities of slaves, because it is the 6th from the 6th; and the enemies and wives of children, because it is the 7th from the 5th; and the death of fathers, because it is the 8th from the 4th; and the religion of brothers and their long journeys, because it is the 9th from the 3rd; and the professions of household intimates, because it is the 10th from the 2nd; and the hidden enemies of the hidden enemies, because it is the 12th from the 12th.

On the twelfth house

Ad-Dawla said the 12th house signifies hidden enemies and deceivers and the envious; and it signifies cows, horses, donkeys, camels, and all animals which are ridden, and the like. And it signifies griefs, sorrows, wailings, weeping, lamentations, whisperings and the like, slanderings, prisons, evil wills. And Sahl said that it signifies cunning [and] evil thoughts. And al-Qabīsī said that it signifies labors and bad characters;[257] and it signifies the end of life, and what happens to women from the conception [of a child] and from [giving] birth (whether good or bad). And al-Andarzagar said, the first Lord of the triplicity of the 12th house signifies enemies; the second, labors; the third, beasts and cattle.[258]

And certain others say that all the Lords of the triplicity of the 12th, and its [domicile] Lord, signify prisons and the incarcerated. And others said that the 8th house signifies the incarcerated. And others said that the 4th signifies prisons. But one did not contradict the other, because the 4th house signifies prisons, since it signifies capture and the act of *capturing* itself.[259] Indeed the 8th signifies prisons, because it signifies the act of *incarcerating* itself. Indeed the 12th signifies prisons, because it signifies the place of the prison, and the *incarcerated person* already captured–and in this they differ. But all the sages agree in this, that the 4th house signifies prisons, because it is the principle of prison and incarceration, since if there is no capture and act of capturing, there is no incarceration nor act of incarcerating. And if there is no capture and act of capturing, and incarceration and act of incarcerating, there is no place of incarceration, nor in which some incarcerated person stays fast. And this house is said to belong to the act of those incarcerated,[260] on account of the fact that it falls from the eastern line,

---

[257] *Ingenia.* Al-Qabīsī (I.68) says "envy, slander, cunning, stratagem."
[258] *Pecora.* Again, cattle or other herd or flock animals, considered *en masse*.
[259] Emphasis mine, here and below.
[260] Lat. *Incarceratis actu*, treating it as an ablative of description.

and because it is in the joy of Saturn, who rejoices in wailing and lamentation and the like.[261]

And the 12th house has these other significations: because it signifies the substance of friends, since it is the 2nd from the 11th; and the brothers of kings, because it is the 3rd from the 10th; and the fathers of the religious, because it is the 4th from the 9th; and the children of the household intimates of enemies, *et cetera*, because it is the 5th from the 8th; and the infirmities of wives, *et cetera*, because it is the 6th from the 7th; and the wives and enemies of slaves, because it is the 7th from the 6th; and the death of children, because it is the 8th from the 5th; and the religion and long journeys of fathers, because it is the 9th from the 4th; and the professions of brothers, because it is the 10th from the 3rd; and the friends of household intimates, because it is the 11th from the 2nd; and the hidden enemies of the native or querent, because it is the 12th from the 1st. And I have found a certain Florentine who used to give the 12th to a pilgrim.

[Summary]

It is necessary to consider and know all of these significations of each of the above-said houses, so that, if a question about any of the aforesaid were made to you, or someone's nativity or a universal question were shown to you, you could judge upon that question regarding all the accidents of the native or querent, and of all the aforesaid persons, under one Ascendant–even though it is most difficult. But it is easier for you to discover any matter which you ought to consider in your judgment, because if you had well the nativity of someone, or his universal question, or even another question, you could judge for him what ought to happen to him regarding all of the above-said significations, and what [would happen] because of all the above-said persons and what [would happen] to all of them from him and because of him.

For you could judge for him what ought to be regarding his own person, his own substance, and those things which are signified by the 2nd house; about his brothers, and about those things which are signified by the 3rd house; about his older parents and about those things which are signified by the 4th house; about his own children and all those things which are signified by the 5th house; about his own slaves and small animals, and about all those things which are signified by the 6th house; about his wives and about all who are signified by the 7th

---

[261] See below–previously, the joys of the planets in the signs were given on the basis of certain elemental affinities with the domiciles; below they will be given joys in the houses, based on what they naturally signify.

house; something about death and about all the things which are signified by the 8th house; something about religion and about all things which are signified by the 9th house; something about his masteries[262] and about all of his greater, feminine parents, and about all things which are signified by the 10th house; about friends and about all things which are signified by the 11th house; something about horses and beasts, and about all things which are signified by the 12th house.

And understand thus about every house, namely about the 2nd, 3rd, and 4th, up to the 12th. And you should know that each of them is its own 1st [house], and has its own 2nd and 3rd, 4th, 5th, 6th, 7th, 8th, 9th, 10th, 11th, and 12th. And it has, following each of them, its own other eleven houses apart from itself, from which it receives its significations, just as the first, eastern [house] receives from its own houses all those which you could well discern from your own industry.

Chapter 6: On the significations of the twelve houses in the contrary direction of the aforesaid approach

First, on the 12th house

Another chapter, namely the sixth, on what are signified by the planets in them, whose approach is in the contrary direction to the aforesaid approach; by which it is known what the planets do in every house in nativities or in questions, beginning from the 12th, going backwards up to the 1st.

For if the nativity of some native were shown to you, or a question were put to you about wealth, and the Lord of the 12th were in the 1st house, it signifies that the native or querent will earn wealth through his own household intimates, or by something of what is signified by the 12th house which was stated to you above.[263]

---

[262] *Magistratibus*.
[263] Bonatti does not explain why he is going against the natural order of houses, but his purpose is clear: to help us balance the use of natural house and derived-house significations in charts. Unfortunately, it is not always evident why he is saying what he does. In the beginning at least, (a) the house Lord signifies the quaesited in a horary chart (or perhaps someone in the life of the native); (b) Bonatti imagines that the querent is asking about the quaesited's wealth, good fortune, and so on; and (c) he combines the meaning of the *natural* house in which the Lord is found, with that of the house as *derived* from the house of the quaesited. So, e.g., if the Lord of the 9th is in the 10th, we combine the meaning of authorities (natural 10th) with wealth (2nd from 9th). However, it is not always clear why Bonatti picks the questions he does, and in some cases it is difficult to say what he is doing.

And if it were in the 2nd, it signifies the native or querent is going to make some short journey or small move because of the benefit of something hoped for, or he is going to go to one of his own absent fellow-villagers, or to one of his own younger blood-relatives. The same will happen to the native in the course of time, in similar acts.[264]

But if it were in the 3rd, whatever the question were about, it signifies that the object will be made secret, hidden in the home, or on some estate. And if it were something to be buried, [it signifies] that it is underground in one of the said places.

If it were in the 4th, its whole signification will be in children or the like. And if the question were about a journey that is not long, it signifies that the journey will not be pleasing to him: for contrary things will happen to him, nor will it be perfected for him to the good. One could say the same, that they will happen to the native in his own like affairs.

Which if it were in the 5th, and it were a question about someone absent, it signifies that he will be in the hands of certain men who are, or once were, his own servants, and thus they are hidden enemies.

Indeed if it were in the 6th, and it were a question about someone absent, it signifies that he about whom it is asked, is in the hands of enemies or robbers or cutters of roads, or people expelled [from the community], or paid men.

If it were in the 7th, and the question were (as was said) about an absent person, it signifies he is dead, or labors under a deadly illness.

But if you were to find it in the 8th, it seems that he is far from that place, or on a long journey, or that some cleric or religious man has him against his will.

If you were to find it in the 9th, it signifies he is in the hands of some authority, or that his own mother is making him stay where he is, against his will.

Which if it were in the 10th, it signifies he is in a place fitting for him, and with his friends and with those loving [him].

Indeed if it were in the 11th, it signifies he is not in a good station, but rather it can be said that he is in the hands of certain people inimical to him because of some envy, who are wishing to harm him, not knowing why; or he is in distresses and labors, or in prison.

---

[264] I am unsure exactly what this sentence is supposed to communicate.

On the 11th house and its Lord

If the Lord of the 11th house were in the 12th and the question were about wealth, it signifies it—for he will earn wealth in his own absence by his own household intimates, or by people of an equal sort.

If it were in the 1st, and the question were about a short journey, it signifies the journey will be useful and lucrative.

Indeed if it were in the 2nd, and the question were about a hidden object, it signifies it is going to arrive in the querent's hands. You should say the same about an immovable object. And if it were a question about elder parents, it signifies their standing according to the nature [or condition] of the planet.

If it were in the 3rd, and the question were about children, it signifies their good condition; it even signifies joy and happiness because of them, and useful garments and every good condition.

And if it were in the 4th, and it were a nativity or a universal question, it signifies the native or querent is going to be liable to anger and full of labor, and beset by infirmities. If it were another, particular question, it will signify the querent is going to lose his smaller animals and slaves and servants, and the like.

If it were in the 5th, it signifies the native is going to be litigious, and that in his lawsuits it will go unluckily for him; it will even come out likewise for a querent. Indeed if it were Venus, it signifies he is going to contract matrimony with beautiful women; indeed if it were Jupiter, it signifies he is going to have good partners and good fortune in mercantile affairs; if however it were one of the others, the aforesaid will happen according to its disposition. For if it were well disposed, it will signify well; if indeed badly, it will portend evil; and it will even signify the deprivation of his goods, or expulsion from them.

Indeed if it were in the 6th, and it were one of the aforesaid malefics, it will signify the querent's death. And if it were in someone's nativity, it will signify he is going to die a bad death. But if it were Jupiter or the Sun, or even Venus, it will signify wealth because of a dowry, or perhaps taking possession of other goods. Indeed if it were Mercury or the Moon, and the question were about a fearful matter, it signifies its weakening, and its annulment.

If it were in the 7th, and it were a nativity or a universal question about a journey, and it were one of the benefics, it signifies journeys will be advantageous and lucrative. If however it were of the malefics, you could judge the contrary.

If it were in the 8th, it signifies rulership and honor is going to come to him, or he is going to adhere to professions of the nature of that significator (insofar as it pertains to him), or to a great man; or that his mother loves him more than her other children.

Indeed if it were staying in the 9th, it signifies that the native or querent often will fulfill his own wishes, and concerning things in which he will have hope, both because of friends and because of other reasons.

If it were in the 10th, it signifies sorrow, alteration, tribulation and prison, and even the taking away of larger animals, both in nativities and in questions.

On the 10th house and its Lord

Indeed if the Lord of the 10th house were found in the 11th in some question or nativity, it will signify the native or querent is going to enter into the family of the king, or of some magnate fit for a kingdom, or that he is going to have wealth suitable for him.

Indeed if it were in the 12th, and the question were about a short journey, it signifies it will not be useful for him, and especially if the journey were to fellow-villagers and to blood-relatives younger than him; and it will render him fearful unless it is because of larger animals.

If however it were in the 1st, it signifies the acquisition of houses and other estates, and for his benefit (both of a querent and a native); and it signifies a good and long life for him, and good fortune from his elders and blood-relatives.

Which if it were in the 2nd, it signifies that the native or querent will be made fortunate in children, and will rejoice because of them, and in consuming [food] and clothing; and in earning substance; and the more so if the Part of Fortune were there.

Indeed if it were in the 3rd, it signifies anger, labor, sorrow, and infirmities, nor will he be made fortunate in smaller animals or in persons subject to him; nor will it go well for him from thence.

Which if it were in the 4th and it were Venus or one of the convertible planets, and it were a question about matrimony, it signifies that it will be perfected. And if it were Jupiter, it signifies the native or querent is going to have good wives and good partners, and good fortune in mercantile dealings. Indeed if it were one of the malefics, it will signify he is going to have lawsuits and discords, or separation in life from the place in which you were to find him, or from his own goods (and the more so if it were of the lighter planets; and more again if the 4th house were a movable sign).

But if it were in the 5th, and it were a malefic, it signifies the native's or querent's bad condition, and his death and destruction. If however it were a benefic, it signifies the native or querent is going to have good fortune in the dowries of women and the taking possession of other goods. And if it were a question about wealth, it will signify his good fortune in foreign lands.

If however it were in the 6th, it signifies long journeys are not good for the native or querent, and [they will be] full of labor and unfortunate, unless it is a journey for domestics or other servants or animals;[265] nor is he fortunate with clerics.

Which if it were in the 7th, it signifies the native or querent is going to acquire honor or an art, and wealth with women and because of women.

Indeed if it were in the 8th, it signifies he is going to fulfill many of his wishes, and that which he hopes for, and particularly concerning the matters of the dead; and especially on the occasion of friends or some fortunate matter.

Indeed if it were in the 9th, it signifies anger and tribulation for the native or querent is going to come from matters about which he was inclined to have good and usefulness, and in which he had trust.

On the 9th house and its Lord

If however the Lord of the 9th house were in the 10th in someone's nativity or question, it signifies the native or querent is going to have a good and decent and honorific intimacy with men, and especially with noble men and magnates, and the household members of magnates, and will contract a stay with them, or he will have it from them or from other magistrates.

Which if it were in the 11th, and it were a question about a journey, it signifies it will be fortunate and fruitful, and the more so, if it were a journey to friends or with friends. It will even signify the native or querent is going to complete many of his own thoughts to his liking, and that he will adhere to some great relation who is known to him.

Indeed if it were in the 12th, it signifies that some immovable and likewise unfortunate (and for him, harmful) things will come down to the native or querent, even though they will not be long-lasting; or that he will be wounded or injured by large animals.

Indeed if it were in the 1st, and it were a question about children, it signifies the querent or native is going to have good and useful children, and [will have]

---

[265] I.e., to purchase or hire such people or things.

fortune in them and because of them, and he will even be fortunate in clothing; and joys coming to him will be lasting; and he will be made happy in all delightful things; and he will live well and honorably.

Indeed if it were in the 2nd, and it were a question about children or domestics, or about smaller animals, it signifies wealth and profit and usefulness because of them; you could even judge the same for the native because of them.

Which if it were in the 3rd, and it were a question about marriage or about a partnership to be contracted, or about a mercantile deal to be made, it signifies the good fortune of all of the aforesaid; and the more so and more certainly, if the significator were made fortunate; and the native or querent will be made fortunate in his blood-relatives, and especially in the older ones, and in fellow-villagers; and he will be made fortunate in lawsuits, and great disputes will happen to him; and he will be made fortunate in partners and in mercantile dealings. Indeed if it were Venus, it signifies he is going to be fortunate in women; if however it were one of the malefics, it will signify the contrary.

Indeed if it were in the 4th, and it were a question about death, it signifies it is going to arrive; and it will be according to the nature of the planet who is the significator of the aforesaid matter. It even signifies that the native or querent will inherit the goods of the dead, and especially the immovable ones; and he will acquire goods from dowries or because of women. And if he did not earn wealth because of one of the aforesaid, it seems that he is going to make money in a foreign land. If however one of the malefics were the significator of death (namely Saturn or Mars), it signifies an unpraiseworthy death; and these things will happen to him in some dwelling.

If however it were in the 5th, it signifies a praiseworthy journey because of children or clothing, or things consumed, or because of heralds or things announced, and he will be made fortunate in journeys of a moderate length.

Which if it were in the 6th, it signifies the native or querent is going to be preferred and set above low-class people and his lessers; and that he will make money because of small animals or at an opportunity [presented] by them.

And if it were in the 7th, it signifies his good fortune in matrimonies or women, and merchant dealings and partners, and likewise in lands that are not his own.

Indeed if it were in the 8th, it signifies the native or querent is going to fall into prison, or a serious or deadly infirmity, and into tribulation. Indeed if he were to get himself involved with large animals, harm and damage will follow from thence, nor will they assist in his usefulness; and it will be feared that they will injure him or dash him against something.

On the 8th house and its Lord

If the Lord of the 8th house were in the 9th, and it were a question about someone absent, it signifies that the absent person is doing well, and especially if his significator were a benefic. Like if it were Jupiter, it signifies that he is enjoying himself with some judges or ecclesiastics; or he is studying in sciences to be learned further. If it were Venus, it signifies that he is enjoying himself with women, or with people freely eating and drinking. If however it were the Moon or Mercury, it signifies that he is enjoying himself with varied and diverse persons, and that he will not remain steadfastly [there], nor firmly in one place or in one land. Which if it were Mars, and he were made fortunate and strong, it signifies that he works by means of some art [in] which iron and fire is worked and comes to be, and the shedding of blood; and it seems that such activity with the aforesaid persons is useful and fruitful for him.

But if it were in the 10th, and it were a question about a short journey, and especially if it were a journey to some magnate or on the occasion of some magistracy, or on the occasion of some matter conveying honor to the querent, it will signify the aforesaid matters are going to come about according to the querent's intention.

Indeed if it were in the 11th, it will signify that his friends are applying themselves to act so that he might acquire some immovable thing that is useful and honorable for him (if the question were about this).

If however it were in the 12th, and it were a question about children, it signifies their bad filial relation,[266] or that they will not live; and if they were to live, he will not rejoice with them nor because of them. It will even signify poison offered in food to the querent or native; and that he will not be made fortunate in clothing; and that, often, embassies and new displeasing things will be conveyed to him.

Indeed if it were in the 1st, it signifies that he will have moderate good fortune in servants and domestics, and in small animals, and that he will not be burdened by many or serious infirmities.

Which if it were in the 2nd, it signifies the native or querent is going to get a woman, on the occasion of which wealth and usefulness will follow; and that he

---

[266] *Filiationem.*

will have good fortune in the merchant dealings of movable things. Nevertheless, if he were to contract a partnership with someone, it will not last long; and he will be litigious with his own family.

Indeed if it were in the 3rd, and it were a question about a short journey, it signifies death on that journey. And if it were a question about a dowry, it signifies he is going to have it, and with neighbors or in the quarter in which the querent lived (but not with respect to an inheritance).

If it were in the 4th, and it were a question about a long journey, it signifies it will be bad, severe, and hard; it even signifies the querent is going to acquire a bad reputation on it. And if it were a question about some cleric, it signifies he is evil and dishonest and having little faith in divine matters. You could say the same about someone absent, if the question were about him.

If however it were in the 5th, it signifies the native or querent is going to have good fortune in children and edibles and clothing. If it were a question about nuptials or a letter, it signifies good heralds, and something good will be contained in the letter.

Indeed if it were in the 6th, and it were a question about fortune, it signifies it will be weak and not well firm; nor will the native or querent be fortunate in friends; nor will they be well truth-telling to him. But he will be fortunate in servants and those serving, and in small animals.

Indeed if it were in the 7th, and it were a question about a prison or about an infirmity (about which it is feared), it signifies the querent is going to see or run into that which he feared or doubted; and this will happen to him because of a women or partner or merchant; and there will be a trouble to be feared from robbers or exiles or people expelled [from the community], or a game or women's betrayal.

On the 7th house and its Lord

If however the Lord of the 7th house were in the 8th in someone's nativity or his question, it signifies the native or querent is going to make money on the occasion of someone's death; or that he will inherit the goods of the dead. And if it were a question about the death of a merchant partner, or a wife or enemy, it will signify it. And if it were a question about someone absent, it will signify that the absent person will take a wife in that absence; and it will be possible that he will be imprisoned on the occasion of a woman.

If it were in the 9th, and it were a question about some journey, it signifies it will be useless and not lucrative, but more likely harmful, and the more so if the

9th were the house of some malefic or there were an impeded malefic in it. Which if it were a question whether a man would be conjoined with some women, or for someone who was inclined to enter into some church, it will signify that. If however it were a question whether someone would find enemies on the road, or about a wife who is suspected of committing adultery with some cleric, or she herself intended to go to some land or to another place, or a cleric whom he said is going to be an enemy of the querent, it will signify that. If however it were a question about someone expelled or exiled, it signifies his return.

Which if it were in the 10th, and the querent feared lest the king or another layperson preferred to him would be inimical to him, or if his enemies will have rule over him, or if the adversaries will win against him in a suit or contention, or if a lord or judge were more favorable to the enemies or adversaries than to him, it will signify that. Indeed if it were a question whether a lord (or other person preferred to him) or physician would corrupt (or do it with) his wife, it will signify that. But if it were a question about contracting a partnership with him, it signifies that the partnership will be good and useful and do honor; and the more so and more usefully so, if the partnership were of immovable things, and that the querent on that occasion will come to some art or to some profession.

Indeed if it were in the 11th, and it were a question about children, it signifies that his children will be fortunate, and he will be made fortunate in them and because of them, and in clothing; in addition to this, if the planetary significator were a benefic and made fortunate and strong, good fortune will follow the querent wherever he would go. You could say the same about friends and about the household intimates of the king and a magnate who is fit for a kingdom.

If however it were in the 12th, it signifies anger and sorrow and an infirmity is going to come to the native or querent—I say this, if the significator were a malefic or made unfortunate. If however it were a benefic or made fortunate, it will signify he is going to get animals both bigger and smaller; and even take possession of, and incarcerate, his enemies.

Indeed if it were in the 1st, and it were a benefic and made fortunate, it signifies the native or querent will be fortunate, so that his station could hardly be improved. If however it were a malefic and made unfortunate, his station could hardly be made worse, nor his being in all actions (except for an expelled man and exile, because for him it signifies return to the land from which he was expelled). Which if it were a woman ejected from the house of her husband, or she absented herself of her own will, and it were a question about this, it signifies she will turn back completely.

If however it were in the 2nd, and it were a question about the death of an enemy or wife or partner, it signifies it. It even signifies the loss of movable things because of robbers, or harm because of enemies or a game, and he would even find that his family will be inimical to the native or the querent.

Which if it were in the 3rd, and it were a question about a journey and blood-relatives, it signifies it will be good and useful, provided that one of the malefics is not there (and especially the Tail of the Dragon). If however one of the benefics were there, and it were a journey by land, its goodness will be increased; and the more so, if the third [sign] were an earthy sign. If however it were by water, a watery sign will be better than an earthy one.

Indeed if it were in the 4th, it signifies that his enemies will be concerned with the querent's immovable things (if it were a question about this). And if it were a question whether the father or grandfather or father-in-law would take a wife, it signifies it is going to happen; it will even be possible that some one of the aforesaid people would bring a suit against him about some matter.

Which if it were in the 5th, and it were a question about a matter which the querent is inclined to have or acquire, it signifies it is made fortunate: it even signifies that his friends will be strong and constant for him; and it will even be possible for him that his children and those who are regarded [by him to be] in place of children, will be inimical to him. And if it were a question about taking a wife, it will signify this. And if he had a suspect wife, it seems that she is not without stain. And it seems that his enemies would take away his clothing, or perhaps robbers will take it away from him; or that his enemies will capture his child.

Indeed if it were in the 6th and it were a question about prison, it will signify it. It seems the same must be said about growing infirm. And if he were to have a suspect wife, it seems she does the deed with a very young man, or that she[267] is otherwise going to be inimical to the querent. And if it were a question about smaller animals, it seems that the enemies will take them away from him. And if a woman asks whether her man is doing it with a young girl of whom it is suspected, it seems that it is true—it even seems that he is going to have children from her.

---

[267] Reading *ipsa* for *ipse*.

On the 6th house and its Lord

If the Lord of the 6th house were in the 7th, and it were a question about infirmity, it signifies it will be because of love (like passionate love).[268] And if it were about someone serving, it signifies the querent will get him, but it does not seem he will be well faithful to him. And if it were about a merchant transaction, it signifies it will be well lucrative, but it must be watched out for if he were to persevere in it, lest it be ended to his harm.

If however it were in the 8th, and it were a question about the death of a servant or a smaller animal, it signifies it. And if it were about a dowry or an inheritance of the dead, or about wealth from blood-relatives (especially those younger than him) or neighbors, it will signify the quaesited thing will come.

But if it were in the 9th, it signifies the querent is going to go on or make a journey because of some immovable thing, and he is going to take possession of it; or he will enter some church or some religion, or is going to have some conversation with clerics.

Indeed if it were in the 10th in a nativity or a question, it will signify good and honorable children are going to come to the native or querent. And if someone were to ask whether his master would be taken sick, or be deposed from his [position of] honor, it seems it must be feared that it will happen so. And if it were a question about a mother or a master (whether she [or he] is taken ill), it seems to signify it.

Which if it were in the 11th, and it were a question about animals, it signifies they are useful. And if it were a question whether a friend would be taken ill, it signifies it; in other things the fortune of the querent will not be well disposed.

Indeed if it were in the 12th, and it were a question about the infirmity of slaves or the incarcerated, or animals, it will signify it.

If however it were in the 1st, and it were a question about people serving, or about lesser animals (what is going to be concerning them), it signifies that they will not last long in his hands; and if they were to remain, they will be taken ill; however it will be useful in the person[269] of the querent.

But if it were in the 2nd and it were a question about entering some church, or about a long journey, it will signify it is good and useful and lucrative.

Indeed if it were in the 3rd, and it were a question about dignity or about an art with fellow-neighbors, or about a mastery[270] with blood-relatives, it signifies

---

[268] *Hereos*. I will follow Hand/Zoller (p. 83) in taking this to be a misprint for *eros*.
[269] I.e., if it were about his own physical condition.
[270] Or professional engagement.

that it will fall to him according to what was asked, nor will it be prolonged for much time besides.

Which if it were in the 4th, and it were a question about stable matters, or about his own blood-relatives older than him, it signifies good fortune in them. But if it were a question about a city, or about a castle, it[271] signifies infirmities are going to come into it, and the habitation of bad men in it, and of those trying and laboring to do evil.

Indeed if it were in the 5th, and it were a question about matters concerning which the querent ought to be happy or rejoice, or about clothing or about pregnancy, it will signify it. And if it were a question about some infirmity, it signifies it is from witches or something worked.[272]

On the 5th house and its Lord

If the Lord of the 5th house were in the 6th, and it were a question whether a child is going to take ill, it signifies it is going to happen; and if it were about taking charge of people serving or small animals (according to how the question was), it will be so signified. Which if the question were about eating or about clothing, it would signify something unlucky is going to happen to the querent from thence. And if it were a question about a herald, it will signify infirmity for him, or anger on the road, and that he will carry a bad letter or embassy.

If however it were in the 7th, and it were a question about the condition of a child, it signifies he is going to copulate, and it seems that he would do this against the will of his parents; and it will be feared lest the child fall into the hands of enemies (if he were to have them), or that he himself would be become a janitor,[273] or he will go back and forth[274] with prostitutes, or perhaps he will adhere to merchants. And if Mars or Saturn were there, or the Tail of the Dragon, or Venus, it will signify evil for all the above-said. And if it were a question about a theft, it will seem that the robber is his son. If however it were a question about someone expelled or an exile, it signifies good for him; for it portends[275] his joy and his turning back to his own land.

---

[271] Omitting *enim*.
[272] *Facturis*, i.e., something caused by human means–its pairing with "witches" (*maleficiis*) suggests magical spells.
[273] *Zanitor*, following Hand/Zoller (p. 84). Perhaps this pertains to *ianua*, "door," as though he will be a lowly doorkeeper, or hanging around idly in doorways.
[274] *Vacillet*.
[275] Reading *portendit* for *protendit*.

Which if it were in the 8th, and it were a question about hereditary goods, and especially immovable ones, it signifies the querent is going to take possession of them. The same is to be said regarding dowry goods. If however it were about someone absent, it signifies he is doing well. And if it were a question whether the inherited goods would arrive into the hands of a child, it will signify it. And if it were about a pregnancy, it will signify the fetus will not be vital.[276]

But if it were in the 9th, and it were a question about a child–whether he is going to enter the church, or he is going to make some great journey–it will signify it (and the more so if it were the child of some cleric), and he will be good and safe. And all of these things will seem to be useful for the querent. And if it were a question on behalf of the Roman Church, it signifies it will rejoice over the quaesited matter, and be happy.

Indeed if it were in the 10th, and it were a question whether a son is going to achieve an art or office, it will signify it with labor and fatigue; and it seems that it will be more over beasts or low-class persons.

Indeed if it were in the 11th, and it were a question about a mercantile dealing or about a partnership to be contracted, or about copulation, and Mars were the significator, it will signify anger and sorrow over all the above-said; and the querent could even be incarcerated on that occasion.

Indeed if it were in the 12th, and it were a question whether a child would be incarcerated or not, and there were doubt about this, it will signify it. If however it were a question about his infirmity, it signifies its prolongation; if about large animals, it will signify good and usefulness from them, but it will be feared that they will be taken away from him by auditors[277] under a certain pretext of rights.

If however it were in the 1st, and it were a nativity or a question about life, it signifies it will be long and honorable, and without danger, and it seems that it is because of the Church.

But if it were in the 2nd, and it were a question about wealth, it will signify it, and especially about movable things, or about some mastery or office, or perhaps from some lord or magnate. And if it were a question about children, it will signify them. And if it were a question about a herald or letter, whether it would come, it will signify it–and with usefulness and honor. But one must beware of children if he were to have children, lest they wound him on the occasion of movable goods. And if it were a question about a family affair, it

---

[276] I.e., it will not have means of life enough to live.
[277] I.e., legal officials.

signifies that all his household intimates will rejoice, and they will strive to make money in good faith.

And if it were in the 3rd, and it were a question about a journey to fellow-villagers or to blood-relatives, it signifies it, inasmuch as it is fortunate in itself for the good; and it signifies joy because of clothing and eating, and it will be useful in all things.

But if it were in the 4th, and it were a question about a secret or hidden matter, it will signify it. And if it were about some lasting thing, it signifies anger and distress and tribulation concerning it. And if it were about the father or grandfather or father-in-law or stepfather, and it was about having a child, it signifies that he will have one. And if the Tail of the Dragon were there, then it would signify detriment and evil, and especially because of fire and the shedding of his tenants' blood. And if it was a question about the end of some matter, joy will follow the querent from it[278] on the occasion of eating or clothing, or betrothal and the like, unless the aforesaid Tail works against the aforesaid. And if Venus were the significatrix, and she were impeded, and the question is about the fear of the city in which the querent lives, or about which he fears, it will be feared that it will suffer detriment from foreigners overcoming it—unless a benefic were in the 2nd from the Ascendant, because then it decreases the malice; if however a malefic were there, the malice is increased, and it will be a worse condition in that matter.

On the 4th house and its Lord

If however the Lord of the 4th house were in the 5th, and it were a question about younger blood-relatives, it signifies their joy and good condition. And if it were a question about their condition in the land in which they are, or their separation, it signifies their separation from that land.

Which if it were in the 6th and it were a question about a general illness of the citizens or inhabitants of the land about which the question were made, or that of another assemblage or society, or even of a particular house or family, or concerning slaves or servants or smaller animals, it will signify it.

If however it were in the 7th, and it were a question about an exile or someone expelled, whether he would return to his own habitation, and by what

---

[278] Bonatti tends to use the verb *sequor* contrary to its proper usage. The Latin reads: "the querent *will pursue* joy from it." This backwards use of *sequor* is found throughout the entire book, but especially in Tr. 9, where I try to follow Bonatti's meaning and point out the distinctions when it arises.

means, and the significator were Mars, it will signify the querent is going to return to his own things by means of iron or fire, or the shedding of blood. Indeed if it were Saturn, it will signify he is going to return with anger and pain and sorrow, and likewise his own labor or that of those living on that land, and this practically after losing hope. Indeed if the question were about the status of stable things, it will signify victory for the adversary or the one litigating with the querent. And if it were a question about commerce being planned out, it will signify it is going to come to the querent.

But if it were in the 8th, and it were a question about someone absent (whether he would turn back or not), it signifies he is going to return. And if it were about the accidents of the city or another land, it signifies infirmities and mortalities are going to enter into it. You may understand the same about any house which is inhabited, and about older blood-relatives. And if it were a question about a dowry or about the inheritance of someone dead or about to die, or about the goods of enemies or wives, or about mercantile dealings, it will signify that they will come to the querent according to what was asked. Indeed if it were about magical objects[279] or evil doings of this kind, it signifies they are in the home. Which if it were an earthy sign in the 4th house, it signifies that they are underground; and if it were a watery one, they will be in a moist place; if however it were an airy one, they will be elevated from the ground; indeed if it were a fiery one, they will be in the furthest elevation of the house.

Indeed if it were in the 9th, and it were a question about some cleric or bishop (or the like), whether he would die or not, it signifies he is going to die. And if it were about one of his own older blood-relatives, whether he is going to enter into some church or into some religion, it will signify that. If however it were a question about a journey, it will signify it will be hard and difficult and unfortunate, unless he is going to go because of some possession. And if it were a question about the querent's reputation [or fame], it signifies it will be low, practically nothing.

Indeed if it were in the 10th, and it were a question about a profession or art or rulership or dignity or the honor of some blood-relative older than him, it will signify it is going to come to him for whom the question was made. And if it were a question about their life, it signifies it is going to be long. And if it were a question about a matter which the querent wants that they should achieve, and

---

[279] *Facturis.* Based on the following sentence, Bonatti seems to be referring to talismans or other magically-charged objects causing trouble.

especially something stable, it will signify it is going to come to them. And if it were about the status of some city or land, it signifies its increase and loftiness.

Which if it were in the 11th, and it were a question about the querent's fortune, or someone else about whose [fortune] it is his business to ask, it signifies it is going to be good. And if it were a question whether public goods will come to the hands of his older blood-relatives, it will signify it. And if it were a question whether the court[280] or the court's heralds, or [those] of an authority or other magnate would enter some city or into someone's home, it will signify it.

But if it were in the 12th, and it were a question for some city or land (what is going to be of it), it signifies its bad condition and betrayal. And if it were on behalf of blood-relatives, it signifies their detriment and bad condition, and it could even be that they would be led away to prison, or they will grow ill with an illness that will be chronic. Which if it were a question about large animals, or about some incarcerated man, or about someone absent, it signifies their return and turning back.

If however it were in the 1st, and it were a question about the person of the querent, it signifies his bad disposition.

If however it were in the 2nd, and it were a question about wealth, it signifies it is going to be, and especially from friends or from stable things. But if it were a question about movable things, it must be feared that they will be taken away from him, and especially by his older blood-relatives.

Indeed if it were in the 3rd, and it were a question about wealth, it signifies that the querent should not pursue it except perhaps concerning larger animals. And if it were a question about the wealth of younger blood-relatives, or even those of equal age, it will signify it because of their own peculiar things or fixed objects.

On the 3rd house and its Lord

Indeed if the Lord of the 3rd house were in the 4th, and it were a question about wealth, it signifies the querent is going to gain stable things because of stable things. And if it were about some city or some castle, it signifies it is

---

[280] *Comes.* In the feudal period this designated the (military) companions of a feudal lord; but it also designated the "court," i.e., all of those who attended a lord. It is also possible that Bonatti simply means "a count."

going to be durable. You could say the same about a house or province, [that it is going] to come after it.[281]

Indeed if it were in the 5th, and it were a question about children, it signifies that he will have them and will rejoice because of them. And if it were about a child's journey or about those things which pertain to the 3rd, or to the 5th house, the question will be good.

Which if it were in the 6th, and it were a question about infirmity or about a matter concerning which the querent could be angered, it will signify it. And if it were about a male or female slave, about a male or female servant, about a dog or a hawk, or a sparrowhawk, or some like thing, it signifies their flight.

But if it were in the 7th, and it were a question whether blood-relatives or neighbors would oppose themselves to him, or whether some one of his own blood-relatives will take a wife, or if a wife would be having [an affair] with some blood-relative [of her own] or a blood-relative of the querent's, or with one of the neighbors, it will signify it.

If however it were in the 8th, and it were a question about death or about a dowry for which the questioner fears, it will signify he is going to encounter what he fears. And if it were a question about the inheritance of someone dead or about the dowry of a woman, or about wealth in the land to which he intends to go, it will signify it (even though with labor and fatigue). And if it were about someone absent, it signifies his turning back (even if not quickly).

Indeed if it were in the 9th, and it were a question about entering the church or some religion, it signifies it. And if it were a question about someone's death, and the significator were a malefic, or a malefic were in the 9th with it, it will signify it (lacking this, not). And if it were a question about a journey, it will signify it will be good, unless the malefics work against it. And if it were a question whether a bishop or other prelate will be friendly to him, it signifies it; you may say the same if it were about stable things, for it signifies good for the querent.

Indeed if it were in the 10th, and it were a question about an art or some other dignity or office, it will signify it. And if it were about a journey of the mother or a magnate, or other person preferred over him, it signifies it. And if it were whether he is going to make or contract a relationship with someone older than him, it will seem that it would come to be.

---

[281] *Post se.* Meaning uncertain. Hand/Zoller (p. 88) may be correct in translating this as "according to its [nature]."

Which if it were in the 11th, and if it were a question whether he is going to be a household intimate of the king or ruler, [or] whether he is going to take possession of royal or public goods, it signifies it; it will even signify fortune to come to the querent, and that he will cherish it.[282] And if it were about a journey, it signifies it will be made fortunate and good.

But if it were in the 12th, and it were a question about blood-relatives, it signifies they are going to become infirm or be incarcerated, and surrounded by betrayal. And if it were about large animals or about an incarcerated man, it signifies good for them.

Indeed if it were in the 1st and it were a question about the querent's life (or that of someone about whom it is his business to ask), it signifies it will be long and useful and good.

If however it were in the 2nd, and it were a question about movable goods, it must be feared that he will be defrauded by his blood-relatives or his fellow-villagers or even by his own household intimates.

On the 2nd house and its Lord

Indeed if the Lord of the 2nd were in the 3rd, and it were a question whether the querent would lose such things as he has, it will signify he is going to lose them, and this will happen because of fellow-villagers or short journeys or blood-relatives.

Which if it were in the 4th, and it were a question about the *census*, it signifies the querent is going to lose it on account of his father or some one of his blood-relatives. And if it were about stable or secret or underground things, it signifies a good status for the querent.

But if it were in the 5th, and it were a question about children, it signifies the querent is going to have them. And if it were a question which he did not want to reveal to you, it signifies that his intention is regarding children or on behalf of the children. And if it were about a herald, it signifies he is going to come. And if he were to fear that his daughter or stepson would take his goods away from him, it will signify it. If however it were about the standing of the family, the question will be good.

Indeed if it were in the 6th, and it were a question whether slaves or servants would take his things away from him, or whether his household intimates would become infirm, it will signify it.

---

[282] Reading *eam* for *eum*.

If however it were in the 7th, and he feared lest his enemies or robbers or expelled people would take his goods away from him, it will signify it. And if it were a question about an expelled man, it signifies he is going to turn back toward his own fatherland. And if it were a question about marriage or about a dowry or about a merchant dealing, it will signify that what he intends will come to him, [but] great usefulness will not follow[283] from thence. And if it were about a game, it signifies it will be harmful to him. You could say the same if it were suspected regarding the wife or the girlfriend, that she was stealing something from him.

Which if it were in the 8th, and it were a question about a dowry or about a deposit[284] or about debts to be recovered or about an inheritance of the dead, and the Lord of the 1st house were stronger than the Lord of the 7th, it will signify it will be acquired. And if it were a question about someone absent, it signifies he is going to turn back.

Indeed if it were in the 9th, and it were a question about the *census*, it will be feared that it will be taken away from him, and especially by the Roman Church.

But if it were in the 10th, and it were a question about wealth, it signifies the querent is going to have wealth from an art or a lord, but it must be feared lest what is earned be taken away from him by an authority or other ruler—and more seriously so if the question were about this.

Indeed if it were in the 11th, and the question were about fortune, it signifies the native is going to be made fortunate. And if it were a question whether the querent is going to gain from the good companions[285] of some lord or magnate, it will signify it; however one must beware lest the wealth be taken away from him by friends.

Indeed if it were in the 12th, and it were a question on behalf of the family, whether they would grow infirm, it signifies it, and with a long infirmity. You would say the same if it were about their incarceration. But if it were about an incarcerated man, it signifies he is going to escape. And if it were about large animals, the question will be good and useful for the querent.[286]

---

[283] Again, Bonatti's own Latin is backwards, and I have translated it according to his meaning.
[284] I.e., money deposited for safekeeping. My sense is that it is about the native's own money which he hopes to recover.
[285] *Comitis*. Again, these were the (military) companions and aids to a lord. Bonatti's meaning seems to be that he will benefit from an association with them.
[286] Bonatti omits to explain what would happen if the Lord of the 2nd were in the 1st.

On the 1st house and its Lord

If the Lord of the 1st house were in the 2nd, and it were a question about wealth, and a benefic were in the 2nd, it will signify it from himself and through himself. And if there were a malefic in the 2nd, it will signify the contrary.

If it were in the 3rd, and it were a question about a journey to blood-relatives or to fellow-villagers, it signifies it will be good and useful.

If it were in the 4th, and it were a question about a possession to be taken hold of, the question will be good; in all other things, it will be the contrary.

And if it were in the 5th, and it were a question about the status of the querent, it will signify it will be good, and that he will rejoice because of children and eating, and he will be made happy from thence, and because of those things which are signified by the 5th house.

But if it were in the 6th, and it were a question about a matter concerning which the querent is going to be angry or distressed, or he had fear about an infirmity to come, or about unfitting labor or [labor] of little note, it will signify he will encounter that which he fears. And if it were about the acquisition of slaves or servants or those serving, or of small animals, it will signify it.

If however it were in the 7th and it were a question about reckoning the value of a woman, or about a mercantile dealing (whether it would come to be or not), it will signify it. And if it were about an expelled man or an exile, whether he would turn back to his own [land] or not, it will signify he is going to turn back; in all other business matters it will signify the contrary.

Indeed if it were in the 8th, and it were a question about an infirm person, it signifies he is going to die, and the more so if Mars or the Moon or Mercury were there, impeded. Indeed if it were about the acquisition of a stranger's *census*, or about a dowry or about an inheritance of someone dead, it will signify it.

If it were in the 9th, and it were a question about traveling, or someone's entering into some church or religion, it will signify it. And if it were about a long journey, it signifies that the journey will not come to be at the appointed time; and if it had been undertaken, it will not be perfected.

If it were in the 10th, and it were a question about some rulership or mastery or dignity, it signifies that what he intends will reach the querent.

And if it were in the 11th, and it were a question about some matter which the querent anticipates, and it is with friends or from friends, and about which he has trust, it signifies that it will come to him according to what he intends.

If however it were in the 12th, and it were a question about prison or about a chronic or melancholic[287] infirmity, or about betrayal or about injury (whether violent, or one to be created or to come to the querent), it will signify it. If Venus or Saturn or the Part of Fortune were there with the Lord of the first, these[288] migitate the aforesaid contrary things (and especially in the matter of someone incarcerated, for it would signify his exit from the prison). But if it were a question about pilgrims or about large animals, it will signify good.

But if the significators were to fall into the aforesaid places,[289] look to see whether they are aspected by the other planets or not, or whether they are joined with them in those places: because the benefics increase good and decrease evil, and the malefics increase evil and decrease good.

On the ease of discovering what is signified by each house

I have introduced all of these things on what is signified by the twelve houses, so that it would be easy for you to discover what is signified by each house. Because occasionally there were some (of whom I have seen many), who believed astrologers ought to operate only by the 1st and 7th houses. They gave the 1st to the querent, and the 7th to the quaesited [person] or to the quaesited matter—which in my judgment was not appropriate. And I did this for your decreased labor (because it was always difficult to seek through all the houses) so that you might discover the significator of every quaesited matter, and because I have not found any predecessor of ours having gotten involved in this (that I ever remember)—not that I believe they were ignorant, but because it was tedious for them to undergo so much work; and they even left it to the industry of the wise.

Whence, if there arose for you a question about some matter, you could know by what house you could discover the significator of the quaesited matter. And I could tell you many other significations of the twelve houses, but I would lead you into such prolixity and confusion, that it would generate irritation for you. Whence it seems to me that these things I have told you can suffice for you, wherefore such questions or such nativities will hardly or never reach you without you being able to do well enough by means of the aforesaid. For you could predict to the native or querent what ought to happen to him from all of the aforesaid, for the whole time of his life, if you were to know well the hour

---

[287] I.e., what we now call "depression."
[288] Omitting *quoniam*.
[289] *Loca*.

of his nativity, and you wanted rightly to give attention to all of the above-said with discernment.

And I will tell you, in its own place and time, how every person ought to be considered, whether he asks for himself or for another, and who ought to ask for another, and how.[290] Because it is looked in one way for him who asks for himself; another way [for him] who asks for another; another, if a citizen or inhabitant of some place asks; another, if an expelled or banned or exiled or absent person asks; another, if a cleric asks; another, if a layperson asks; another, if a cleric asks about a layperson, and *vice versa*; and another if a king asks about a subject, and *vice versa*; another if a king [asks] about the common people, another if it is the reverse; another if the Pope [asks] about a bishop, another if the bishop [asks] about the Pope; another, if a bishop [asks] about his own clerics, another if a cleric [asks] about his bishop; another if a master [asks] about a slave, another if it is the reverse. And understand thus with all diversities of persons, the which diversities and houses (which are given to them) I will tell you after this in the business of judgments, for thus every person will discover the matter of the question and judgment.

Chapter 7: On the numbering of the houses and why they begin from the 1st and go toward the 4th, and from the 4th to the 7th, and from the 7th to the 10th, and from the 10th to the 1st

So that it might be satisfactory for a question and the querent about the numbering of the twelve houses, if someone wished to say that [while] they are to be numbered, it does not happen according to the right order. For we number them beginning from the 1st, going under the earth toward the 4th, and from the 4th toward the 7th, and from the 7th toward the 10th, and from the 10th toward the 1st, the which numbering or computation of houses seems to happen from the right to the left. For indeed it seems that we ought to number them from the 1st, going toward the 10th, and from the 10th to the 7th, and from the 7th to the 4th, and from the 4th to the 1st. For then we would advance according to the direction in which we write, beginning from the left, going toward the right.

The reason why this was, is this: because even though the heaven turns from the east to the west by means of the first motion, still the planets (which imprint

---

[290] See throughout Tr. 6 for these matters.

in inferior bodies) are moved from the west to the east by means of the second motion (which is from the right to the left) in the contrary direction of the first motion, wherefore it is against the succession of the signs. For the signs ascend from under the earth (which is the left of heaven) to that which is above the earth (which is its right).

But perhaps you could say that the planets sometimes run in the direction of the first motion (namely when they are retrograde). To which it can be responded thus, that the motion of retrogradation it not natural, but rather accidental.[291] Nor however is it totally with the first motion, but rather it is always according to something contrary to the first motion, namely from the motion of the circles carrying them off[292] toward the east, in the contrary direction of the first motion.

Chapter 8: Which houses are strong, which stronger, which weak, which weaker, and which middling

Above I have made mention to you about the twelve houses which are named "towers" or "cusps," and about what is signified by them, from the 1st up to the 12th by going forward, and from the 12th up to the 1st by going backward in succession. Now it remains to be stated which of them are strong, which stronger, which weak, which weaker, which middling.

The strong ones are the four angles, namely the 1st house (which is the eastern angle), the 10th (which is the southern angle), the 7th (which is the western angle), the 4th (which is the northern angle). And of these four, two are stronger than the others—namely, the 1st and the 10th.

The weak ones are four, which are cadent from the angles: namely the 3rd (which falls from the angle of the earth, which is the 4th house), the 9th (which falls from the southern angle, which is the 10th house), the 12th (which falls from the eastern angle, which is the 1st house), the 6th (which falls from the western angle, which is the 7th house). And of these four, two are weaker than the others—namely, the 6th and the 12th.

Indeed the remaining four, which are the 2nd, 5th, 8th, and 11th, are middling, but still they have greater participation with the strong ones (because they go toward them) than with the weak ones. Because even though they are bordering

---

[291] That is, retrograde motion is only apparent, because the planets are always moving consistently on the circles of their epicycles—it only appears backwards to us.
[292] *Deferentium*, whence we get the astronomical term "deferent."

on [the cadents], just as with the angles, still [the succeedent houses] recede from them and go toward the strong ones. For the 2nd, which succeeds the 1st, goes toward it; the 5th, which succeeds the 4th, goes toward it; the 8th, which succeeds the 7th, goes toward it; the 11th, which succeeds the 10th, goes toward it.

And Sahl said that the more worthy and stronger places[293] of the circle are the angles; the less worthy and less strong are the succeedents; the ones weaker than the rest of the other places, are the cadents. And he said that the angles (namely the 1st, 10th, 7th, 4th) signify present things; the succeedents[294] (namely the 2nd, 5th, 8th, 11th) signify what is to be, and what succeeds that which is present. Indeed the cadents[295] (namely the 3rd, 6th, 9th, 12th) signify what already was and what is going away, and no longer is.

Of the aforesaid angles, the eastern angle (namely the Ascendant) is stronger and more worthy; and a planet which is in it, is stronger—and especially if it were to have some dignity there (whether domicile, or exaltation or bound or triplicity or face—unless it were in the excepted cases,[296] or if the Lord of the 7th were in the Ascendant, and likewise). Then the angle of the Midheaven (namely the 10th) succeeds in strength, whence a planet which is in the 10th house is said to be less strong than one which is in the Ascendant, except in [worldly] dignities or magistracies or professions or other lay offices, and whose which pertain to laypeople (as is said elsewhere). And again the one which is in the western angle (namely in the 7th house) will be somewhat less strong again than one which is in the 10th. And one which is in the angle of the earth (which is the 4th house) will be thus far less strong than one which is in the 7th.

And after the angles, the stronger ones are the succeedents,[297] as I told you. But the 11th house is stronger than all the other succeedents, and it follows after the 4th in strength; but a planet which is in it will be less strong that one which is in the 4th. And the 5th succeeds the 11th in strength, whence a planet which is in the 5th will be somewhat less strong than one which is in the 11th, with the

---

[293] *Loca.* But Sahl's translator uses *loci.*
[294] *Succedentia*, which is only used for neuter terms—this either means succeedent signs, or succeedent "places" (*loca*). Bonatti continues this way of referring to the kinds of houses below.
[295] *Cadentia.* See above note.
[296] See below. Bonatti means that while a planet in one house will be quantitatively stronger than one in another, it may not be stronger in the *particular signification* that the other planet has. So a planet in the 1st house may be generally stronger than one in the 10th, but it will not be stronger in signifying *profession* as will the one in the 10th.
[297] *Succedentia*, see above.

peculiar significations of each house being excepted, in which its Lord is stronger than the other (insofar as the significations are to be distinguished).

But even though the succeedents may be said to be stronger than the cadents, the 9th, which is of the cadents, is stronger than the 2nd is, or the 8th, which are [both] of the succeedents. And a planet which is in the 9th will be somewhat less strong than one which is in the 5th, but stronger than one which is in the 2nd or 8th. And the 3rd house succeeds the 9th in strength, and precedes the 2nd and the 8th in some cases, whence a planet which is in the 3rd will be less weak than one which is in the 2nd.[298]

Whence, the aforesaid seven places[299] are better, stronger, and more praiseworthy than the rest of the others: namely, the Ascendant, which is stronger than the 10th; and the 10th, which is stronger than the 7th; and the 7th, which is stronger than the 4th; and the 4th, which is stronger than the 11th; and the 11th, which is stronger than the 5th; and the 5th, which is stronger than the 9th; and the 9th, which is stronger than the 3rd.

After these seven places,[300] the stronger or less weak one is the 3rd, because it is the house in which the Moon rejoices; for then the 3rd prevails over the 2nd and the 8th, like in journeys and the like, just as it was said in which houses the planets rejoice.[301] Then the 2nd, because it ascends after the 1st; but in the 8th house there is said to be great misfortune, because it is the house of death, nor does it aspect the Ascendant. But the two houses left over, namely the 6th and the 12th, are evil and very weak, and unfortunate, and they are said to be worse than the rest of the houses. And every planet which is in them will be of no advantage, because the 6th from the Ascendant does not aspect the Ascendant, and it is cadent from it, and it is the house of infirmity and of all vices [or defects] and of all diseases, both separable and inseparable. And it is the place[302] of the joy of Mars, who rejoices in burnings, the shedding of blood, and in all evil doings which are worked by iron or fire. Likewise the 12th house is cadent from the Ascendant, nor does it aspect it, and it is the place of hidden enemies not openly turning against [the native or querent], and it is a place of distress,

---

[298] See below, but Bonatti is still unclear as to exactly what situations favor the 3rd over the 2nd and 8th.
[299] *Loca.*
[300] *Loca.*
[301] Does this mean that the 3rd is given greater weight generally in such questions, or just when the Moon is in it, or what?
[302] *Locus.*

grief, labor, and sorrow, and wailing and lamentation, and it is the place of the joy of Saturn, who rejoices in wailing, sorrow, labor, and lamentation.

Chapter 9: That the planets go against the firmament, namely against the first motion

Abū Ma'shar said[303] (and the philosophers agree in this), that all the planets run in a peculiar motion of their own against the motion of the firmament, unless by chance they are retrograde—which happens to the three superior planets (namely Saturn, Jupiter and Mars) and to two inferior ones (namely Venus and Mercury). Indeed retrogradation does not happen to the luminaries, but quickness of course and its slowness does happen to them.

Indeed the Tail and Head of the Dragon run in the contrary of the motion of the planets, namely against the succession of the signs. For the planets go from Aries into Taurus, from Taurus into Gemini, from Gemini into Cancer, from Cancer into Leo, from Leo into Virgo, from Virgo into Libra, from Libra into Scorpio, from Scorpio into Sagittarius, from Sagittarius into Capricorn, from Capricorn into Aquarius, from Aquarius into Pisces, from Pisces into Aries. But the Head and the Tail go in the contrary of this motion, for they go from Aries into Pisces, from Pisces into Aquarius, from Aquarius into Capricorn, and so on up to the end of the signs, by retrograding. And again, Cancaph[304] said, for the Head of the Dragon is nothing else than the intersection of the circles of the luminaries with one another, in two opposite places; whence in those places, or around those places[305] by 12° or thereabouts, the eclipse of the luminaries takes place.

Chapter 10: On the colors which the houses signify

Since the aforesaid twelve houses signify the above-said, someone could perhaps reckon that they do not signify anything else. But it is not so, or rather they signify not just the aforesaid, but they signify diverse colors in turn. For the 1st house and the 7th, signify whiteness; the 2nd and the 12th signify greenness; the 3rd and 11th signify saffron; the 4th and the 10th redness; the 5th and 9th signify a honey color; the 6th and the 8th signify blackness. Whence if it were

---

[303] Undoubtedly in *Gr. Intr.*
[304] Unknown astrologer, but probably the Indian Kankah. See Introduction.
[305] *Loca.*

necessary for you to look for any matter in terms of color, look to see in which of the houses you were to find the significator, and according to that house, judge on the color of the thing which you were to seek.[306]

Chapter 11: In which houses the planets rejoice

Abū Ma'shar[307] and al-Qabīsī[308] said that every one of the seven planets has a certain accidental power in one of the above-stated twelve houses, which is called a "joy."

> For Mercury rejoices in the 1st, because the 1st house signifies the body of the native or querent; and therefore Mercury rejoices in it, because he signifies knowledge, and that is a thing which is more fitted to the person of the native or querent than any other; for it alone can ennoble a man, which no other accident can do.

> The Moon rejoices in the 3rd, because the 3rd signifies short and quick journeys, and those which are changed quickly and are repeated; whence, because the Moon signifies even fast and quick changes from one proposition to another, from one thing to another, therefore she rejoices in it, because no other house signifies this.

> Venus rejoices in the 5th, because it is the house of joy and delight and dancing, and she signifies this; therefore she rejoices in it, because the rest of the houses do not signify this.

> Mars rejoices in the 6th, because it is the house of deception and infirmities and slaves, and he signifies slaves and deceivers and liars and those speaking falsely; and therefore he rejoices in it, because the rest of the houses do not signify this.

> The Sun rejoices in the 9th, which is the house of religion, because he naturally signifies religion; and therefore he rejoices in it, because the rest

---

[306] See for example the question of racing horses in Tr. 6, Part 2, 12th House, Ch. 2.
[307] *Abbr.*, I.121.
[308] Al-Qabīsī, I.70.

of the houses do not signify this, even if he himself signifies other things.[309]

Jupiter rejoices in the 11th, because he is a benefic, and signifies fortune and wealth, and is naturally a significator of money and profit, and the 11th house signifies that.

Saturn rejoices in the 12th, because it is the house of grief and sorrow, labor, lamentation and tears, and Saturn rejoices in these, and the like.

Chapter 12: On the significations of the houses, or of the angles [and] the succeedents, and [the significations] of the Lords of the angles, succeedents, and cadents

It was stated in the signification of the twelve houses, that the angles signify strength and perfection, and the hastened and more quick arrival of matters; and the angles and their Lords signify the greatness of honor and value and fortune.

Indeed those cadent from the angles signify weakness and detriment and misfortune, and the covering of things (apart from the 9th and the 3rd, which signify appearance; indeed the 6th and 12th signify hiddenness and covering up, and the baseness of things, and disgrace, and a hastened fall).

Indeed the succeedents of the angles signify medium strength and fortune. For the 11th, which succeeds the 10th, is stronger and more worthy than the others, and signifies medium fortune because of friends, and because of something in which someone would have some trust, or because of another reason among those which are signified by the 11th house. The 5th house, which succeeds the 4th, signifies medium fortune by donations and by reason of children and gladness and happiness, or because of another reason among those which are signified by the 5th house. Indeed the 2nd, which succeeds to the 1st, signifies medium fortune because of substance and underofficials and household intimates, or even some one of those things which are signified by the 2nd house. The 8th, which succeeds the 7th, signifies medium fortune because of substance which is inherited from the dead, which certain people call "inheritances."[310] And al-Qabīsī said[311] that it signifies [medium fortune] because of

---

[309] Reading *alia* for *aliud*.
[310] *Almaverith*. See above.
[311] Al-Qabīsī, I.72.

secret things or at least another reason of those which are signified by the 8th house.

Chapter 13: On the signification of the Lords of the angles, and concerning the angles, and first on the Lord of the first [angle] in the 1st

When the Lords of the angles are in the angles, they signify these things: wherefore if the Lord of the first [angle] were in the first [angle], it signifies the native's good fortune, and his acquisition through himself, by his own industry and the exhaustion of his own body, and through his own family, through his own study, and through his own concerns, and through those things which are signified by the 1st house.

If however it were in the 10th, it signifies his good fortune through his own magistracies, and through offices or positions of civil authority, and through lofty and higher professions, and even through the king and communicating with kings or magnates, and the like; and even by those things which are signified by the 10th house.

If however it were in the 7th, it signifies his good fortune through assemblages and contracts which he will make with men who will be useful to him, and even through wives, and because of women and partners, and through those things which are signified by the 7th house.

If however it were in the 4th, it signifies his good fortune because of the father or grandfather or father-in-law, or because of some inheritance which will reach him (whence he will gain wealth), and through the lengthening of rivers or other waters, and the planting of trees, and the building of houses, and because of ancient things and [things having] roots, or through hidden treasure which he will find underground, and the like; or through those things which are signified by the 4th house.

On the Lord of the 10th in the 10th

Indeed, if the Lord of the 10th were in the 10th, it signifies good fortune through a great kingdom, and through a king and higher magisterial offices, and through those things which are signified by the 10th house.

And if the Lord of the 10th were in the 7th, it signifies good fortune through the king or a kingdom, and through victory in contentions, and through those who have people contending against them; and because of the reasons of women, or through those things which are signified by the 7th house.

If the Lord of the 10th were in the 4th, it signifies good fortune through a kingdom and through the collecting together of tributes, and through the reasons of tributes or their occasions, and by the cultivation of lands and the buildings of cities, castles, and the like; and by the draining out and divisions of the waters and rivers, and through the guarding of cities, castles, and the like; and through ancient things and diggings under the earth, or through some one of the things which are signified by the 4th house.

If however it were in the 1st, it signifies good fortune by means of a kingdom or through a praiseworthy and famous matter, and through the skills of his own person, and through a stay with kings and magnates and their proximity; and because of a common person or through those things which are signified by the 1st house.

On the Lord of the 7th in the 7th

If the Lord of the 7th were in the 7th, it signifies good fortune through business transactions and assemblages and exchanges. And if it were a woman, through nursing and nourishing, and [if a] man, through women and partners, and through the activity of sowing, and the like, or through those things which are signified by the 7th house.

If it were in the 4th, it signifies good fortune by assemblages of women, and women will earn wealth for him, and for his usefulness; and by the business dealings of fathers and grandfathers, and their purposes, and by reason of inherited things, and the planting of trees and vineyards, and the cultivation of the land, and the like, or by those things which are signified by the 4th house.

If the Lord of the 7th were in the 1st, it signifies good fortune and profit and business dealings through the employments of medicine, and through astronomy, and through matters and through labors in spiritual matters, and skills, or through those things which are signified by the 1st house.

If however the Lord of the 7th were in the 10th, it signifies good fortune through employments of the king, or through those things which are signified by the 10th house.

On the Lord of the 4th in the 4th

If the Lord of the 4th were in the 4th, it signifies good fortune through the employment of chief offices, and the mechanical arts. And if he were of a clan of farmers, it signifies his good fortune through the cultivation of the land because of the produce or profit, through the purposes of fathers and the like, and ancient matters, or through those things which are signified by the 4th house.

If however the Lord of the 4th were in the Ascendant, it signifies good fortune from the cultivation of the earth and produce, through skill and profoundness of counsel, and through those things which are signified by the 1st house.

If[312] however the Lord of the 4th house were in the 10th, it signifies good fortune because of the cultivation of lands and from the produce, or from profit through the employments of kings and magnates or nobles and the wealthy, and by the fruits of magisterial offices and their employment, and the like; or through those things which are signified by the 10th house.

Indeed[313] if the Lord of the 4th were in the 7th, it signifies good fortune and wealth or profit and success from the cultivation of the earth, and because of profit through the purposes of wives, partners, and enemies and contentions, and by business dealings, and similar things which are signified by the 7th house.

On the signification of the Lords of the succeedents in the succeedents

Indeed the Lords of the succeedents in the succeedents (any one of them in any succeedent) signify medium fortune[314] through those things which are signified by that succeedent, just as was said about the Lords of the angles in each angle, according to what is signified by it.

On the signification of the Lords of the cadents in the cadents

But the Lords of the cadents in the cadents (any one of them in any cadent) signify misfortune and impediment through those things which are signified by

---

[312] Omitting the title "On the Lord of the 4th in the 10th," to keep symmetry with the other passages.
[313] Omitting the title "On the Lord of the 4th in the 7th," to keep symmetry with the other passages.
[314] Omitting an extra *in succedentibus*.

that cadent, just as was said about the Lords of the angles in every angle, according to what is signified by it.

These things are those which the Lords of the aforesaid houses signify in the aforesaid houses, but it was exemplified by the Lords of the angles, as an example for the Lords of the succeedents and the Lords of the cadents.

Chapter 14: On finding the significator of a quaesited matter

And in addition, so that you may not fall into error nor into ambiguity concerning the significations of matters which are signified by each house, I will teach you to find the planet which would be the significator of the matter which you seek. For the Lord of the sign is not always the significator of the matter which is signified by that house concerning which it is asked; rather it is sometimes some planetary Lord of the house, and [sometimes] another who is not the Lord of the domicile is stronger in that house.

For that one is said to be stronger, who has more dignities or strengths there, and who was of more strengths in the house of the matter, or who signifies that matter about which there is a question. And that planet is called the significator, which al-Qabīsī[315] called the *al-mubtazz*[316]–that is, "the victor." And it is called the victor, because it exceeds the other planets in strengths in the house sought– an example of which is this.

A certain question was made[317] about substance, the Ascendant of which was the first degree of Pisces. Aries was the 2nd house (which is the house of substance), namely its sixth degree; thus it seems that Mars, who is the Lord of Aries, would be the significator of substance–but it is not so Mars has only six strengths there, because he has five there from [his rulership of] the domicile and one [from his rulership of] the face, and so there are six strengths of Mars there. And that same sign is the exaltation of the Sun, who has seven strengths there: four from the exaltation and three from the triplicity; and so the Sun has the aforesaid seven strengths. Whence [the Sun] remains as the significator of substance and not Mars, on account of the greater number of strengths which

---

[315] Bonatti is dealing with al-Qabīsī, I.77 in this explanation and the following example.
[316] Lat. *almuten, almutem, almutez*, from Ar. المبتزّ, meaning "one who has gained victory," or the "victor." See Introduction.
[317] This example is based on al-Qabīsī, I.77. I note that Bonatti *never* explicitly uses this method himself, although he often speaks of an *al-mubtazz*. Usually he cites other authors' uses of the term, which often involve other standards of determining the *al-mubtazz*. See, e.g., Māshā'allāh's alternative weighting system in Tr. 8, Part 1, Ch. 1.

the Sun has there. But even though the Sun is the ruler over substance in this question, Mars is his participator, but he would be less able there than the Sun is. And if the Sun were so impeded that he could not be the significator, then the signification will come down to Mars (and likewise to Jupiter, if Mars were weak so that he could not be the significator). And the Moon will always be a participator there.

Moreover, Jupiter has something to do there (whence he has some kind of participation with them), for he has two strengths on account of the bound which he has there; and he is even a participator for another reason, because he is the natural significator of substance.

And the twelfth degree of Taurus was the 3rd house in this question. Whence if the question were about brothers, or about one of those things which are signified by the 3rd house, it is necessary for you to look then to the planet who was stronger in it. And understand thus about the rest of the houses and about the rest of the things signified by them. And you even ought to look, in a question about substance, at the Part of Substance, which you could discover thus: see which planet is the significator of substance,[318] and see in what degree of any sign it is, and subtract that from the degree of the house of substance, and what remains is the place of the Part of Substance, just as you will find when we treat of the Parts in their own place.[319] But I would give you an example here of the 2nd house of this question (which is the house of substance), which was the sixth degree of Aries. And Mars, who is the Lord of Aries, was found in the eighth degree of Scorpio. Now you must subtract Scorpio from Aries (but you cannot do this, because you cannot subtract 8 from 1). Add 12 signs to the 8, and subtract 8° of Scorpio from the 12 signs and 6°, and there will remain to you 4 signs and 28°; and you will begin to project from the sixth degree of Aries (which is the beginning of the house of substance), and the Part of Substance falls in the Leo, in the twenty-eighth degree of that same Leo.[320] And you will do thusly with the Part of Fortune and the other parts. But

---

[318] Bonatti is being misleading here–he means the *Lord* of the house of substance, not the "significator" (which he has just defined as being identical with the *al-mubtazz* of the degree of the cusp).
[319] See Tr. 8, Part 2. But Bonatti's method here is not the same. The method here is to take the distance from the Lord of the 2nd house to the cusp of the 2nd house (in the order of signs), and project that distance from that same cusp. But the method in Tr. 8 is to project the distance from the *Ascendant*, as it is in al-Qabīsī (V.5).
[320] Bonatti has gotten this wrong. The distance between Mars and the cusp of the 2nd is 148°. But 148° is the location of 28° Leo itself, i.e., only if we project from the first degree of Aries, which is not what was instructed. Projecting from the cusp of the 2nd yields 4° Virgo. At any rate, this procedure is at odds with Bonatti's own instructions later, and his general theory of

the Part of Fortune is taken in another (and easier) way, just as will be stated in the Treatise on the Parts. And you will do thusly with the rest of the houses, namely with the 3rd and the 4th and the 5th, *et cetera*. And thus you will find the significator of the matter which you seek, always by determining that significator which is of greater strength in the house signifying the quaesited matter.

Chapter 15: On accidental powers

It is said of the planets that they would be in their "likeness," (but having observed the method according to what will be stated in the Treatise on the Parts), which al-Qabīsī and the other sages call *haym*[321]—namely when a diurnal planet is in the day above the earth, and in the night below the earth, and a nocturnal one in the night above the earth and in the day below the earth. And a masculine planet when it is in a masculine sign, and a feminine one in a feminine sign. If it were so, a planet is said to be in its own "likeness." Because diurnal things rejoice in the daytime, nocturnal ones in the nighttime, masculine ones in masculinity, feminine ones in femininity. Whence if a planet were the significator or some matter, and it were in its own likeness, it will perfect the matter which it signified, better and more completely, than if it were not in its own likeness. And *haym* is a certain strength, and then a planet will be somewhat stronger than when it is not in its own *haym*, just like one who is in a station in which he makes money and in a certain way he satisfies his intention, and profits, and fortune seems to favor him.

---

the Parts, which dictates that three positions must be used–in this case, the third position would be the Ascendant, from which the 148° ought to be projected. Perhaps Bonatti got interrupted while writing and forgot to add the degrees of the cusp of the 2nd.
[321] For example, al-Qabīsī I.78. See Introduction.

TREATISE 3: PLANETS

On the natures of the seven planets, and what is peculiar to them, and what they signify about the condition of any matter according to their being, and according to their natures, and what they imprint in inferior things according to the diversity of the qualities of their motions

[PART 1]

Chapter 1: On Saturn–what he would signify

After we have arrived at the completion of what was intended regarding the circle of signs and its division, and its accidents, what must be made to follow [is] a recalling to mind of the seven planets, and to narrate their natures, and what is signified by them, and the impressions which they imprint in inferior things—and first, concerning Saturn.

Al-Qabīsī said[1] Saturn is a masculine, diurnal planet, and he works at intemperate coldness and dryness. And he is a significator of fathers and grandfathers

---

[1] In what follows, quotations from al-Qabīsī, Dorotheus and Māshā'allāh (unless otherwise noted) all come from al-Qabīsī, *Intr.* II.1*ff.* All quotations from Abū Ma'shar come from *Gr. Intr.* (various Treatises).

and all ancestors who are signified by the 4th house—but this is more by accident than by nature, for he naturally signifies the person or body of the native, on account of the fact that the first thing which happens to a man is the [physical] person through which being is given to him.

And Saturn is in the first circle of the planets, and is the first planet in their order, and whom all others follow, and is even the first one who exercises his operation in a conceived child after the falling of the seed into the womb, by binding and uniting together the matter from which the conceived child is formed. For the operations of the fixed stars, which are the principal agent [in the cosmos], are not perceived manifestly in these things, but only [those] of the planets, which are the secondary agents.

Indeed al-Qabīsī (and others who said it), [said] that Saturn is a significator of fathers, and of old things, and the burdensome things they have in light of his slow and burdened motion, and his heaviness; and therefore they made him the significator of older parents and of ancient things and burdensome things, not without suitable cause.

Which if he were the significator of someone's nativity, and he were oriental, and the nativity were diurnal, the native will not easily reach to the full amount of his natural life; but he could reach up to the beginning of old age (which is from the sixtieth year onwards), unless something else impeded against nature—just as we see the majority of men die before the required time, as by iron, fire, a fall, [falling] ruins, drowning, and by many others of the causes which are not of the consideration of nature, nor of its intention (just as was said above). If however he were oriental and the nativity were nocturnal, it signifies that the native's life will be up to the end of old age, unless the aforesaid impede, as I said, concerning which it will be spoken below in the Treatise on nativities.

And he said [Saturn signifies] everything which signifies the severity of intemperate cold and dryness. And of the humors, he signifies melancholy. And of the complexions of bodies, he signifies melancholy, and perhaps the melancholy will be with an admixture of phlegm, and with slowness and heaviness of limbs of the native's body, so that he will not be light in gait nor lightly jumping, nor will he learn how to swim (or like things which make for showing the lightness of the body). And he will be stinking and have a bad odor; as if it is of a goat-stink; and [Saturn] makes men eat much. And if a Saturnian man undertook to esteem someone (which rarely happens), he will esteem him with true esteem. And if he undertook to hate someone (which often happens), he will hate him with an extreme hatred, and will hardly or never desist from that hatred.

And Albuaz said that if he were of good condition, it signifies profoundness of knowledge, and good and deep counsel, such that another will hardly or never know how to improve on it.

And of professions he signifies ancient things and those full of labor (and heavy and valuable [or expensive]), and aquatic works or those which take place near water (like mills, bridges, ships, and the like) and the bringing forth[2] of waters, and the cultivation of the earth (like fields, planting trees, the building of houses—and especially of the houses of religious men wearing black clothing)—if he were made fortunate and of good condition. If however he were made unfortunate and of bad condition, he signifies old and low-class things, like working with hoes,[3] the digging of base pits, and in stinking places, and the carrying of stones and cement to walls by the neck, and especially to underground walls, or those of cities, and which are next to pits, and the making of many things out which come to be of brick, and the like. And often such people live in labor and distress and poverty, and they eat bad and stinking foods.

And al-Qabīsī said that he signifies low-class sailors[4] if he were of bad condition. And if he were of good condition, he signifies great and wealthy sailors (namely those who are enriched by navigation), and he will be of true esteem, and ample and patient [or enduring]. And if Saturn were of bad condition, the native [will be] undistinguished, sad, grieving, of bad suspicion, eager to suspect every evil, and in rousing men by whisperings and evil incitements. And if he were of good condition, he signifies old and durable things, as are inheritances which come from any source (and especially from the dead), and estates which are acquired[5] by him by lawful means more so than by wicked means. Indeed if he were of bad condition, it signifies that the native will make use of putrid and dirty and marshy waters, and stinking and old [waters] which stand in one place for a long time, like in fishponds and the like; and waters of bad and convertible taste; nor will he abhor to drink them, and he will willingly spend time in swamps or near them; and he will eat rotten fish and rotten meats, nor will he seem to sense any harm from thence.

---

[2] *Productiones*, suggesting the channeling or diversion of waters from rivers and streams.
[3] *Ligonisationes*. A *ligo* is also a mattock or spindle used in mills, so at any rate hard physical labor is meant.
[4] Al-Qabīsī does not distinguish between low-class and wealthy sailors, as does Bonatti.
[5] Reading *acquirentur* for *acquirent*.

And of infirmities, he signifies epilepsy or falling sickness; he signifies phlegmatic and melancholic diseases, and [diseases] of freezing up, hard ones, earthy ones, and locking up; and he often signifies diseases which are not cured, like leprosy, white morphew,[6] morphew,[7] deep (and hollow and hard) fistulas, and in places of nerves, and other like illnesses. And it signifies that these diseases will happen to the native if Saturn were the significator [of his nativity], and he were of such a condition. And in the questions of infirmities, he will often signify such illnesses.

And he signifies faraway and laborious pilgrimages. And it will hardly come to be (when he is of bad condition), if he himself were the significator of the journey, but that the journey would be full of labor, and rough, and practically intolerable. And he signifies hard and rough prisons.

And he signifies that [the native] will collect into his custody the debts of those pledging their property to each other, but he will not much care to make the arrangements between them.

And he signifies the heaviness of the body, and [its] slowness and labor and the affliction of the mind, and evil thoughts, and the substance of the dead which remains behind them; and fathers and grandfathers, and brothers older than the native, and slaves and eunuchs and low-class persons.

And if Saturn alone were the significator of someone's nativity, so that another is not complected with him, it will be the native's natural duty to work with leather and to work his labors from them.

On the complexion of Saturn with Jupiter and the other planets

Which if Jupiter is joined to him, it signifies the working of papers[8] in which the books of churches and divine words and treatments of divinity are written; and in which words about higher and celestial things are written, like the judgments of the stars (both theoretical and practical), and of all lofty arts, and judgments of the laws, and the like.

And if Mars is joined to him, it signifies the working of leather from which shoes come to be.

---

[6] *Albaras.*
[7] *Morphea*, a kind of skin lesion with hardened skin and a colored halo.
[8] I.e., of parchment.

And if the Sun is joined to him, it signifies the working of leather which is taken up and put together by sewing, like pelts and cruppers[9] and the like.

And if Venus is joined to him, it signifies the working of leather from which come to be drums, cymbals,[10] and all instruments which make a sound of delight and games, and the like.

And if Mercury is joined to him, it signifies the working of leather, namely of parchments on which writings are written, which come to be for perpetual memory, like wills, instruments of purchases and sales, and the like; and parchments on which the calculations of expenses are written, which happens in the courts of magnates and the wealthy, and of others who want to have a record of their expenses; and on which are written the calculations of merchants and money-changers, and the like.

And if the Moon is joined to him, it signifies the working or preparation of the leather of forest animals, and even of domesticated ones and carcasses, and those similar to these.

Whence, if the native wished to carry out works of leather, judge for him according to what you were to see concerning the complexion of Saturn with one of the planets; and according to that method, let him get involved in the working of leather.

And of sects, he signifies the Jewish faith, namely the Old Testament, and every sect which confesses the unity [of God]. And if he were of bad condition, it signifies belief in unity with much hesitation or doubt. And Māshā'allāh (who was one of the most experienced astrologers, and very sharp in this science) said that therefore it signifies the Jewish faith, because it is of the more ancient ones, and no positive law is found older than it, and all other laws and all sects confess it, and it confesses no other law; nor will [the native] confess any sect, inasmuch as all other planets are joined to Saturn, and he is joined to no other of the planets.

---

[9] *Subtelas*. A crupper is a belt-like piece of leather going under the tail of a horse, in order to keep the harness from slipping.
[10] In the post-Roman period the metal symbols also evolved into tuned drums.

And he signifies black clothing, and those who naturally use black vestments (both religious or cloistered, and others). And of metals, he signifies iron [and] lead.

And Abu Bakr said[11] that he signifies the interiors of the ear, and the spleen and stomach. And of colors, he has black. And of tastes, the astringent and the acidic.[12] And of days, Saturday; and of nights, that which precedes Wednesday.

And the quantity of his orb is 9°. And the years of his *firdārīah* are 12; his greatest ones, 464; the greater ones, 57; the middle ones, 43 ½; the lesser ones, 30. And his greater years are said to be 57, because they are considered according to the quantity of degrees of the bounds which fall to him as his bounds, out of the degrees of the twelve signs. Indeed the middle ones are said to be 43 ½, because they are considered according to his greater years added with the lesser ones (which are 87 [in total]), half of which is 43 ½. Indeed the lesser ones are considered from his slow course, because he completes it in 30 years; and his lesser years draw that number from thence (namely, 30). His strength in the regions of the circle is in the northern parts.

And Māshā'allāh said that Saturn signifies, of the figures of men, a man between black and saffron, who, when he walks, merges his eyes on the ground; heavy; when he walks he joins his feet together, and holds them curved;[13] having small eyes, dry skin, nervous; having a beard sparse in whiskers; thick lips, clever, ingenious, a seducer, a killer (and especially secretly). And Dorotheus said that it signifies a man very hairy in body, with joined eyebrows. And of the Parts, he has the Part of Strength and Stability.[14] And it signifies the employments of lands and inheritances, and those who are in charge of works; and boldness and labor and skills, and the reasons for death.

And ad-Dawla said Saturn makes a man to be swarthy, having sparse hairs in the beard; filthy; more often working in the water; grave, lazy,[15] never or hardly laughing. And those whom Saturn has as subjects (namely those of whom he is the significator), often suffer fissures (which the vulgar man calls "rays") in the heels; he renders a man to be of a grayish color; sometimes he makes the chest thin, and the hairs on the head rough and unkempt; he orders that filthy

---

[11] I do not currently find this in Abu Bakr's *Liber Genethliacus*.
[12] *Acetosum*.
[13] In English we call this "pidgeon-toed."
[14] In Tr. 8, Part 2, Ch. 2, he assigns Saturn the Hermetic Lot he calls the "Heavy Part." Traditionally, the Hermetic lot of Saturn is called the Lot of Nemesis.
[15] Reading *piger* for *pigrus*.

clothing (more likely black) be put on him; in the end this must be done, because Saturn always seems to be sad and to have a bad will.

Whence, if you wished to judge something about some Saturnine man, either in his own nativity or in his own question, consider the above-said, and you will judge according to them. Which if perhaps someone asked why Saturn introduces these significations, and these impressions, given that this [explanation] would seem more likely to be natural than [that of an] astrologer); still it seems the reason could be assigned: namely that the motion of the eighth sphere is found to be from the east to the west—not insofar as it has [such a] being, but insofar as it is fitted by nature[16] to be able to be moved. And it is said to have an external mover; and as it seemed to certain people, it is moved by the first cause. Indeed the planets are moved from the west to the east, in the contrary direction of the first motion (or the motion of the eighth sphere). And they are said to have an internal mover, namely an Intelligence (as it seemed to certain people). And with this, discord and contrariety and rebellion and enmity[17] must arise, out of which hatred and malice tend to emerge and rise up; and Saturn is more close to that contrariety, and therefore he signifies this more than others who are removed from this contrariety.

[And of regions he signifies the Sind, Hind, and all the cities of Ethiopia and their mountains.][18]

---

[16] Reading *natura* for *nata*.
[17] Reading *inimicitia* for *inimicitias*.
[18] I have added this line from al-Qabīsī, since it is omitted in the manuscript but Bonatti follows al-Qabīsī.

Chapter 2: On Jupiter—what he would signify

Al Qabīsī said Jupiter is benefic, masculine, diurnal, and is a natural significator of substance, because substance is the second accident which happens to a native after his emergence, and of necessary things that which first occurs to him; and so Jupiter is the second planet, because in the order of the planets he is the first one after [Saturn]. And Jupiter is likewise the second planet who exercises his own operation in a conceived child, namely by bestowing spirit and life to it. And he works at temperate, airy, and sanguine hotness and moisture. And of age, he signifies youth up to the end of that age which is called youth, and it is from the fourteenth year (or from the twenty-first) up to the fortieth or forty-fifth year.

And of professions, he has those which pertain to the law, and judging justly and honestly. And he will give regard, when he sees some people altercating or litigating amongst themselves, to making peace between them, and producing concord in them, and to being always eager for good things. And he signifies an abundance of substance. And of business dealings, those which come to be without seduction. And he signifies the soul, life, happiness, and religion and truth, patience, and every good, beautiful, and valuable precept, and whatever pertains to honesty. And he signifies the abundance of Venus.

And of infirmities, he signifies whatever is of increased blood by means of an increase which is not excessive (so that he would not exterminate nature) nor of inflamed or convertible blood. And he is a planet of wisdom, intellect, and good work.

Which if Jupiter were well disposed, and he were oriental and in an angle, the native will be of good quality, benign, just, he will honor old men, and he will be a sound advisor, a helper of those in need, of good fame, he will love his friends, [and] he will have a good intellect. But if Jupiter were made unfortunate, according to Ptolemy[19] the native will be inexperienced in doing well, turned toward devilish operations, he will be eager under a certain type of pretended sanctity; he will stay in the houses of prayer, will willingly live solitarily, and in crypts and cavernous places, and caves, and on that occasion he will predict future things; he will not esteem anyone, he will have no friends, he will abhor children, with men he will flee conversation, nor will he want to be honored by anyone; he will be unfaithful, none would be able to confide him; he will even be evil, weak, foolish, full of labor, making wicked choices.

On his complexion with Saturn and the other planets

Which if he is joined with Saturn, it signifies the knowledge of nigromancy, and the art of magic, and incantations and exorcisms, and the like.

But if Mars is joined to him, it signifies the knowledge of medicine (and especially surgery).

Indeed if the Sun is joined to him, it signifies the knowledge of sects, and prudence in contentions and disputations, and he will know how to defend the right faith, and to attack heretics of the faith and of the arts; nor will he permit a false conclusion to come to him. And in all things he will be a good and organized disputer, nor a prattler.

And if Venus is joined to him, it signifies the composition of sounds and of other delightful sciences. For the native will be a harp player, trumpet player, and wise in musical instruments.

If however Mercury is joined to him, it signifies the knowledge of arithmetic, and of all things which pertain to number; and the knowledge of writing beyond other writers (if he wished to study in it), and philosophy (namely astronomy), and all other *quadrivial* sciences.

If however the Moon is joined to him, it signifies the knowledge of the management of waters and their measure, and that of lands, and swimming-places, and the bringing forth of rivers, and the like.

---

[19] Based *Tet.* III.14.

And of the quality of the mind, he signifies generosity and modesty and justice. And of sects, he signifies plurality and pretense [or insincerity], for he whose significator were Jupiter (when the Moon is joined to him) wants himself to have this sect and that, and he will observe neither; nor however will his intention be evil.

And Cancaph[20] and Vettius [Valens][21] said that he signifies the liver, the stomach, the left ear, the arms, and the belly (namely from the navel below), and the lower parts of the pubic region; and he signifies the intestine.

And of colors, the ashen, and green, and those similar to these. And of flavors, he signifies a sweet flavor.

And the quantity of his orb is 9°. And of days, he has Thursday; and of nights, he has that which precedes Monday. And the years of his *firdāriah* are 12. And his greatest years are 428; the greater ones, 79; the middle ones, 45 ½; and the lesser ones are 12. And his strength is in the west of the circle. And his greater years are said to be 79 because they are considered according to the quantity of the degrees of the bounds which fall to him as his bounds out of the degrees of the 12 signs. Indeed the middle ones are said to be 45 ½, because they are considered according to the number which is arrived [at] out of the putting together of his greater and lesser years, which make 91–from which the halves fall to 45 ½ as a portion. Indeed the lesser years are considered according to his course in the eccentric, which he accomplishes in 12 years. And from thence his lesser years (namely, 12) drew their number.

And Māshā'allāh said that of the figure of men he signifies a white man, having eyes not exactly black, unequal and short nostrils, bald, having blackness in one of his teeth, of a beautiful stature, a good mind, good manners, a beautiful body.

And Dorotheus said, having big eyes, and wide pupils, a curly beard. And of the Parts, he has the Part of Blessing and Profit.[22] And he signifies faith and an appetite for the good. And of works, wholesomeness and security, and participation.

And of regions he has Iraq,[23] Babylonia, Isfahan,[24] Persia, Ctesiphon,[25] al-Ahwaz.[26]

---

[20] Unknown astrologer, but see Kankah in the Introduction.
[21] This bears a passing resemblance to *Anth.* I.1, but I am not sure what Bonatti's source is.
[22] Also called the Part of Blessedness and Aid in Tr. 8, Part 2, Ch. 2. It is the Hermetic Part of Jupiter, and taken from the Part of Things to Be (also known as the Part of Spirit) to Jupiter, and is cast from the Ascendant.
[23] *Alchirat*. In Tr. 7, Bonatti spells this more accurately as *Alirach*.

And Sacerdos[27] said Jupiter makes a man good and honest; he gives him to have a round beard, beautiful eyes, two larger teeth in front of the rest, and sometimes to a little extent, different ones; in the face of this man a golden color admixed with white, gladly wearing beautiful clothing, having hair on the head sometimes long and beautiful; in condition, [he is] of religious men; he looks at the ground while walking.

Chapter 3: On Mars—what he would signify

Al-Qabīsī said Mars is a masculine, nocturnal, malefic planet. He works intemperate heat and dryness through his own nature; fiery, choleric, of a bitter taste. And he is the natural significator of brothers and pilgrimages. And Mars is therefore naturally the significator of brothers, because brothers are the third accident which happens to a native after conception (namely, after the nativity), and which the native loves more among all those things which can happen to him first; and so Mars is the third planet which there is in the order of the planets; and he follows Saturn, third in their order. And Mars is likewise the third planet who exercises his operation in the conceived child, namely by operating in it through blood, and reddening him. And he is the significator of pilgrimages, because in pilgrimages happen many inconveniences to pilgrims, and many distresses and plunderings and ungodly labors, and the like—which are likened to the significations of Mars.

---

[24] *Azomi.*
[25] *Almaden.*
[26] *Alandes.*
[27] Unknown astrologer.

And he has, of the age of men, completed youth (namely from the twenty-second year up to the forty-fifth, so that both [years] are included). And of professions, every profession which is exercised by iron and fire, as is striking iron with hammers on an anvil, or by other means; and to practice the work of craftsman, bakers, furnace-tenders, butchers, barbers, and the like.

On his complexion with Saturn and the other planets

Which if he is joined with Saturn, it signifies the work of craftsmen which is only done with iron, and especially iron tools with which the work of lands is practiced, like hoes, motors, ploughshares, and the like.

If however he is joined with Jupiter, it signifies the works of craftsmen which come to be from copper ore and lead, like works of pewter, and the like.

Indeed if the Sun is joined to him, it signifies works of craftsmen which arise from gold not having been worked much hitherto, like the imperial coins of the area of the Byzantines,[28] gold florins, medallions of buillion,[29] and every other work from raw gold.

And if Venus is joined to him, it signifies the works of craftsmen which come to be for the ornaments of women, like rings, necklaces, and the like.

And if Mercury is joined to him, it signifies the works of craftsmen which come to be for stitching conjoined things, and for joining them together (which are awls, needles, and the like).

Indeed if the Moon is joined to him, it signifies the works of craftsmen through which scales, dishes, balances, bowls, silver goblets, and vessels with which drinks are measured in taverns come to be, and with which people drink in the courts of the wealthy, and the like.

---

[28] *Bizantii, termini, augustani.*
[29] *Medaliae massannicinae. Massa* can refer to boullion, otherwise I am uncertain what this refers to.

On his significations when he alone is the significator

And if he were the sole significator, he signifies the work of medicine, both surgery and the other side of medicine. Which if none of the planets is complected [with him], he signifies the work of medicine which is by the opening of veins, like phlebotomy, and the opening of abscesses, and the draining of wounds, and the like.

And al-Qabīsī said that if Saturn is complected with him, it signifies the work of the medicine of wounds, and the like. And if Jupiter is complected with him, it signifies the work of natures[30] and the cure of the eyes. And if Venus is complected with him, it signifies the work of ornaments which pertains to barbers, like the cutting of hair on the head, and beards, and the cutting of nails. And if Mercury is complected with him, it signifies the cutting of veins. And if the Moon is complected with him, it signifies the extraction of teeth, and the purging of the ears, and the like. And if he were the significator by himself alone, it signifies injuries of the unfortunate, and that he will willingly injure lesser people; and the shedding of blood, wounds, killings, burnings, decapitations, abuses, thieves, tavern-keepers, robbers by daylight, the proud, liars, perjurers, scoffers, forgers (both of coins and papers), and oppressions through power, by killing those he can; and rage, and cutters of roads, and rushing, and the leaders of an army, and shamelessness [or immodesty], and fickleness, nor will he be ashamed of any evil which he will have done; and it signifies pilgrimages outside the land, and outside his own fatherland, and an abundance of sexual intercourse.

And if he were of bad condition, and he were the significator of a woman, she will miscarry [or abort]; and sometimes she herself will be culpable for the miscarriage. And it signifies middle brothers, and the knowledge and discernment for the care of beasts, for he will be in charge of a pen.[31]

And of infirmities, he signifies hot fevers, namely those which arise from choler not inflamed,[32] and without cause; and true (and even not true) madness; and bloody pustules, impetigo, white morphea,[33] and unusual rednesses which come to be in the body apart from nature, with stinging [or roughness] and a

---

[30] *Opus naturarum.* Uncertain meaning.
[31] *Archimandrica.* Normally this was the term for an Eastern Orthodox abbot, from Gr. *arch-* and *mandra* (a pen or enclosure), but Bonatti cannot truly mean this to be an attribution of Mars. Moreover, al-Qabīsī (II.14) says "the management of riding animals."
[32] *Non adusta.* I take this to mean fevers that are not due to local inflammatory infections.
[33] *Albaras.*

stink; and itching, and lentigoes,[34] and illnesses eating the flesh of the body (like the royal disease, cancers, and the like); and it signifies migraine, and erysipelas,[35] and the like.

And he even signifies that the native will eat rotten meats, and not well cooked. And it signifies quaking fear, and horrible thoughts disturbing men, which move and impede and render them useless. And he signifies whatever was with the inflammation of heat. Of the qualities of the mind, he signifies agitation and its confusion.

On his complexion with Saturn

Which if he is joined with Saturn, it signifies extreme hatred and envy, and the native will be very jealous; and he will rejoice and be happy if he were to see evil and some tribulation or some harm come to someone. And of sects, he loves that in which there is discord and war, and he will willingly adhere to it; and he will quickly be changed from sect to sect, and from one faith into another; nor will be persevere well in any of them, unless perhaps by accident, by constraining his own will. And he will experience uncertainty, and change with speed from obligation to obligation, just as do certain people who always are held by debts, and remain enmeshed in them; nor do they know how to get themselves out of them, but when they avoid one, and get themselves out of one, they run into another. And when they want to satisfy one [debt] with creditors, they take from another and always remain involved in them, and in distress because of them. And thus they do this thing, [and] thus they destroy the same thing; and they change their wills and make others, and never remain long nor persevere in the same proposition; but they will be all of these things at once.[36]

And [Abu 'Ali] al-Khayyat[37] and Abu Bakr[38] said, wherefore [Mars] has, of the parts of the body, the gallbladder, kidneys, veins, spermatic ducts, and the back. And of colors he has redness, and of flavors the bitter.

And the quantity of his orb is 8°. And of days, he has Tuesday, and of nights he has that which precedes Saturday. And the years of his *firdāriah* are 7. His

---

[34] A lentigo is a flat patch of increased pigmentation on the skin, cured nowadays by treatments such as bleaching creams.
[35] *Ignem sacrum*, "holy fire," St. Anthony's disease. An erysipelas is a skin lesion that is hot, fleshy, with fluid that crusts.
[36] *Sub unitate*, lit. "under unity."
[37] Source unknown.
[38] Source unknown.

greatest years are 214; and the greater ones are 66; but the middle ones [are] 40 ½; the lesser ones are 15. And his greater years are said to be 66 because they are considered according to the quantity of the number of degrees which fall to him as his bounds from the number of the degrees of the twelve signs. Indeed the middle ones are said to be 40 ½, because they are considered according to the quantity of one-half of the number of the aggregation of the greater and lesser years, which is 81–the which having been divided, are 40 ½. But the lesser ones are considered in another way than in the aforesaid, because he goes through his epicycle eight times in fifteen years, and thence they drew its number, namely 15, because in no other number of years does he do this. And his strength is in the direction of the south.

And Māshā'allāh said, wherefore he signifies, of the images of men, a man red in the face, having red hair on his head; a round face, easily [doing] every unbecoming thing, having saffron eyes, a horrible look, bold, having a sign and mark on the foot. And Dorotheus said that he signifies a man of sharp gaze.

And of regions, he has Jerusalem and the land of the Romans up to the west. And of the Parts, he has the Part of Boldness.[39] And he said that he signifies perseverance and agreement; of the mind, [passionate] love,[40] cleverness, pride, boldness, saying no, and sharpness, and hastening in all matters.

Ad-Dawla said Mars gives a man to have a curved body, and thick, and he will make a schismatic man, that is, a weed, and sowing discord among men. In his face, the color red mixed with black (that is, Martial), as if it would be said he has a brown color, like those who go into the Sun and heat, so that he is neither black, nor is truly red, but he has a horrible color; and he sometimes has freckles[41] on his face, and sometimes sparse hairs in his beard, as though like those castrated.

---

[39] See Tr. 8, Part 2, Ch. 2.
[40] *Convenientiam animi amorem.* It is difficult to know exactly what is meant. It could also mean "agreement, the love of the mind..." Hand/Zoller (p. 115) read: "a suitability of the soul to amorous love," which is not grammatically possible. Al-Qabīsī reads: "agreement, vanity..." and totally ignores love (*amor*).
[41] *Grana rubea*, "red granules."

Chapter 4: On the Sun–what he would signify

Al-Qabīsī said the Sun is a masculine, diurnal planet, benefic by aspect (indeed, a malefic by corporal conjunction). He works heat and dryness through his own nature. And he is naturally a significator of fathers, if the nativity were diurnal. And therefore the Sun is naturally a significator of fathers, because the 4th house is the significator of fathers, and the Sun is the fourth planet from Saturn, following after him (namely, the third one after him in their order); and even because he is the fourth planet who exercises his own operation in the conceived child, namely by operating in it through natural heat, or something like it in giving spirit and official members to the conceived child, and vital soul and the features of the face. And [the father] is something which the native loves above other things (apart from brothers), of those things which can happen to him before children, with the exception of the two aforesaid things after the nativity.

And he signifies light and splendor, and beauty, and intellect and faith. And he even signifies a great kingdom, and all other lay dignities, both of magnates and others. And this, because he is posited in the middle of the others (just like a king), and the others stand next to him–certain ones on one side, certain ones on the other side (namely the superiors to his right, the inferiors to his left). And he has power in all planets, because he burns them all up. Moreover, his motion is practically uniform, and is not varied nor altered, but always keeps the same similar advancement annually. And his motion is most noble above the motions of the other planets, nor does he go retrograde like others go retrograde. But it could be said that the Moon does not go retrograde; which is true, but even though she does not go retrograde, still she receives such slowness that it can practically be equated with retrogradation. But you could say that the

Moon sometimes eclipses the Sun; to which it must be said that even the Moon sometimes signifies kingdoms and magistracies.

And he naturally signifies the king of the Romans,[42] who has power over the king of Babylon by law, of which[43] the Sun is naturally the significator. And the Sun even has a certain prerogative over the Moon, namely because the Moon is neither a splendid or luminous body, but rather she receives whatever light or splendor she has from the Sun; and therefore she renders less and impedes less. Why this is so, dare not be said, lest perhaps certain people—or rather many fools in tunics—should rise up, wanting to use true reason and a purpose consonant with truth, which they do not know. Indeed the wise among them are not ignorant of it, nor do they rebuke astrologers, but rather they commend them and esteem them; but the fools among them would say that it is heresy, not knowing what heresy is.

And of the age of man, he signifies the end of youth, which is from the forty-fifth year up to the sixtieth. He participates with the generality of the planets in the disposition of years. And of professions he has the kingdom, rulership, and the chief place. And he even signifies those who know well how to joust with lances, and to throw javelins, the hunt, and the hunt which is by means of poisoning (as sometimes do those who poison arrows with which they kill wild animals). And he signifies the purging of the body with every kind of purging with which men's bodies are purged, inside and out.

And of infirmities, he signifies hot and dry infirmities appearing on the bodies of men.[44] And of substance, he signifies much gold, and especially the raw. And al-Qabīsī said that he signifies all kinds of substance. And of qualities of the mind, loftiness and subtleness, and that which pursues honesty and generosity and glory, and the prolixity of the mind. And of sects, he signifies good worship, and the like. And al-Qabīsī said that he signifies the command of the voice and the strength of speed.[45]

---

[42] I.e., the Byzantines.
[43] I.e., of Babylon.
[44] This could be the reason Bonatti says that Mars does not signify fevers with inflammation—because the Sun signifies public and visible things, i.e., "on the body." This line in Bonatti comes from al-Qabīsī.
[45] *Imperium vocis atque fortitudinem celeritas.* Al-Qabīsī says: "widespread fame and excessive power."

On his signification with Saturn and the other planets

Which if he is joined with Saturn, he signifies the management of an estate, and a chief position of this kind.

And if he is joined with Jupiter, it signifies a chief place in faith and religion, and it even signifies all judgment between men, judging the works of lesser people or the oppressed, and the like.

If however he is joined to Mars, it signifies the leadership of an army, and the searching out of wars, for the native will be powerful in these.

Which if Venus is joined to him, it signifies a kingdom through the allegiance of powerful men, and through women.

Indeed if Mercury is joined to him, it signifies the counselors of kings and those taking care of books and great works of inheritances.

And if the Moon is joined to him, it signifies the work of legates and the revealing of counsel, and things similar to these.

And Vettius [Valens][46] and ['Umar] al-Tabarī[47] said that the Sun signifies the image of a man's countenance, and particularly the right eye of men and the left one of women. And Ben[48] and Abu 'Ali said that it signifies, of members, the heart, the marrow, and the thighs. And of infirmities, those which appear in the mouth like cancers and others which eat the flesh of the mouth; and every detriment of the mouth, and the coming down of water in the eye.[49] And his virtue and authority is especially in the head. And the Hindus said,[50] wherefore when he is in the Ascendant, he will be burning up. And he whose significator he was, will have a sign on his face.

And of colors, he has the imitative color,[51] which seems to participate with every color; and according to certain people, he signifies the color white. And of

---

[46] Again, this bears a resemblance to *Anth*. I.1.
[47] Source of citation unknown. This is the first time Bonatti mentions al-Tabarī; he is unaware that Omar of Tiberias and 'Umar al-Tabarī are the same man.
[48] Unknown astrologer.
[49] I.e., a cataract.
[50] Unknown Indians cited in al-Qabīsī, II.22.
[51] According to Burnett's translation of al-Qabīsī, "transparent."

flavors, he has the sharp. And of days, he has Sunday, and of nights that which precedes Thursday.

And the quantity of his orb is 15° in front and in back. And the years of his *firdārīah* are 10. And his greatest years are 461, and according to certain people if he were to exceed them, they will be 1,000.[52] And his greater years are 120, because they are considered according to the quantity of the number of degrees which fall to him as his bounds, by the number of the degrees of the twelve signs—because even though the Sun does not have bounds assigned through the signs as the five wandering planets have, still he has virtue in the aforesaid half of the circle of signs (which is from the beginning of Leo up to the end of Capricorn, and those [degrees] are 180), which the planets have in their own bounds. But because two domiciles of the two malefics are in that half, 60 years are taken away from him (30 for each of their domiciles), and exactly 120 remain, out of which the trine aspect results. Indeed his middle years are extracted in another way than the others are extracted. For his greater years are halved, and to one half are added his lesser years,[53] and they make 79; the which having been halved, makes 39 ½–and those are the middle years of the Sun.[54] Indeed the lesser ones are considered from the number of the degrees of his exaltation in the nineteenth degree of Aries (as was said above), and from that is the number of the Sun's lesser years. And his strength is in the direction of the east.

And Māshā'allāh said, wherefore he signifies, of the figures of men, him who would have a color between saffron and black, covered with redness; of short stature; bald ([or] as in certain authors, curly),[55] and having a beautiful body. And Dorotheus said the figure of the Sun and the Moon is like the figure of the planets who are with them, and of him who is more worthy in their places. Therefore, if you wished to know the figure of the Sun, know that it is saffron, having a portion of red in the hair on the head; his eyes somewhat saffron.

---

[52] The years are 1,461 (as al-Qabīsī confirms). Since the difference between Bonatti's number and al-Qabīsī's is exactly 1,000, a confusion in sources must be to blame.
[53] The lesser years are 19.
[54] Both here and in the section on the Moon, Bonatti has misread John of Spain's translation of Abū Ma'shar (*Gr. Intr.* VII.8). The correct value for the middle years is 69 ½. Abū Ma'shar says the years are "39 ½ (and according to certain people, 69 ½." These other "certain people" are correct. The greater years (120) added to the lesser years (19) yield 139, which, divided in half, yields the value of the middle years, 69 ½.
[55] Al-Qabīsī's Māshā'allāh says "bald, with curly hair" (II.23).

And of regions, he has Samarkand[56] and Khorasan,[57] and Persia, and the land of the Romans.[58] And of the Parts, he has the Part of Things to Be and of Divination.[59] And he is the significator of natures,[60] and of the spirit of wisdom, and elation, and perfection, of faith too, and of the sciences, and joy.

And ad-Dawla said the Sun makes a man full of flesh, having a beautiful and white face, and eyes sometimes large; in whose face the color white is commingled with citrine; indeed the Solar man has a beautiful and full beard; he even wears long hair on the head.[61]

Chapter 5: On Venus—what she would signify

Abū Ma'shar and al-Qabīsī said Venus is a benefic, and she is a feminine, nocturnal planet, and she signifies women and wives. And if the nativity were diurnal, as al-Qabīsī says, she signifies mothers. And as Sacerdos says, she signifies younger sisters. And she is naturally a significatrix of children, because children are signified by the 5th house, and Venus is the fifth planet from Saturn, namely the fourth after him, following him in their order. And even because she is the fifth planet, who exercises her own operation in a conceived child, namely by completing the sex of a male and female (of whatever sex the conceived child were), and by perfecting the nose and eyebrows and the whole disposition of the face for it. And because Venus is the planet of delight and joy, and the 5th house is likewise attributed to children, and she signifies them because children

---

[56] *Conacant.*
[57] *Oracen.*
[58] I.e., the Byzantines.
[59] See Tr. 8, Part 2, Ch. 2.
[60] Hand/Zoller (p. 117) read: "of the natures and spirit of wisdom, glory..."
[61] Presumably like a lion's mane.

are an accident in which a native will rejoice more, and nature is delighted more in them than in other things. Indeed, in the Treatise on nativities it will be described more broadly what must be said about them; but I will tell you something of them now.

Because if you wished to know the being of the native, and you wished to know what would happen to him from women (namely from the mother or wives or younger sisters, and the like), see in the hour of the nativity if Venus is the *al-mubtazz* in the nativity: then you would know it will be generally well for him from women. And if she were not the significatrix of the nativity, [so] that she is not the *al-mubtazz* over it, see how and from where she aspects the Lord of the first.

> For if she were to aspect him from the seventh, from the trine aspect, the native will be loved by his wives with a perfect love. And if she were to aspect him from there by a sextile aspect, he will be loved by his wives, but not with a perfect love—but rather there will sometimes be altercations and disputes between them, and sometimes they will love each other, but sometimes not; now this, now that. And if she were to aspect him from the seventh by the square aspect, then the native will rejoice little with his wife, and often there will be some kinds of altercations between them, and they will not be united well together. Indeed if she were to aspect him from the opposition, the native will never rejoice with his wife (this will be feared more with the first one), nor will it be well for him from her; and there will always be quarrels and disagreements between them.

And if Venus were to aspect the significator of the nativity from the 10th house by one of the aforesaid aspects, say that it will be so for the native from the mother, just what I said it would be for him from the wife. Because if Venus were to aspect the significator from the 7th house, from a good aspect, say that it will be good for the native from the mother; indeed from a bad [aspect], say that it will be bad for him from the mother.

And if Venus were to aspect the native's significator from the 4th, from one of the aforesaid aspects, say that it will go thusly for him from his younger sisters, according to the aspect by which she aspected him—in the manner you stated concerning the mother.

And Venus works coldness and moisture through her own nature, with a moderate mixture. And she likewise signifies, of the age of a man, adolescence, and especially in bare youth, which is from the fourteenth year up to the twenty-second. And she has, of professions, knowing how to make instruments of praises,[62] and of games and playing at draughts and playing at dice. These will be the offices of him whose significatrix is Venus, and which are drawn nearer to by him, and which he will know better how to do if he wished to get involved in them; and if he were to get involved in other things, he will not learn more, nor will he know [them] so well as he would these. And he whose significatrix were Venus will be living in leisure, and he will know better how to conduct his own life, and how to live more delightfully and in a more courtly way than another who is much worse[63] than he. And he will be a fornicator and wholly a child of fornication, and he will freely practice every venereal pursuit, and he will abound in sexual intercourse, so that sometimes his nature[64] will be exterminated for that reason. And he will know how to put together crowns and garlands, and all ornaments, and particularly womanly ones; and he will freely wear ornaments on his own body, and he will go around covered with beautiful and clean clothing; and he will know how to work gold and silver and how to make necklaces, and all such things which pertain to the ornamenting of the body, and especially those which pertain to the ornamenting of women (if he were to adhere to those professions).

And this is what sometimes does not permit certain people to reach the perfection of their professions or offices: because they perform arts and offices which do not naturally belong to them; and they never learn them perfectly; and they learn whatever they take from them, with labor; but those which pertain to them naturally, they learn easily and well.

And Venereal men are of games and laughter and dancing, and gladness and joy, and freely using food and drink in company; and Venereal men get drunk more quickly than others, and they trust in others, and often are deceived by them. And Venus signifies esteem, generosity, love, and justice, and the like. And Venereal men spend time in the houses of prayer, so that they may appear to be what they are not; and they restrain their faith, and long to hear the

---

[62] *Laudorum.* Perhaps "instruments of worth," but I confess I do not know exactly what Bonatti means.
[63] Perhaps, "in a lower condition"?
[64] *Natura.*

sounds of musical instruments, and they are strong in them more so than other men.

On the complexion of Venus with Saturn and the other planets

Which if she is joined with Saturn, it signifies the sound of singing, lamentations, and those by which the dead are bewailed, and which men use when they build, and the like.

If however she is joined with Jupiter, it signifies that the native will be taught in the sounds of ecclesiastical reading and old songs, and in every song pertaining to clerics and the religious, and those using [them] in the houses of prayer, and altars, and the praise of the Lord Jesus Christ.

Which if she is joined with Mars, it signifies the sounds or singing of the laity and of the masters of battles, and songs which arise in battles, like the tuba, the bugle, cymbals, and the like. And it signifies the sounds or songs in which the mention is made of capture, imprisonment, labor, killing, and the clashing or arms and ships, as happens in the commemorative celebrations of ancient deeds, as the deeds of Troy, France, Rome, Britain, and the like are remembered; for the native will know how to sing those songs.

Which if she is joined to the Sun, it signifies that the native will know the sounds or songs which come to be with the wood [instruments] which men use in the presence of kings and magnates, like rotes,[65] viols, cytharas, sambucas,[66] lutes,[67] and the like.

And if Mercury is joined to her, it signifies the sounds by which melodies arise and verses are composed, like lyres, and the like.

---

[65] *Rottae*. This seems to be the Latinized form of Fr. *rote*, a small hand-held harp resting on the knee.
[66] *Sampucae*. This seems either to be a small shrill harp, or a wooden flute made of the elder tree.
[67] *Leuta*.

If however the Moon is joined to her, it signifies songs which sailors use in navigation and in the erecting or raising up of their sails in high, and the like.

And of infirmities, she signifies cold and moist infirmities which happen often in the genital members or around them, and the like. And she signifies that a native will be fit for knowing how to adapt and prepare those things which pertain to beauty, like cloaks, the vestments of women and their ornaments, and which are decorated in ornaments like with gold, pearls, fringes, and the like.

And of the quality of the mind she signifies sweetness, and signifies friendship and eating, and the longing for eating and drinking and sexual intercourse, and the like. And of sects, she signifies idolatry, and those [sects] in which eating and drinking are practiced.

And Vettius [Valens] and Cancaph said that she signifies, of the body, the haunches, the spine of the back, sperm, and its course [or descent]. Indeed Albuaz and ['Umar] al-Ṭabarī said, wherefore she signifies fat, the kidneys, and the navel and the belly; the vulva too and the womb. And of colors, she has white; and of flavors, the rich [or greasy]. And of the days, she has Friday; and of the nights she has that which precedes Tuesday.

And the quantity of her orb is 7° in front and so many in back. And the years of her *firdārīah* are 8. And the greater ones [are] 82, and the middle ones 45, the lesser ones 8, and the greatest (according to al-Qabīsī) are 1,151. And her greater years are said to be 82 according to the number of the degrees of the twelve signs which fall to her as her bounds, according to which number they are considered. Indeed the middle ones are said to be 45, because they are considered according to the number of half of her greater and lesser numbers put together; the which having been put together, they make 90, half of which is 45. Indeed the lesser ones are 8, which draw their number from the fact that Venus goes around her epicycle five times in eight years, which she cannot do in another number of years. She goes around the eccentric in 348 days. And her strength, in the regions of the world, is to the right of the west.

And Māshā'allāh said that she signifies, of the figures of men, a white man tending to blackness; having a beautiful body, beautiful hair on the head; having a round face, and short whiskers, and beautiful eyes (and their blackness is greater than whiteness). And Dorotheus said, having a beautiful face, beautiful eyes (their blackness more than it should be) and much hair on the head. And he said that it signifies a white man put together with red; [and] thick; and he shows benevolence.

And of regions she has the Hejaz[68] and Yemen,[69] and the whole land of the Arabs, because her significations appear more in those parts than in others.

And of the Parts she has the Part of Desire.[70] And she signifies friendship and esteem and patience, and games, and the conjoining of males to one another by foul and prohibited and wicked and abhorrent means.

And ad-Dawla said Venus makes the hair on the head beautiful, and beautiful eyebrows. But the Venereal man indulges in sweet and smooth words; he has eloquence through all sweetly flowing [words]; he joins mouths with his girlfriend. But he is zealous in his own countenance, and the composition of his whole body; he moves himself lightly in going around or in doing something; he is of medium stature, and wanton.

Chapter 6: On Mercury—what he would signify

Al-Qabīsī said Mercury is a commingled, masculine, diurnal planet. He is inclined through his own nature to that with which he is complected (of the planets and the signs), so that if he is joined to a good planet, he is made good; and if he is joined to a malefic, he is made bad. And if he is joined to a masculine planet, he is said to be masculine; [and if to a feminine one, feminine];[71] and if to a nocturnal one, nocturnal; and if to a diurnal one, diurnal.

---

[68] Lat. *Alhegem.*
[69] Lat. *Alyemen.*
[70] The Hermetic Lot is called the Lot of Eros; in Tr. 8, Part 2, Ch. 8, it is called the Part of Love and Concord.
[71] Clause omitted in the text, but Bonatti clearly means to include it.

And he signifies younger brothers: whence, look in the nativity of some native, and see how Mercury behaves with the Lord of the first or with the significator of the nativity;[72] for if Mercury were to aspect him from a trine or from a sextile aspect, it will be well for the native from his own younger brothers (and especially [if] with reception). And if he were to aspect him from the square aspect or from the opposition, it will be well for him from them, especially if reception [were to] intervene. Say likewise concerning the corporal conjunction. You may understand the same about his aspects with the Moon.

And the Mercurial man esteems his girlfriends more so than his wives; and he will more willingly cling to them. And Mercury signifies a valuation of, and thinking about, the love of God, insofar as it is from his own conscience, even if he is otherwise wanton in illicit things; and he will have a good belief, and will spend time devoutly in temples and other oracles of the churches; and he will be of good faith and Catholic opinion. And if Mercury alone were the significator of the nativity, and he were in his own nature, so that none of the planets is joined with him, nor does one even participate with him, the native will be of his own understanding in the beginning of youth, and he will grow in his own will, and in the manners peculiar to him, and this will happen to him in the first ten years of his youth (namely adolescence).

And al-Qabīsī said that he signifies terrestrial things, and the increase of things by growing, and of age he has youth and advancement in it; and that he signifies, of works, works which generate the cognition of truth, and rhetoric, for he will be organized in his speech. And Mercury signifies geometry and the knowledge of doing business, and he will know how to arrange many business dealings; and he will get involved in many of them, and he will know how to lead them to effect. And he will have a thought about many matters, and he will be acquainted with matters of selling[73] and other matters in which there is benefit. And if he were made a cleric, he will be a good and pleasing preacher. And Afla[74] said that he signifies philosophy, and augury, and writing, and proverbs; he will be good moral philosopher; he will even learn arithmetical

---

[72] The text is unclear as to whether or not the "significator of the nativity" is synonymous with the "Lord of the first" or not. This distinction between (a) the Lord of the Ascendant, (b) generic phrases like "the significator of the native," "the significator of the nativity," and so on, and (c) specialized planets like the *hilāj* and the *al-kadukhadāh*, permeates Tr. 9.

[73] *Res venales.* This can also refer to bribes. It is sometimes difficult to tell which Bonatti means when he uses this phrase.

[74] Unknown. Perhaps ad-Dawla?

science. For the Mercurial man will be a good prover [of things], and he will work especially at that.

On his complexion with Saturn and the other planets

Which if he is joined with Saturn, it signifies the work of apportioning and measuring lands, and dividing possessions and inheritances between partners and the heirs of the dead. And the knowledge of counting and estimating which it behooves someone to have for making some building, like a tower and a house, or something similar; and the knowledge of organizing looms, like those who weave woolen or linen cloths, or a *pignolatum*,[75] and the like.

Which if he is joined to Jupiter, it signifies the work of counting and making the melodies of churches' books; and he will know other songs equally well, and jumping in games, and the like.

Which if he is joined to Mars, it signifies that the native (for whom he was the significator) will know how to bring an army forth, and he will know well how to organize them and to pay off those doing battles, and the renderings to warriors which they should receive; and that he will know well how to do battle and, well to strike those with whom he did battle, with lances and swords, maces, and other deadly arms, and the like.

Which if he is joined to the Sun, it signifies he is in charge over a number of kings, and the substance of lords, magnates, and nobles, and the wealthy; for he will know how to arrange their affairs, and how to rule their families, and how to represent family affairs.

Which if he is joined with Venus, it would signify that he will know the numbering of the sounds of chords of musical instruments (like cytharas, viols, the pipes of organs, harps, drums, and the like).

Which if the Moon is joined to him, it signifies that the native will know how to serve in the courts of kings, magnates, nobles, and others, like

---

[75] A generic term for a woolen garment, a contraction of *pannus laneus*.

putting down dishes in the presence of those reclining; cutting bread and meat in front of them, and the like.

And of infirmities, he naturally signifies infirmities of the soul, as magnanimity is by making small things out to be big, and faintheartedness by magnifying small things; and horrible thoughts, and disturbance of the mind, and uncertainty, so that sometimes he will seem to be out of his mind, and the like. And if he with whom he is joined, were well disposed, it signifies the good quality of soul; and if he were badly disposed, it signifies a bad quality of soul.

On Mercury, if he were made fortunate

If however Mercury were made fortunate, his goodness and fortune will be according to the goodness and according to the fortune of him who makes him fortunate, and according to the place in which [Mercury] himself were well disposed. And if he were bad and made unfortunate, his badness and misfortune will be according to the nature and according to the condition and according to the misfortune of him who makes him unfortunate; and according to the place in which the malefic was (or he who makes him bad).

And al-Qabīsī said that of sects he signifies the worship of true unity, and of rational laws, and of like things; and it signifies with pretended sanctity and pretense, pretending himself to be better than he is, but not with heresy. And Albuaz and Ebrianus[76] said that of the body of man he signifies the navel, and the thighs, the legs, nerves, veins, and arteries. And of colors he signifies every commingled and varied color. And Vettius [Valens] said that he signifies *alezeminium*,[77] which is a certain color like the color of a lily of the field. And of flavors, he signifies the acidic.

And the quantity of his orb is 7°. And of days, he has Wednesday; and of nights, the one which precedes Sunday. And the years of his *firdārīah* are 13. And his greater years are 76; the middle ones 48; the lesser ones, 20; the greatest ones, 460. And his greater years are said to be 76, because 76 degrees fall to him for his bounds, of the degrees of the twelve signs, according to which number they are considered. Indeed the middle ones are said to be 48 because they are considered according to half of the number of his greater and lesser years put

---

[76] Unknown astrologer.
[77] Unknown color. But the metal aluminum is named after the crystal *alumen* or "alum," which is whitish; if this is the origin of *alezeminium*, perhaps the *Lilium candidum* or "white lily" is meant?

together (which are 96) and divided into two halves (of which one half is 48). Indeed the lesser ones are 20, because Mercury is found to make sixty-three revolutions in his epicycle in twenty years, which he does not do in another number of years—and thence they drew that number; and he goes around the eccentric in approximately ten months. And his strength in the parts of the world is in the north.

And Jafar said[78] that Mercury, from the middle of his retrogradation up to his second station, signifies childhood.

And from his second station up to the corporal conjunction of the Sun, he signifies youth and esteem and friendship and concord, and his seeking and imitation of love.

And from the conjunction of the Sun up to his first station, he signifies old age.

And from his first station up to the middle of his retrogradation, it signifies decrepitude and contrariety, and dissembling [or carelessness], and slowness, and modesty (except for in acquiring money), and taking possession of things in all ways he can—the native will accumulate them by moral *and* wicked means.[79]

And if Mercury were in the middle of his retrogradation, and he were the significator of some native, the native will be of moderate quickness, on account of the weak wits which he will have.

And if he were near his second station, it signifies that the native will be of quick wits, but not extreme quickness; and he will have a good talent in knowing how to uncover men's way of thinking with flatteries, so that they will reveal their secrets to him.

And if he were joined to the Sun by body, and he were direct, and were someone's significator, it signifies that the native will be of quick and

---

[78] It is unclear which astrologer is meant; probably not the author of the astrometeorology material in Tr. 10.
[79] *Phas et nephas.*

expansive (and broad and great and deep) wits, and of good memory; and the same will happen concerning the other planets, except for the Moon.[80]

And Māshā'allāh said that Mercury signifies, of the figures of men, a man having a color not very white nor very black, having a high forehead, a long face, a long nose, beautiful eyes not totally black, a black beard sparse in whiskers, and having long fingers.

And of regions he has Daylam[81] and Makran[82] and all regions of the Indians. And of the Parts he has the Part of Business,[83] because he signifies businessmen on account of the excessive mental agitation of worry which he signifies; and on account of the eagerness which thrives in him, in inquiring into diverse things. And he signifies fear and disturbances, and war, and enmities, and seditions and contrarieties. And he even signifies advancement and a profession, and subtlety in all works, and in all inquiries about which the native might wish to get involved. For he will know how to search for what he wants, subtlely, from every man; and how to seek, subtlely, for all things taken together which are inquired into by anyone in terms of sayings or deeds.

And Sacerdos said Mercury gives a man to have a slender body. But the Mercurial man is wise, freely devoting his leisure time to reading; often of average stature, acquiring friends enough, [but] not easily keeping them.[84] And he said that he has a beautiful beard, but sparse and short, sometimes having thin lips (and likewise the nose).

---

[80] I believe Bonatti means that the same statements about the native's wit will pertain to other planetary significators' relations to the Sun.
[81] Lat. *Aqualem*.
[82] Lat. *Magidem*.
[83] In Tr. 8, Part 2, Ch. 2, this is called the Part of Poverty.
[84] Hand/Zoller (p. 124) seems to omit the *non*, saying he keeps them easily.

Chapter 7: On the Moon—what she would signify

Abū Ma'shar and al-Qabīsī said the Moon is benefic, feminine, nocturnal; she works coldness and moisture through her own nature, and she is a significatrix of mothers. Whence if the nativity were nocturnal, she signifies what will happen to the native from the mother. Whence you ought to consider how the Moon behaves with the significator of the native: because if she were to aspect him with a good aspect (namely a trine or a sextile) or she were to receive him with perfect reception, it will be well for the native from the mother. If however she were to aspect him with a bad aspect, it will be ill for him from the mother. And understand the same about the mother from the child—because if the significator of the nativity were to receive the Moon, it will be well for the mother from the native; if however it were to aspect her badly without reception, it will be ill for the mother from the native.[85]

And al-Qabīsī said that there is temperate phlegm in her. And she signifies the childish age, and the beginning of growth (namely the first four years from the nativity), on account of her repeated and quick changes in the manner of the changes in the time of childhood. And the same philosopher said that of works she has legations and commissions, and the works of waters and lands, and the cultivation of the land, according to the quantity of her goodness or her badness. And she signifies the chief place, for she knows how to represent the matters of kings and princes and magnates if [the native] were in charge of them, and the like, if she were then made fortunate and in a good aspect of the Sun or the Lord of the 10th house, namely by a trine or sextile. And of substance, she signifies silver. And she signifies fortune in the cultivation of the earth, if she were to have dignity in the 4th house at the hour of the nativity.

---

[85] Perhaps this is only in a nocturnal nativity, as Venus signifies mothers in diurnal ones.

And of faith she signifies religion, wherefore Lunar men often become religious, and especially in youth. But sometimes they do not well observe their promises to God, and they rarely persevere well in religions; and from thence arise the tales of the common people.

And of infirmities, she signifies epilepsy, and a twisting of the countenance, and those [infirmities] which pertain to paralysis, and especially the particular [kind],[86] and particularly those which arise in the tongue and lips and eyes. And she signifies the agitation of the limbs which arise from some illnesses, which often happens because of cold and moist illnesses (as phlegmatic ones are). And she signifies the quality of the mind according to her commingling with the planets; wherefore if she is joined with a good planet, the quality of the native's mind will be good; indeed if she is joined with a malefic, its quality will be bad.

On the complexion of the Moon with Saturn and the other planets

Which if she is joined with Saturn in the nativity of some male or female, it signifies that the native will have a hatred for men,[87] and he will pretend that he esteems them, and he will be jealous, and he will rejoice in others' harms, and he will be pained at their advantages; and it will seem to him that every good thing of another is a harm to him.

And if she is joined with Jupiter, it signifies that the native will be cautious, and he will be honest and benign in all things; and he will lead a good and fine and honorable and pleasing life, and one praiseworthy in every way.

And if she is joined with Mars, it signifies that the native will be a whisperer, and jealous; and he will apply himself in malices and whisperings; and in sowing weeds among men in all things; and those which are harmful to others, nor will he care if they are not useful to him, provided that he believes them to be harmful to others–but with this proviso, that reception breaks the above-stated malice.

But if she is joined with the Sun from a trine or sextile aspect, or with reception, what is signified will be fulfilled more completely; and it signifies that the native or querent will get involved in arranging regal matters

---

[86] I.e., confined to a particular part of the body.
[87] Bonatti means humans generally, not only males.

and those of magnates and nobles and the wealthy who are fit for a kingdom.

If however she is joined with Venus, it signifies that the native will be courtly and benign, and sweet, and of a good mind and honest manners; and he will be quick and light and have a quick movement; and he will act with divine offices, nor will he speak evil about anyone; nor will he say something uncouth[88] to anyone and have it be his own fault.

Indeed if she is joined with Mercury, with reception, it signifies that the native will be an eloquent preacher, and that he will adhere to writing and rhetoric; and he will be organized in all of his own speech, and in every one of his statements, both metered and prosaic. If however [it were] without reception, from a trine or sextile aspect, it will be below this. Indeed if from the square aspect or the opposition, he will be talkative, and will spout many empty and useless words; nor will he want to give others their turn to speak; and he will interrupt their words, nor will he want that his own should be interrupted. And Vettius [Valens][89] and Albuaz said, wherefore she signifies the thinking and novelty of the mind, and the weakness of wits and sense; and a heaviness of the tongue, and honest women. Whence you should consider, in the nativities of women, if she were joined to Mercury as was said, because then she signifies that the woman will be honest and good, and of a good mind; and she will gladly nurse children, and she will be fortunate in this; and she will be an assistant[90] of those giving birth, and she signifies mothers and maternal aunts, and a purveyor of foods, for the native will know how to supply foods to others.

And Toz the Greek[91] and Albuaz said, wherefore then she properly signifies the lung and the brain. And of colors, she signifies citrine. And of flavors, the salty.

And she signifies the right eye of women and the left one of men. Whence you should consider in nativities if the Moon were impeded: because it signifies an impediment of the eye, which will happen more if she were impeded in Aries

---

[88] *Rusticitatem*, literally, something a rustic or person from the country would say.
[89] I do not find this in Valens, but this is virtually identical to al-Qabīsī, II.37.
[90] Reading *assestrix* for *astitrix*, with Hand/Zoller.
[91] Unknown astrologer.

(in men it impedes the left one, and in women the right one). For either he will be born with an impeded eye, or his eye will be impeded before his natural death by an inseparable impediment, and sometimes the native will wholly lose the eye.[92]

And of days, she has Monday; and of nights, that which precedes Friday.

And the quantity of her orb is 12°. And the years of her *firdārīah* are 9; her lesser ones, 25; the middle ones, 39 ½. (And certain people wanted to say that it was 66, to whose opposing view I do not see a reason why I should assent.)[93] But the greater ones [are] 108; the greatest, 420. And her greater years are said to be 108 because she has her virtue in that half of the circle of the signs which is from the beginning of Aquarius up to the end of Cancer, which the other planets have in their bounds, and they are 180; but 60 are taken away from her on account of the two domiciles of the two malefics (which are Aquarius and Aries), and again 12 years are taken away from her, on account of the fact that her half takes away 12° in its elevations from that which are the beginnings of the first clime, up to the end of the seventh clime (which is attributed to the Moon), whence only 108 remain.[94] Indeed the middle ones are said to be 39 ½ for the reason by which the middle years of the Sun were said [to be what they are]; nor are the aforesaid 12° taken away then.[95] Indeed the lesser ones are 25, and this because when the Moon is at the end of 25° of Aries, which belongs to each luminary (for it touches the nineteenth degree of Aries, which is of the exaltation of the Sun, and it touches the third degree of Taurus, which is of her exaltation), and account of the taking away of the aforesaid 12 years from her greater years, it adds a second half of them (6) to the lesser years of the Sun, and thus there come to be 25 years. And her strength in the parts of the world is in the "right of setting."

---

[92] Based on *Tet.* III.13.

[93] The correct value is 66 ½. Bonatti has misread the already confused version in Abū Ma'shar (*Gr. Intr.* VII.8), which gives 66 ½ but then says "according to certain people, 39 and a half." Bonatti seems to have gotten these two values switched, and overlooked the "and a half," thus yielding his erroneous 39.

[94] The reader should consult Hand's footnote (Hand/Zoller, p. 212 n.725), where he plausibly shows where this 12° comes from in the ascensional times of the climes. But as he rightly points out, it is unclear why the 12° should be subtracted.

[95] This explanation is based on Bonatti's reliance on Abū Ma'shar. The middle years are derived rather simply: the greater years (108) added to the lesser years (25) equals 133, which, divided by two, gives the correct mean: 66 ½.

On the forms which the Moon signifies

And Māshā'allāh said that she signifies, of the figures of men, a white man, snowy, commingled with redness, benevolent eyebrows, having eyes not wholly large; a round face, a beautiful stature. And of lands, the Turks[96] and *Exthomama*[97] and Daylam.[98]

And Sacerdos said the Moon gives a man to be of no service, because by day and night he desires to run around here and there, nor does he remain stable anywhere easily–which is true, if she were slow in course in the nativity, without perfect reception, and she were joined to a planet quick in course (and especially of the inferiors). And he said, the Lunar man has a round face, an average stature. But there is a great alteration of the eye, or he was pierced through the eye. And he said that he is a squinting [or envious] man, or the orb of the eyes is entirely higher.[99] And that I might explain it clearly and briefly to you, the other one of the eyes will by no means lack a defect.

And Sarcinator[100] said in a certain treatise of his, the Moon signifies his years of childhood, from the beginning of the New Moon up to seven days; and from the seventh day up to the fourteenth, she signifies the years of youth; and from the fourteenth up to the twenty-first, she signifies the years of old age; and from the twenty-first up to the end of the [lunar] month, she signifies the years of senility.

And when she is under the rays of the Sun, she signifies secrets and hidden things; she even signifies things that should be hidden–whence it is good to handle and do then those things which ought to be hidden, namely those which we want to be concealed from the people, before she is separated from the Sun. Indeed [we should hide] those which we want to be hidden for the time being, after she is separated from the Sun, [but] before she exits from under the Sun's rays.

And from the beginning of the [lunar] month up to the opposition, she signifies all that is going to be; and from the opposition up to the end of the [lunar] month she signifies all that must be destroyed. And from the beginning of the [lunar] month up to the Full Moon, she and the Sun signify accusers. And

---

[96] Lat. *Artore*; John of Spain, *Arcoch*.
[97] Al-Qabīsī reads: "al-Gilan, Armenia…" John of Spain reads: *Timanam*. Some variants in the Latin manuscripts read *Erthenium* and *Ectheia*, apparently referring to Armenia.
[98] Lat. *Adila*.
[99] *Vel omnino altior orbis oculorum*. I am not clear of the sense of this phrase.
[100] Unknown astrologer; his treatise may be a *Pentedeca*, mentioned by Bonatti in Tr. 5 (32nd Consideration).

from the beginning of the [lunar] month up to the opposition, she signifies wealth and holding on [to it]; and from the opposition up to the end of the [lunar] month, she signifies payments and dispersion; wherefore if the nativity were at the beginning of the [lunar] month, the native will be intent on wealth and retaining however much of the earnings there is in it. And if it were at the end of the [lunar] month, the native will be intent on spending, and he will disperse substance so that his method of spending will decline into wastefulness. And it signifies, in the beginning of the month (with respect to [horary] judgment), the manager and the quaesited matter, and the prosperity of the manager, and of the quaesited matter; and at the end of the [lunar] month it signifies the contrary, as al-Qabīsī says. And in the opposition it signifies contrariety.

And if there were 15° between the body of the Moon and the opposition of the Sun, it signifies the existence[101] of the beginning of contrariety and its cause. And if she were separated from the opposition of the Sun, it signifies the causes of salvation from the enmity.[102] And in her exit from under the Sun's rays, she signifies an exit from hiddenness, and the detection of hidden things, and things similar to these. And in her entrance under the rays of the Sun, she signifies fitness for being hidden, and especially those things which we want more to be hidden and to be concealed. And from the hour of her separation from the Sun, she signifies fitness[103] for going out from hiddenness. And from the hour of her exit from under the rays of the Sun, she signifies opening, and arrival from absence; for then it seems to signify the arrival of someone absent, if a question were made about someone absent when the Moon were so disposed.

On the signification of the Moon in the square aspect of the Sun

Al-Qabīsī said, while she is in the [first] square aspect of the Sun[104] she signifies descending from a height into the lowest point, just as often happens to those who have great dignities and high magistracies, and they are deposed unwilling from them, and with blame. And the same thing happens in the second square aspect; and the second square aspect is even worse than the first,

---

[101] *Esse.*
[102] Reading *salvationis* (following al-Qabīsī's text) for Bonatti's *erectionis* ("building up"). It could be that by *erectionis* Bonatti meant something like "putting things back together after the enmity."
[103] That is, she is fitted or adapted for matters involving something emerging, as in elections.
[104] That is, at the end of her first quarter. The second square below is on the other side of the Sun at the end of the third quarter.

because even though it signifies a diminution of status in the first square aspect, still it signifies the appearance of matters and wealth, and the increase of holding on to [things]; but in the second square aspect, it signifies the contrary.

On the signification of the Moon from the conjunction up to the half of her light

Ptolemy,[105] Arthephius,[106] and al-Qalandar (who were found to have been very strong in this science) said that the Moon, from the conjunction of the Sun up to the [first] half of her light[107]–her nature is moisture, because then she signifies moisture. And from the half of her light up to the fulfillment,[108] it will be a hot nature, because then she signifies hotness. And from the fulfillment up to the second half of her light, her nature will be dryness, because then she signifies dryness. And from the second half of her light, her nature will be coldness, because then she signifies coldness.

Moreover, they said that the rest of the planets (namely Saturn, Jupiter and Mars), from their rising up to their first station,[109] will be in the nature of moisture, and they signify youth (namely, what is from the fourteenth year up to the forty-first). And from their first station up to the opposition of the Sun, when they are in the middle of their retrogradation, they are in the nature of heat, because then they signify hotness; and they signify completed age (namely that which is from the forty-first year up to the sixty-second). And from the opposition of the Sun, namely when they are in the middle of their retrogradation up to their second station, they are in the nature of dryness, because then they signify a not-true dryness; and they signify old age (namely that which is from the sixty-second year up to the ninetieth). And from their second station up to their concealment under the rays of the Sun, they will be in the nature of coldness, because then they signify coldness; and they signify senility or decrepitude, namely that which is from the ninetieth year up to the end of a man's life (which can sometimes be up to 120 years–and few are found who go beyond this, even though certain people sometimes lie about this).

Whence only the inferiors (namely Venus and Mercury), from the middle of their further longitude up to their first station, signify what the Moon does in the first half of her light. And from the first station up to the middle of their

---

[105] *Tet.* I.8.
[106] Unknown astrologer.
[107] That is, up to the first quarter.
[108] I.e., the Full Moon.
[109] I.e., after they have left the Sun's beams and appear oriental in the morning, until they begin to go retrograde.

nearer longitude, they signify what the Moon signifies from the middle of her light up to its fulfillment. And from the middle of their nearer longitude to their second station, they signify what the Moon signifies from the fulfillment up to the second half of her light. And from their second station up to the middle of their further longitude, they signify what the Moon signifies from the second half of her light up to the conjunction of the Sun.

Indeed, the Sun, from the beginning of Aries up to the end of Gemini, signifies childhood. From the beginning of Cancer up to the end of Virgo, he signifies youth. From the beginning of Libra up to the end of Sagittarius, he signifies completed age. From the beginning of Capricorn up to the end of Pisces, he signifies old age.

And Arthephius and al-Qalandar said that the Sun signifies the soul, and the Moon signifies thoughts. Whence you should consider in someone's nativity, if the Sun were well disposed and in a good place form the Ascendant: because it signifies that his soul will be naturally benevolent. And if he were badly disposed, and in a malign place from the Ascendant, it signifies that his soul will be naturally malevolent (but by accident he could constrain and emend his bad will because of his own free will—as happens sometimes, and oftentimes in these religions and in religious people, and even in other discerning people thinking on malevolent thoughts). And if the Moon were well disposed, as was said concerning the Sun, the native's thoughts will be on the good and for the good. And if she were badly disposed, his thoughts will be evil, and on evil and for evil.

And they said that Saturn signifies grief and sorrow and wailing and lamentation, and labor, and evil. And Jupiter signifies wisdom, reason, and honesty, and good. And Mars signifies anger, furor, and contrariety, and changing more to evil than to good. Venus signifies delight, games, and joy, and gladness. Mercury signifies reasonability, discernment, dialectic, and learning. And the Moon is said to be a pedagogue, and has signification over every matter, and participates with every planet in nativities, questions, journeys, and the beginnings of all things, and their middles and ends, because she is the mediator between the heavens and the other planets, and the elements. And even though the heavens or supercelestial bodies act in elements, still this always comes to be with the Moon mediating, because she is located between the other planets and the elements, so that [the elements] cannot be corrupted nor changed from them or from one of them, without that changing or altering the virtue crossing through her rays or through her power.

Chapter 8: On the Head and Tail of the Dragon— what they would signify

Indeed the Head of the Dragon is naturally a benefic, and of a masculine nature; but by accident it is sometimes a malefic. For its nature is composed of the nature of Jupiter and of the nature of Venus, and this signifies increase and matters which are susceptible of increase, namely a kingdom and dignities and substance, and loftiness, and good fortune. And ad-Dawla and al-Qalandar said that the peculiar property of the Head is to increase, except in the giving of years (for it takes away one-twelfth of them if it is with the significator[110]). Whence if it were with benefics, it increases their fortune; and if it were with malefics, it increases their malice, and then it is accidentally a malefic. And the years of its *firdārīah* are 3.

Indeed its Tail is naturally malefic, and of a feminine nature; but by accident it sometimes becomes a benefic. And its nature is composed of the nature of Saturn and Mars. And it signifies decrease, namely dejection and a fall and poverty, and the decrease of every good thing and every fortune. And the same philosophers said that the peculiar property of the Tail is to diminish: which if it were with benefics, it decreases their fortune; and if it were with malefics, it decreases their malice; and then its good fortune comes to be accidentally. Whence it is said that the Head becomes a benefic with benefics, and malefic

---

[110] I.e., with the *al-kadukhadāh*. But in Tr. 9, Part 2, Ch. 2, Bonatti says the Head and Tail each subtract one-fourth of the years, not one-twelfth. This may be a misprint.

with malefics; indeed the Tail a malefic with benefics, and a benefic with malefics. And the years of its *firdārīah* are 2.

Chapter 9: What any one of the planets would do in the conception of children

Here I will put down certain things about that which the planets do in the conception of children.

For Sacerdos said that in the first month Saturn coagulates matter, and he binds it together, and dries it out, but not by making it wither. Whence if Saturn were well disposed, then the preparation of the conceived child will be well ordered and well disposed, so that every one of the other planets could operate well what pertains to it in the conceived child, according to its being and according to its disposition. If however Saturn were then badly disposed, his compacting or uniting of the conceived child's matter will be badly disposed, nor could the form or disposition of that conceived child ever be well ordered, even if the other planets are well disposed.

In the second month, Jupiter bestows the spirit and members. Whence if Jupiter were then well disposed and of good condition, the limbs of the conceived child will be well disposed and well ordered, and everywhere formed in a natural path; and his spirit and his breathing will be good, and he will inhale and exhale sweetly, and well, without labor and an impediment of respiration. If however Jupiter were of bad condition and badly disposed, it will be the reverse.

In the third month, Mars operates in it through the blood, by reddening it, and leading it in the form of blood. Whence if Mars were then well disposed and of good condition, the blood of the conceived child will be good and pure, and well nourishing the conceived child's body, and hardly and most rarely superabounding so that it might incur injury (unless perhaps on account of a disorderly life), so that he could carry out the force of nature. If however Mars were then badly disposed, it will be the reverse.

But in the fourth month, the Sun gives or completes the more principal members for him, and gives the heat to the limbs, and strengthens natural heat, and increases it, and sets it aright for all of its operations to be carried out. Whence if the Sun were then well disposed, the natural heat of the conceived child will be good and useful, and well preserving the native, and well perfecting all his operations, and most rarely permitting itself to be conquered by unnatural heat; and it will be long lasting in the native's body. Indeed if the Sun were then badly disposed, it will be the reverse.

Indeed in the fifth month, Venus completes the ears, nose, eyebrows, and the whole disposition of the native's face, and the testicles, and she assists the operation of the other planets. Whence if Venus were well disposed then, the conceived child will be charming, having beautiful eyes, beautiful eyebrows, a beautiful nose, beautiful ears, and the whole disposition of the face blessed with gladness. Indeed if Venus were badly disposed then, it will be the reverse.

Indeed in the sixth month Mercury composes the kidneys, tongue, lungs, and perfects all apertures, and all hollow places of the body not yet completed; and all of these will be completed according to the disposition of Mercury.

Indeed in the seventh month, the Moon opens all the channels of the lungs, and perfects them if anything is missing, and she perfects the windpipe, the arteries, and the vulva.[111] She divides, with her limits, all the members of the body not yet divided.[112] Whence if she were then well disposed, all of these will be suitable, each one of them for the office deputed to it. Indeed if she were badly disposed, it will be the reverse.

And this (namely the impediment of the Moon) is the reason why certain children are born impeded in some part of their body. For this happens on account of the impediment of the Moon, and the impediments happen in the member which is deputed to that sign in which the Moon were then impeded. And if she were in the first half, it signifies that the impediment will happen on the right side of the native. Indeed if she were in her last half, it signifies that it will happen on the left side of the native. And because in these seven months each planet has worked its virtue, and what belongs to it in the conceived child, if the child is born it can be vital by rights. And I have seen many who were born at the end of seven months after conception, and they lived for a long time. And my father (who lived to 107, according to his report) was one of those, just as his mother used to report.

Then the disposition reverts to Saturn, who solidifies and draws together and condenses the infant's members with his coldness in the eighth month. Thence it happens that if a child were born then, he will not live—and this happens on account of the intemperate coldness of Saturn disposing [this] condition to the native then.

---

[111] Reading *vulvam* for *uvam*.
[112] I am not sure what Bonatti means here.

But in the ninth month Jupiter reigns, who then draws out the members of the infant with his own moderation, separating [the child] from the uterus of the mother with the cutting of the umbilical cord in a healthy manner, and so then children who are born then are believed to be vital.

But it could be said that Hermes [said] (with whom Ptolemy assented), that the conceived child's periods in the uterus are namely the greater (which consists of 288 days), the middle (which is of 273 days) and the lesser (which consists of 258 days)–and none of these are divided by any number of the above-said months. To which you could respond that Ptolemy and Hermes considered those births which commonly occur–not considering which children should be vital or not, but only the common periods of infants in the uterus. And likewise they spoke of those who go beyond the seventh month in [gestation]. Nor even was their rule so general without it being able to be repealed by a special [case]. For they could not cross the street with a dry foot,[113] nor is it part of my interpretation to dispute over these things, because it seems well enough that each [opinion] can be observed and made smooth.[114] But thus far we must return to what was proposed according to the intention of this work.

Chapter 10: How the native's life would be disposed according to the years of nourishing of each planet

And there is something to be said about the disposition of the native's natural life: how each of the planets would dispose [it] from its beginning up to its end. The order of which is such:

For the Moon, who is nearer to the earth and is said to be faster than all the planets, and beginning from the inferiors is the first of the planets in order, disposes the life of the native from its beginning for four years (which are the years of her nourishing). And this disposition is said and reputed to be like nourishing.

Then Mercury disposes for ten years, which are his years of nourishing.

Then Venus disposes for seven years, which are [her] years of nourishing.

---

[113] The meaning of this saying seems to be that even they could not ignore the plain facts.
[114] This seems to mean that the opinions can be harmonized if looked at in the proper way. See Bonatti's continuation of this discussion in Tr. 9, Part 1, Ch. 6.

Then the Sun disposes for nineteen years, which are his years of nourishing.

Then Mars disposes for fifteen years, which are his years of nourishing.

Then Jupiter disposes for twelve years, which are his years of nourishing.

Then Saturn disposes for thirty years, which are his years of nourishing.

Indeed if the native were to go through these, the disposition returns to the Moon; after that, to Mercury; and so on to the rest of the planets, as was said. Whence, in whichever disposition one of the aforesaid dispositors were well disposed in that time, the native's life will be disposed well, and *vice versa*. And it adds to or takes away (in those years) from the significator of the native in that time, according to its disposition and its condition.

Chapter 11: Which of the days and which of the nights each planet would have, and why they are denominated from it, and on the unequal hours, and on the masculine and feminine hours

Each of the planets has its own day and own night deputed to it, whence if some day or some night were deputed to some planet, the first hour of that day or night will belong to that planet from which it is denominated; and the second will belong to the planet who succeeds it in the order of planets.

For example, Sunday belongs wholly to the Sun, wherefore the first hour of Sunday belongs to the Sun. Monday belongs totally to the Moon, wherefore its first hour belongs to the Moon. Tuesday belongs wholly to Mars, wherefore the first hour of that day belongs to Mars. Wednesday belongs wholly to Mercury, wherefore its first hour belongs to Mercury. Thursday belongs wholly to Jupiter, wherefore its first hour belongs to Jupiter. Thursday belongs wholly to Venus, wherefore its first hour belongs to Venus. Saturday belongs wholly to Saturn, wherefore its first hour belongs to Saturn.

Moreover, I say that the first hour of Sunday belongs to the Sun; and the second one belongs to Venus, who succeeds him in the order of planets. The third one to Mercury, who succeeds Venus. The fourth one to the Moon, who succeeds Mercury. Then it begins from the top, and its fifth hour belongs to

Saturn, from which it is begun after the Moon. The sixth belongs to Jupiter, who succeeds Saturn in order. The seventh to Mars, who succeeds Jupiter in order. Again, the eighth to the Sun, who succeeds Mars. The ninth to Venus, who succeeds the Sun. The tenth to Mercury, who succeeds Venus. The eleventh to the Moon, who succeeds Mercury. The twelfth to Saturn, who (as it was said) succeeds the Moon. And thus you have the twelve hours of the day, both equal and unequal.

On the equal and unequal hours of the night

Just as every planet has its own day deputed to it, so each of them has its own night deputed to it, and named after it. For the entire night which follows on Sunday,[115] is said to be Jupiter's; the second Mars's; the third the Sun's; the fourth Venus's, the fifth Mercury's, the sixth the Moon's, the seventh Saturn's, the eighth Jupiter's; the ninth Mars's, the tenth the Sun's; the eleventh Venus's, the twelfth Mercury's. And thus you have the twelve hours of the night, both equal and unequal.

On the masculine and feminine hours

Of the hours (both of day and night), there are even certain masculine ones and certain feminine ones. For the first hour of each day, and the first hour of each night, is said to be masculine; the second feminine; the third masculine; the fourth feminine; the fifth masculine; the sixth feminine; the seventh masculine; the eighth feminine; the ninth masculine; the tenth feminine; the eleventh masculine; the twelfth feminine.

Whence you should consider the hour of the nativity of any male, to see whether it is masculine; because if it were so, it makes for a good condition of masculinity; and if it were feminine, it does not make for a good condition of masculinity, for it feminizes the native a little bit. And if it were a feminine hour in the nativity of a female, it makes for a good condition of femininity, and makes her be in the nature of femininity. And if it were a masculine hour, it makes her come down a little bit toward masculinity, and makes her in a certain way the nature of a virago, even if not wholly so.

---

[115] That is, the hours beginning after sundown on Sunday, up through sunrise on Monday morning.

Chapter 12: On the shapes or figures which the signs give to a native

It was spoken concerning the shapes or figures which the planets give to those whose significators they are. But it even remains that something else be said about the assistants of their figures or shapes, which it seems in a certain way pertains to the *hīlāj*[116] (which is called the "root of life").[117] For just as the planets bestow their figures to natives, so do the signs. For each one does not give a complete form to the native through itself, but both together, namely the one with the other; because a planet cannot give an image to the native through itself without a sign, nor the sign through itself without a planet, any more than a mother could generate a child without a father, nor a father without a mother. For someone cannot be born without some planet being the Lord of the sign then ascending, and so it is necessary that each participate with the other in the nativity of any native. Whence the signs modify[118] the planets, so that the figure of the native is not wholly such as the planet gives. And thus the planet modifies the sign, so that the figure of the native is not wholly such as the sign gives; and sometimes one assists the other. These are the figures which the signs give men:

For Aries makes a man having a long neck, and a long face, much hair on the head, eyes sometimes grave [or heavy], small ears, and a body often curved [or bent].

Taurus makes a man having a full face, sometimes curved [or bent]; and if he did not have a full face, he will have a grand nose; and if he did not have a naturally grand one, in the space of time he will have long nostrils by accident; black and grave [or heavy] eyes; shaggy or raised hairs on the

---

[116] This is what is usually written in Latin as *hyleg* or *ylem*, from the Ar. هيلاج, equivalent to the Gr. *aphetês*, the planet or degree signifying the life of the native, and used in longevity calculations. But Bonatti sometimes uses the term in an extended way: for instance, as a significator of the father in a nativity (Tr. 9, Part 3, 4th House) or as a special significator in electional figures (Tr. 7, Part 2, Ch. 17).

[117] According to this section, the *hīlāj* gives a shape, along with the sign; the *hīlāj* itself is not the overall "significator of the native," but its assistant. However, at the end of this chapter, he speaks of the significator of the nativity and its sign as though it might be the same as the *hīlāj*.

[118] *Derogant.* This is an interesting choice of verbs. *Derogo* also means to "restrict, repeal, take away from," as when a ruler's decrees are restricted and modified. The language suggests that the sign and planets are not merely partners, but that the sign restricts and channels the planet somehow.

head; a thick and fat neck, almost more than is decent; modest, who looks at the ground when walking; proceeding honestly, not stable [but] almost wandering, but you should not trust your wife to [be with] him in secret.

Gemini makes a man having an average stature, a full chest, an agreeable person.[119]

Cancer makes a man having a disarranged body, and thick skin over his whole body; and it renders a man thin above, thick below, having twisted teeth, small eyes.

Leo makes a man active, and very noted, and intelligent, thick above, thin below; nor is he made unsuitable [or not handsome] from thence; magnanimous; thin legs.

Virgo makes a man having a beautiful person, and a good will, beautiful eyes, and a decent face.

Libra makes a man having an agreeable face, average flesh,[120] who even will love women.

Scorpio makes a man having a ruddy and small face, much hair on the head, small eyes, long legs, big feet, quickly changeable; in whose mouth truth is hardly or never found; growing angry, a litigator; and having lawsuits and quarrels with everyone (and doing it practically for nothing).

Sagittarius makes a man having long hips, and a long face, and a full jaw[121] on the face; a subtle mind and often more beautiful from the back than from the front; thin hair on the head, and sometimes a belly bigger than it ought to be; and he delights in riding horses.

Capricorn makes a man having thin legs, a dry body, a face like a goat's, much hair on the head.

---

[119] "Person" should be understood in terms of bodily form, not personality.
[120] I.e., average "build." Note that I will translate this word (*carnosus*) as "fleshy" in Tr. 9.
[121] Reading *mola* for *mila*.

Aquarius makes a man tall and vain, haughty and arrogant, who even will be a great expounder [or interpreter], and often he is wasteful, and a devastator of goods; having a beautiful and colored face, and sometimes one leg longer than the other.

Pisces makes a man having a full chest, a small head, a beautiful and blooming beard, and a full jaw[122] of the face in relation to his head; a white color, having round eyes, magnanimous.

But most often it happens that men are not found so made, and this is by accident, and not by nature; wherefore sometimes the significator of the nativity is found to be so disposed that it contradicts the sign, and does not permit its significations to be perfected as it should be perfected according to the nature of the sign. And sometimes it is found so disposed, and so weak, and so remote from the power of completing its significations, that the sign contradicts him in such a way that his significations are not perfected as they ought to be perfected by the nature of the planet. You however, from your own industry can consider these things, why they happen, and how. For I cannot write all the particulars taken together which can happen in future times.

Chapter 13: On the diverse accidents which happen to men

There are certain accidents which happen to men, about which I have not found anything stated by any of the philosophers whence my mind would be put at rest. Nor do I believe, nor does it seem like to truth, that this was on account of the fact that they were ignorant of it, but rather that it seemed to them a sprawling and prolix matter, whence they feared lest it would generate irritation to listeners; and they even left it to the industry of the wise, such as are these: for we see a small child born of a large father and large mother, and a large child born of a small father and small mother; and a black one from a white one, and a white one from a black one; a thin one from a fat one, and a fat one from a thin one. We see certain ones fat, others muscled, others thin, others between both. We see some fat ones strong, and honest, and bold, and easy, and proceeding lightly, others from the same one, weak and heavy, and proceeding heavily, vile and timid; some wise, some foolish, even natives from

---

[122] Again, reading *mola*.

the same parents both wise and foolish; some arrive to great riches and dignities and fame from low-class and poor ones; indeed some arrive to the greatest depression and poverty from magnates and nobles, so that they are reputed to be practically as nothing. We see some who in no way are likened to their fathers, whence sometimes the mothers are accused concerning this (when they are not culpable); some who are likened to their fathers; some who are likened to their grandfathers or great-grandfathers (both maternal and paternal); and some different ones we see practicing at one and the same time one and the same art, and some of them are enriched by it, and some are impoverished from the same thing (and sometimes they know [the art] better and create fewer expenses), and living miserably, but they do not become enriched; certain ones the contrary. We see some, when they are not very wise, whose words are listened to and believed, and reputed to be more wise than [the words] of those who are sometimes wise, and the vice versa. We see some who always remain healthy, some always infirm, some semi-healthy, some for whom medicine and the cures of doctors are successful in their infirmities, some for whom they are harmful. We see some who abound in riches and lack children, some who abound in children and lack riches; some who abound in both, some who lack both; some who abound in the aforesaid for a time, some who lack the aforesaid for a time; some who at some time abound in children, and see their death and are saddened because of them; certain ones who abandon them and the children inherit their goods after death.

Likewise, there are some [men] who carry out womanly tasks, and certain women who carry out manly tasks, and they make war and do many things which pertain to men, such as was a certain Maria of Cremona,[123] who wore male arms as a man does, like hunting spears (and she used to hunt boars); and the daughter of Girzavensis who was called Fredona; and many others. And some who are the best singers and have voices sounding well, and some who knew nothing of how to sing; and some who knew very well how to play musical instruments, and use them. And some who neither knew nor were capable of knowing it, but they knew how to do other things, better than other men. And we see some rejoice on one day and be saddened on the next, even without an obvious reason; and some rejoice on a good day and are saddened on a bad ones, and some be saddened on a good day and rejoice on a bad day. We see some stuttering, some talkative, some wise having few words, and not

---

[123] *Maria Cremensis.*

well organized, some having many words and well organized; some many [words] and not well organized (both wise and not wise).

And we see many other accidents happening to men about which it would be difficult to make individual mention; but whence they come, and why, I will make mention to you, and I will expound to you in the Treatise on nativities, with the help of God.

And even though the work might seem sprawling, still it will be of such great usefulness, that it will not generate irritation in reading or in studying it; and certain extraordinary and practically unheard of things will be stated there, such as are these; because we see that no face of a man is so like the face of another without there being some unlikeness between them, and the like.

PART 2: On the Particular Judgments of the Stars

On those things which happen to the planets in themselves, and what happens from one to another

Chapter 1: On those things which happen to the planets in themselves

In this second Part of the third Treatise, we must speak about certain accidents which happen to the planets in themselves and to one another, and I will speak to you as someone who has already been introduced, and not by way of introducing. And, following in the footsteps of the philosophers, I will tell you first about those things which happen to the planets in themselves. And these things are about those accidents, namely when a planet is ascending in its circle of the *awj*,[124] and when it is descending in the same circle, and when it is neither ascending in it nor descending.[125]

And Al-Qabīsī said the signification of those things which happen to the planets in themselves, is like when a planet is ascending in the circle of its *awj*, in less light and magnitude and course. For when a planet is in the more remote part of its eccentric from the earth (in which its *awj* is), it appears then in less light and magnitude of its body, and it seems slower in course: not that it runs less in one day than in another, in terms of it running through the line of its epicycle, but on account of the location of the parts of the epicycle it appears so.

And when it is in the opposition of its *awj*, namely in that part of its eccentric which is more near to the earth, then it appears in a greater light and magnitude of its body, and faster in course. In the more remote part of its eccentric it seems slower in course on account of the greater span of degrees in that part than in the other. Indeed in the nearer part of [its course], it seems faster in course on account of the lesser span of degrees in that part than in the other. Because it runs faster through a lesser span than a greater one, when [in actuality] it always runs equally [fast], as I said.

---

[124] Lat. *auge*, from Ar. اوج, "the summit" (see al-Bīrūnī, *Instr.*, §171). The *awj* is the point on a planet's deferent that is furthest from the earth. It is usually presented as a native Arabic word, but note its similarity to Lat. *augeo* (stem *aux-*), "to increase, to exalt."

[125] A rather good explanation of the terms found here, along with a diagram, can be found in the ARHAT edition of the *Abbr.* (1997), p. 16. But see also Kennedy (1958).

Whence it seems then to be of a faster course in the direction of the eighth heaven, than it comes to be in the direction of its eccentric. Indeed in the more remote part it seems slower of course in the direction of the eighth heaven therefore, because it goes through a greater span of degrees which are in that part than in the other, more slowly than [it does through a] lesser [span]. For the degrees of the eccentric are greater on the side of the *awj* than on the one opposite it, which happens on account of the declination of the center of the eccentric from the center of the earth, which is the center of the eighth sphere.

And some, not making sense concerning the *awj*, but perhaps equivocating on it by speaking broadly, thought that the *awj* was the more remote place on the epicycle. But the true *awj* is simply the more remote place on the eccentric, and not the epicycle. On the epicycle only the further longitude and the nearer longitude are considered. The further longitude is that part of the epicycle which is above the line of the eccentric. Indeed the nearer longitude is that part of the epicycle which is below the line of the eccentric, and so in this the *awj* and longitude differ from one another. Moreover, that the *awj* is considered in the epicycle is evident by this: because the epicycle goes around the whole eccentric. Whence sometimes it is in the *awj* (namely in the more remote part of the eccentric), sometimes in opposition to the *awj* (namely in the nearer part of the eccentric), sometimes between these places (namely [between] the *awj* and its opposite). And the epicycle goes around all the signs, but the *awj* of the eccentric stays always fixed in one sign and in one place, and thus solely in the eccentric is the *awj* considered.

Indeed the *awj*es are as follows as I tell you in the present work. For the *awj* of the Sun and the *awj* of Venus is in one and the same degree, namely in the eighteenth degree[126] of Gemini and in its fiftieth minute. The *awj* of Mars is in the second degree of Leo, namely in its fifty-first minute. The *awj* of Jupiter is in the fifteenth degree of Virgo, namely in its thirtieth minute. The *awj* of Saturn is in the first degree of Sagittarius, in its fifth minute. The *awj* of Mercury is in the eighteenth degree of Libra, namely in its tenth minute. Indeed the *awj* of the Moon is not distinguished as the other *awj*es of the other planets are distinguished, because she does not withdraw from the average of her course[127] in her equations[128] as happens with the other planets, which happens on account of

---

[126] The text simply says "18," but the numbers for the other longitudes are written out, so I have treated this as being "the eighteenth degree."
[127] *A medio cursu suo*. Here and the equivalent phrases below I translate *medio* as "average."
[128] *Aequationibus*.

the course of the center of the eccentric in the small circle, whose center is the center of the orb of the signs.

When a planet is in the middle of the circle, so that as much of the circle of the fixed stars is above the planet as there is below or in front of or behind the *awj*, then it seems equal in body and light; in all other places it appears in either greater or lesser light and body. And when it is going toward the *awj*, and there are 90 equal degrees or less between it and the *awj*, then it begins to appear with less light and body, and thus it keeps being made smaller step by step, until it reaches the *awj*, which is the more remote part of the eccentric. And when it undertakes to separate itself from the *awj*, it begins to appear in greater light and body, and so it does not keep being made bigger insofar as it is in view[129] up until it is elongated from the *awj* by 90 equal degrees (which are considered in the circle of signs) and appears equal, just as was said. From that point forward it is made greater in light and body in a more perceptible way than before, until it reaches the opposite of the *awj*, which is the part of the eccentric closer to the earth. And if the equated argument of the planet were from one degree up to six signs, it would be an increasing number or course. And if were from six signs up to twelve, it will be a decreasing course. And if it were exactly six signs, or exactly twelve, the planet will be neither increasing nor decreasing [its] course.

And thus is considered in the epicycle the direction and retrogradation, and station, and quickness and slowness of the course. For when a planet is in that part of the epicycle which is above the eccentric, it is called direct. And when it is in that part of the epicycle which is below the eccentric, it is called retrograde. And when it is in the places of the contact of the line of the eccentric with the line of the epicycle, it is called stationary. And when it is between those two places of contact (namely from the top of the line of the diameter of the epicycle which is a little distant from the line of the eccentric), it is called slow in course.

But because this work is not about the consideration of this topic, I will cease speaking about it more, and return to [my original] proposal, and especially since all of this is discussed widely in al-Farghānī,[130] whose intention was to treat of the supercelestial bodies and their diversity. And when the equated equation of some planet is added on top of the middle of its course, then it increases the course or number. And when the equated equation is subtracted from the middle of the course of the planet, then it decreases its number or

---

[129] *In aspectu.*
[130] Lat. *Alfraganus.* See Introduction.

course. And the equation is considered according to the epicycle, and not according to the eccentric.

And when Saturn or Jupiter or Mars goes[131] over the average of his course, he is said to be decreasing[132] their course or number. However, the average course of Saturn in one day is 2' and 35 thirds.[133] The average course of Jupiter is 4' 59". The average course of Mars is 31' 26". And when each of them goes as much as is its average course, it is said that its course is equal, that is, neither increasing nor decreasing. And when in one day the Sun or Venus or Mercury go more than the average of the course of the Sun, which is 59' 8", it is said to be increasing its course; and when it goes less than 59' 8" it is said to be decreasing its course. And when the Sun is near his *awj* before or after by 90°, his course is said to be equal or average. And when it is less than 90° his course is said to be slow. And when he is distant from it either before or behind, by more than 90°, his course is said to be quick. And when he goes exactly 59' 8" his course is called equal. And when in one day the Moon goes more than 13° 10' 35", she is said to be increasing her course. And when she goes less than 13° 10' 35", she is said to be decreasing her course. And when she goes exactly 13° 10' 35", her course is called equal.

Chapter 2: When the planets are northern, and when southern

However it happens to the planets that they are sometimes northern [in latitude], sometimes southern. However a planet is made northern when it crosses its *jawzahirr*[134] (this is the place in which the line of the eccentric of the planet cuts the path of the Sun). Whence, when it crosses from the south into the north, its crossing is through the place of the contact of its eccentric with the eccentric of the Sun. And as long as it stays in that part of its eccentric which is on the northern side of the path of the Sun, it is called northern, until it comes to the other place of contact, which is opposite to its crossing, and returns to the part of the eccentric which is on the southern side of the eccentric of the Sun. And in all of that half, it is called southern. And when it has crossed the aforesaid first place of contact, up through three full signs, it will be

---

[131] Reading *vadit* for *vadunt*.
[132] *Minuens*. This should probably read, "increasing."
[133] I.e., 11" (35/3 = 11.666).
[134] Lat. *genzahar, zenzahar*, Ar. الجوزهر (al-Bīrūnī, *Instr.*, §177). According to Wright, the Arabic derives from Pers. *gaviz'har*. Every planet has a *jawzahirr*, but of course the Moon's (i.e., its Nodes) are of greatest interest to the astrologer.

"northern-ascending," and from three signs up to the sixth it will be "northern-descending." And when it has transited the aforesaid place of contact again, returning to the south up to three full signs, it will be "southern-descending," and from three up to six full ones (which is the place of its *jawzahirr* from which it begins to be northern), it will be "southern-ascending." These are the things which happen to the planets in themselves.

Chapter 3: On those things with happen with the planets to each other, namely to one of them from another

In this chapter we must treat of those things which happen to one planet from another (that is to one another), according to the sayings of the philosophers. And among the first things to be discussed is about the things which happen to Saturn, Jupiter, Mars, Venus, [and] Mercury from the luminaries, and in relation to the luminaries.

And Ptolemy said[135] that when a planet sees itself face to face, then the planet is said to be in the *al-muwājahah*[136] of a planet. *Al-muwājahah* means viewing face-to-face, [though][137] this statement of Ptolemy's seems somewhat rough; but it must be understood this way, namely that when a planet is occidental of the Sun it is said to be in the "facing" of the Sun. And take care lest you be deceived in the fact that Ptolemy said "occidental," lest by this you understand that a planet sets after the Sun, as occidentality is understood elsewhere. But by "occidental of the Sun" Ptolemy understood when a planet is on the western side [of the Sun], so that it would set *before* the Sun sets.[138] And

---

[135] *Tet.* I.23. Bonatti's explanation here is not quite Ptolemy's, but it must be admitted that Ptolemy's own explanation is less than fully clear.

[136] Lat. *almuguea*, from Ar. المواجهة, "the facing" (al-Qabīsī, III.5; al-Bīrūnī, *Instr.*, §449), a translation of Ptolemy's *idioprosôpon*, *Tet.* I.23. I will translate this as "facing." It seems to me that "facing" must be based on the symbolic chart of the beginning of the world (the *Thema Mundi* described in Firmicus Maternus (*Mathesis* III.1). In that chart, the zodiac is divided into a solar half (Leo to Capricorn) and a lunar half (Aquarius to Cancer). In Bonatti's description, the domiciles that are used to measure the required distances for the "facing" of the Sun are all on the solar side, and in an actual chart a planet must be "eastern" (*orientalis*) of the Sun or setting before it, to be able to be in its "facing."

[137] *Hoc enim*.

[138] Ptolemy gives as an example Venus, if she should "make a hexagonal interval relative to the lights while being west relative to the Sun and east relative to the Moon, in keeping with their houses from of old." I am not sure how this works out for all the planets in Ptolemy, but Bonatti seems to be right that Ptolemy wanted (at least Venus) to be "western" (*occidentalis*) of the Sun. In all of the following examples, the planets are posited in signs that will make them set before (and so be western of) the Sun.

Ptolemy understood that when he said "face to face," that is when there comes to be between a planet and the Sun as much as there is between the domicile of the Sun and the domicile of the planet. May you understand by this when a planet is distant from whatever place from the Sun as much as there is between its domicile and Leo (which is the domicile of the Sun).

For example, let it be put that Saturn is distant from the Sun by as much as there is between Leo and Capricorn (which is a domicile of Saturn), namely so that the Sun is in one sign (whatever one it is) and Saturn is in one sign that is distant from him by as much as there is distance [between] Capricorn and Leo, namely so that one is in the sixth sign from the other, just as Capricorn is the sixth sign from Leo. And there is between them by signs and degrees and minutes as much as there is between the two signs,[139] by reckoning one of them in number, the other being excluded, which is five whole signs: then Saturn will be in the "facing" of the Sun.[140] For example, let it be put that the Sun is in the twelfth degree of Leo, and Saturn is even in the twelfth degree of Pisces: thus Saturn is in the sixth sign from the Sun, by the reckoned sign in which each of them is, namely Leo, Cancer, Gemini, Taurus, Aries, and Pisces. Now Saturn is distant from the Sun by as much as there is between Leo (which is the domicile of the Sun) and Capricorn (which is a domicile of Saturn), so that five whole signs fall between them: because from the twelfth degree of Pisces up to the twelfth degree of Leo are five whole signs, namely Aries, Taurus, Gemini, Cancer, Leo, just as there fall five whole signs between Leo and Capricorn (which are [Virgo], Libra, Scorpio, Sagittarius, and Capricorn). For from the twelfth degree of Leo up to the twelfth degree of Cancer is one whole sign. From the twelfth degree of Cancer up to the twelfth degree of Gemini is one whole sign, and thus there are two signs. From the twelfth degree of Gemini up to the twelfth degree of Cancer is one whole sign, and there are three signs. From the twelfth degree of Taurus up to the twelfth degree of Aries is one whole sign, and thus there are four signs. From the twelfth degree of Aries up to the twelfth degree of Pisces is one whole sign, and thus there are five whole

---

[139] This is not accurate from Ptolemy's perspective. Bonatti is probably following Plato of Tivoli's translation of Ptolemy (1138 AD), which says that there should be so much "in longitude [or length]" (*ex longitudine*) between the planet and the luminary, which accounts for Bonatti's attempt to measure it exactly. But Ptolemy only reckons the distance in terms of whole signs.

[140] Bonatti greatly complicates the example with his forwards and backwards counting. Simply put, if Leo is the first sign, then Capricorn is the sixth from it: here, if Pisces is the first sign, then Leo is the sixth from it.

signs. For the sign is not completed in the sign in which it begins, but it is completed in the sign following after it.

Likewise it is necessary that for Jupiter to be in the "facing" of the Sun, that there falls between him and the Sun in signs, degrees and minutes, as much as there is between Leo and Sagittarius (which is a domicile of Jupiter), and this is four complete signs–namely so that Jupiter is in the fifth sign from the Sun. For example, the Sun is in some sign, let us put him in Gemini. Now it will be necessary that Jupiter be in Aquarius, so that he is distant from the Sun by four whole signs, neither more nor less. For Aquarius is the fifth sign from Gemini in a similar degree and minutes. The Sun, therefore, is in the third degree of Gemini; so from the third degree of Gemini up to the third degree of Taurus is one whole sign, and from the third degree of Taurus up to the third degree of Aries, is one whole sign, and thus there are two whole signs. And from the third degree of Aries up to the third degree of Pisces is one whole sign, and thus there are three signs. And from the third degree of Pisces up to the third degree of Aquarius is one whole sign, and thus there are four whole signs, and so Jupiter will be in the fifth sign from the Sun.

Likewise so that Mars is in the "facing" of the Sun, it is necessary that he be in the fourth sign from the Sun, so that in signs and degrees and minutes there fall three whole signs, just as there fall between Leo and Scorpio (which is a domicile of Mars); and as was said by including one and excluding the other, like with the rest. So let it be put that the Sun is in the fourth degree of Aries: now it is necessary that Mars be in the fourth degree of Capricorn, because between the fourth degree of Aries and the fourth degree of Capricorn are three whole signs. For from the fourth degree of Aries up to the fourth degree of Pisces, is one whole sign, and from the fourth degree of Pisces up to the fourth degree of Aquarius is one whole sign, and thus there are two whole signs. And between the fourth degree of Aquarius and the fourth degree of Capricorn is one whole sign, and thus there are three whole signs: and thus Mars will be in the fourth sign from the Sun.

With Venus however, "facing" is not considered as it is with the other planets. Because she is not elongated from the Sun as much as there is distancing her domicile from the domicile of the Sun. But she is said to be in the "facing" of the Sun when she sets before the Sun sets, and is in [her] furthest elongation from the Sun, so that she cannot be more elongated from him.

Concerning Mercury however, it must be said that for him to be in the "facing" of the Sun, it is necessary that he be in the second sign from the Sun, so that one entire sign falls between him and the Sun, just as there is one complete sign between Leo and Virgo (which is a domicile of Mercury). So let it be put that the Sun is in the ninth degree and twelfth minute of Capricorn; now it is necessary that Mercury be in the ninth degree and twelfth minute of Sagittarius, because between the ninth degree and twelfth minute of Capricorn and the ninth degree and the twelfth minute of Sagittarius, is one entire sign.

Indeed the Moon is not said to be in the "facing" of the Sun, for the reason that the luminaries are not said to be in the "facing" of a luminary; and it would even have been necessary that she be far from the Sun by exactly one sign for her to be in the "facing" of the Sun, if he were supposed to receive her, and if she could receive the "facing" which could bring in or confer perceptibility.[141]

On "facing"

Indeed with the "facing" of the Moon it must be considered (and it is necessary for you to know) that just as a planet who is in the "facing" of the Sun is occidental from the Sun (that is, that it sets before the Sun),[142] so it is necessary that, on the other hand, the planet who is in the "facing" of the Moon be oriental from her in such a way that it sets *after* the Moon, and not before her— and [that] the Moon set before it and not after it.[143]

And Ptolemy said[144] that when a planet is distant from the Sun by as much as its domicile is distant from the domicile of the Sun, and from the Moon as much as its domicile is distant from the domicile of the Moon, or it were safe from their rays,[145] then it is in "facing".

---

[141] *Quae posset inferre vel conferre sensibilitatem.* The meaning is unclear, especially since it is unknown whether *quae* refers to the Moon or "facing".
[142] I.e., "western" of the Sun.
[143] I.e., so that the planet will be "eastern" (*orientalis*) of the Moon, and so set after her. In this way, "facing" the Moon is a mirror image of the Sun's. The distances used to measure "facing" the Moon are based on the domiciles on the lunar half of the zodiac, but in practice the planet has got to be on the other side of the Moon, i.e., setting after her.
[144] Again, *Tet.* I.23. Ptolemy is responsible for this ambiguity, since he first says the planet ought to be in the relevant distance from the Sun *or* the Moon, but in his Venus example says Venus should be west relative to the Sun *and* east relative to the Moon.
[145] By "or" Bonatti seems to be clarifying the preceding points (setting before the Sun and after the Moon), not introducing a third condition.

On the "facing" of the other planets

Indeed concerning the "facing" of the other planets, the wise did not take care to make mention, because they did not believe there was great power in it. However, each of the other five planets has its own "facing." For the "facing" of the three superiors is considered just as the "facing" of the Sun is, and that of the two inferiors is considered just as the "facing" of the Moon is. And each of them can be in the "facing" of another, namely when it is distant from it by as much as its domicile is distant from the other's domicile which is nearer to it. And always, an inferior receives "facing" from a superior, except for Saturn, who receives his "facing" from Mercury.

Chapter 4: On the *al-'ittisal*[146] of the Planets

And there is another condition of the planets toward one another, namely the corporal or aspectual conjunction or application, which al-Qabīsī calls *al-'ittisal* or "continuation." For the corporal conjunction is when a planet is joined to a planet in the same sign; indeed the aspectual one is when two planets are in two different signs aspecting each other by a trine or sextile or square aspect,[147] and the light [planet] is in fewer degrees in its sign that the heavy one is in its own, however so that there are 6° or less between them (namely, between the rays of one and the body of the other).[148] For example, let it be put that Venus or Mercury is in the fourth degree of Aries, and Mars or Jupiter or Saturn is in the tenth degree of Gemini or Cancer or Leo in front of it, or in the tenth degree of Aquarius or Capricorn or Sagittarius behind it: then Venus or Mercury is joined to it by aspect until it reaches its aspect degree by degree. And understand the same about the corporal conjunction, like if Venus or Mercury is in the fourth degree of Aries, and one of the superior planets is in the tenth degree of Aries: thus the light one is joined to the heavy one by body, and it is

---

[146] Lat. *Alitisal* (sometimes *Alitifal*), Ar. الإتصال. Al-Qabīsī (III.11) uses this word for "application," but other sources (like Plato of Tivoli's Latin translation of the Arabic edition of Ptolemy) use "continuation" (*continuatio*) as a synonym for "application."

[147] Here we get an unambiguous statement that corporal and aspectual conjunctions *cannot* be out-of-sign, even though the conjunction (whether corporal or aspectual) is measured by degrees. The conjoinings must be in signs which *themselves* are configured in classical aspects (e.g., Aries and Gemini are in a sextile configuration).

[148] This statement (from al-Qabīsī III.11) seems to derive from the Greek doctrine that planets have a 3° orb (or that there must be 3° in distance), so that when planets are within 6°, their orbs will touch.

said to be always joined to it until it completes its conjunction with it in the same minute. But after it has transited him by one minute, it is said to be separated from him.

What I told you about Venus and Mercury, understand about all the others, because always the light one is joined to the heavy one, and the less heavy is joined to the more heavy, until Saturn is reached: for Saturn, because he is heavier than the rest, is joined to none of the planets (as is said elsewhere), but all are joined to him.

However, al-Qabīsī said[149] that a planet is not said to be joined to a planet unless it is joined to it degree by degree (whether the conjunction were corporal or aspectual)–but he understood it to be the action of perfecting a matter. Indeed Māshā'allāh,[150] whom the sages trusted very much, said that after a planet projects its rays upon a planet,[151] it is said to be joined to him; which is true, unless another planet prohibits their conjunction. Otherwise one planet is conjoined to another, and the effecting of matters is signified by that. Whence, when one planet projects its rays upon the rays[152] of another, and is distant from it by as much as are the orbs of each, it is said that one "seeks the conjunction of the other," and it signifies the effecting of the quaesited matter, unless another planet destroys or impedes, and the conjunction is said to be burdened. And when they are distanced by as much as there is of the orb of one planet, it is called a "complete conjunction"; and unless something impedes (as I said), it signifies the effecting of the matter. And when the orb of the light of one touches the body of the heavier one, it is said that the heavy one is in the degrees of the light one. And all these things are considered both by aspect and in the corporal conjunction.

Chapter 5: When the planets are said to be oriental, and when occidental

Saturn and Jupiter [and Mars],[153] after they go out from under the rays of the Sun (as al-Qabīsī says), are called "oriental," and are said to be increased in

---

[149] Again, al-Qabīsī III.11. Al-Qabīsī's point was that planets will be in an effective *applying* conjunction or aspect up until the exact degree, when (as Bonatti rightly notes), the aspect will perfect.
[150] Source unknown, but perhaps based on *OR*, Ch. 1.
[151] *Super planetam.*
[152] *Super radios.*
[153] The 1491 and 1550 editions omit Mars.

strength up until they are then elongated from the Sun by 30°, just as a sick man who, after a crisis, is increased in his strength and full health, until he resumes his former vigor and returns to the state in which he had been before he began to fall ill, and stays more carefree. Then from those 30° up to another 30° they are said to be "oriental-strong," because then they are in greater safety from the Sun than they could ever be: for they do not fear him then in anything, just as he who has escaped an illness does not fear it, and has already resumed all his powers, or rather after the complete freeing and resumption of his powers he is sometimes made more fleshy and stronger than usual (if however his complexion is well disposed to be able to take them on).

And when they have transited the Sun by 60°, namely so that the Sun is that much elongated from them, they are called "oriental, going toward weakness" until they come to the elongation of 90° from the Sun, and then they are called "oriental-weak" until they come to retrogradation. And after they have undertaken to go retrograde, they are called "oriental-retrograde" until they are in the opposition of the Sun degree by degree. And after they have transited the degree of the opposition of the Sun until they come to direct [motion], they are called "occidental retrograde." Then, from the degree of their direct [motion] up to the sixtieth degree after direction, they are "occidental-strong"–not that they are truly strong, but less weak. Then from the said 60° up until their longitude is 30° from the Sun, they are said to be "occidental, going toward weakness." Then, up until they come to the beginning of combustion, they are said to be "occidental-weak." And after they have undertaken to enter under the rays of the Sun until they come to his degree, they are said to be "occidental-combust." And all of these [degrees] are considered according to the zodiac and its degrees, and not according to the eccentric or according to the epicycle.

Chapter 6: Of the two inferiors, when they are oriental and when occidental

Indeed Venus and Mercury, when they are being separated from the Sun, and they [are] retrograde, are called "oriental-weak." And after they begin to go direct, until they are near the Sun (so that there are so many degrees between them and the Sun as there had been between the Sun and them when they undertook to go retrograde), they are said to be "oriental-strong." Then, up until the middle of those degrees which remained between the aforesaid place and the rays of the Sun, they are said to be "oriental-weak." And after they begin to enter the rays of the Sun until they are in the same degree with the Sun, they are said to be "oriental-combust." Then, up until they have traveled all the other degrees of combustion, they are called "occidental-combust, going toward appearance." And after they begin to appear from under the rays of the Sun in direct [motion] up until the fifteenth degree after appearing, they are said to be "occidental-strong." Then, up to the middle of the degrees which there are between that place and their first station, they are called "occidental, going toward weakness." Then, up to the beginning of their retrogradation, they are said to be "occidental-weak." Then, up until they come to the rays of the Sun, they are said to be "occidental-retrograde" or "[occidental]-most weak." And after they undertake to enter under the rays until they come to the degree of the Sun, they are said to be "occidental-combust." And every planet, after it has gone out from under the rays of the Sun, until it is joined to another planet (whether by body or by aspect), is said to be in its own light.[154] This is the condition of the planets with the luminaries.

Whence you ought to consider in nativities or questions, and look at, the significator of the native or the querent, to see whether it signifies good or evil. For if it were to signify good, and were in a good place of its epicycle or its eccentric, it will signify the good completion of how much there is of it. And [look to see] if they were oriental-strong superiors, and were ascending to their further longitude or to their *awj*, or were fast in course, and especially if they were northern–because then the matter will come to be better and more perfect and faster, and with less labor. If indeed they were oriental-weak, or going toward weakness, or they were descending in one of the aforesaid circles, they signify the effecting of the matter but with labor and obstacles, and more slowly and with worry, and with some kind of diminution; and this is so in nativities just as in questions. Indeed if they were occidental, they will subtract the good again. And if they were occidental-weak, they will subtract more again from what is signified. And if they were retrograde or combust, they will subtract more again, and they will give what they ought to give with labor and obstacles and worry and distress, and especially if in addition they were southern.

---

[154] This is version (b), a planet in its "*own* light," based on al-Qabīsī III.10. See Introduction.

Chapter 7: On the *dastūrīya* or *haym* of the planets

Al-Qabīsī said[155] that a planet is then said to be in its *dastūrīya*[156] when it is in its *haym*, or in its "likeness": this is when a masculine planet is in a masculine sign, and a feminine one in a feminine one; and a diurnal one in the day above the earth and in the night below the earth; and a nocturnal one in the night above the earth and in the day below the earth; and in the day it is oriental from the Sun, and in the night occidental from the Moon.[157] And like if a planet is in one of the angles of the Ascendant, and one of the luminaries is in one of the angles in a square aspect to that planet. As for example, let the fifth degree of Taurus be ascending, which is then the 1st house: then it is necessary that a planet be in the 4th house, or in the 10th from the Ascendant, so that as it is in the angle of the Ascendant (namely in the fifth degree of the sign facing that domicile, so that three complete signs fall between those domiciles and the Ascendant, and one luminary be in a square aspect to that planet, namely so that 90° fall between them (namely between the planet and the luminary).[158]

And there is said to be *dastūrīya* in another way, and it is interpreted as "dextration"[159] or "security." This is when a planet is oriental of the Sun in the day, and occidental of the Moon in the night. Namely, it is oriental of the Sun when it rises before him; and occidental of the Moon when it sets before her, namely so that there are 60° between the planet and the Sun or Moon. And likewise let the luminary be in its own *haym*, namely the Sun in the day above the earth, and

---

[155] Al-Qabīsī, III.6.

[156] Lat. *dustoria* (Ar. دستورية), a term of art generally explained in Latin texts as meaning "security." The Arabic concept is a distortion of the Greek doctrine of *doruphoria*, i.e., with being a "spear-bearer" or "bodyguard" (thus offering "security" to the planet receiving it. Al-Qabīsī says a planet's *dastūrīya* is when (a) it is in its *hayyiz* ("domain") and (b) angular, and the luminary whose authority it is, is both (c) in its own *hayyiz* and (d) in a square aspect to that planet. For example, suppose that Jupiter, in a day chart, were above the earth, in the 10th, in a masculine sign–he would be in *hayyiz* (likewise if he were below the earth in a masculine sign in a nocturnal chart). Now, he would be in his *dastūrīya* if the Sun were, say, in the 7th, in a masculine sign. See Introduction.

[157] In what sense does he mean "oriental" and "occidental"? Note below that Bonatti uses the terms again and defines them for his example; but since it is "another way" *dastūrīya* can take place, it is unclear whether the definition in the other way is meant to apply to the current one.

[158] But note that the earlier definition required *dastūrīya* to be with a luminary also in its own *hayyiz*. Moreover, older definitions did not usually require exact 30° divisions.

[159] *Dextratio*, lit. "being on the right side." I note that in English we speak of one's "right-hand man" as someone who provides support and security.

in the night below the earth,¹⁶⁰ and the Moon by necessity has it thus in the night above the earth, and in the day above the earth.

And therefore the wise said that it is when a planet is safe from the rays of the luminaries: because after a planet enters under the rays of the Sun, so that it is covered by them, it is said to be burned up [combust] until it goes out from under its rays and appears. And when it begins to enter under the rays, it is said to be beginning to be burned, or to have fallen into a burning fire, while it is under the rays near the Sun by 12°, going toward him (if it were the inferiors), or separated, going away from him by 2° or less; or, if it were of the superiors and the Sun were to go toward it, and it were near him by 12°, or he were to leave it behind him by 2° or less, it is said to be oppressed. And when it is with the Sun in one degree, so that there are 16' or less between them, both by latitude and longitude (which rarely happens), it is said to be united, and then it is made strong, because it is said to be in Sun's forge, that is, in his heart. And many of those dealing with the stars, and particularly in my time, agreed in this, that when a planet is distant from the Sun by 16' or less, it is made strong, and is said to be in the heart of the Sun. Indeed I am in agreement with them, but not purely and simply. Because for a planet to be in the forge or in the heart of the Sun, it is necessary that it be distant from the Sun by less than 16' according to longitude and latitude—and this was the intention of the philosophers. Because if a planet is distant from the Sun by less than 16' in longitude, and according to latitude it is distant by more than 16', nevertheless it is combust, because the distinction between combustion in latitude and combustion in longitude is practically imperceptible.¹⁶¹

And al-Qabīsī said that when a planet has transited that same union, namely that the three superiors remain after the Sun by 5°, and the three inferiors are elongated from him by 5°, [the planet] is said to have escaped (whether they are direct or retrograde).¹⁶² And the philosophers spoke on this with greater caution, and for more established certainty, lest they could be deceived in something. I however believe a planet to have escaped after it is separated from the Sun by 2° or more, whether it were in front of or in back of him.¹⁶³ And a

---

¹⁶⁰ By definition the Sun is always in its *haym*, since his being above or below the earth defines night and day.

¹⁶¹ The fact that it is imperceptible is not a valid reason for latitude to be included; rather, it is a reason not to be hasty in attributing *kasmimi* (usually spelled "cazimi") to a planet.

¹⁶² In other words, when the superiors are in an earlier degree than the Sun's (after he has passed them), and the inferiors are in a later degree (by secondary motion), having already passed the Sun.

¹⁶³ This is an important statement about Bonatti's own practice.

planet is said to have "escaped" by similarity with a sick person whom fever has let go, nor however has he yet gotten better so that he could be said to be freed; nor is he fully freed. However, he is out of danger while he gets better, after which he is said to be freed. And so it is with a planet when it enters combustion: it is like one who begins to grow ill. And when it is in extreme combustion, it is like a sick person when he is in a state of paroxysm, which comes to be when a fever is going to come upon [him], and it is already in the process of happening. And when it is separated from the Sun up to 2°, it is like a sick person whom a crisis has come over, nor is yet completed (like sweat, sleep, flux, and similar things making a crisis). And when it is from those 2° up to another 3° (namely the remainder to 5°), it is like a sick person whom a crisis has come over, and it is already completed. And when it is from those 5° of elongation from the Sun, until it goes out from under the rays, it is like a sick person whose sickness ceases and is visibly diminishing; and [when] it is wholly freed from combustion, [it is] like a sick person completely freed from sickness, but [who] has not yet resumed his previous powers, however is safe from the illness.

Chapter 8: On the three superiors, after they have appeared from under the rays of the Sun

And after Saturn, Jupiter and Mars have appeared from under the rays of the Sun, and are wholly outside of combustion, so that they appear in the morning in the east before the Sun, they are called "oriental-right" until they come to the opposition of the Sun. And their strength is increased up until they are elongated from the body of the Sun by 30°. And from thence up to another 30°, so that their longitude from the body of the Sun is 60°, they are "oriental-strong." And from those 60° they are "oriental, going toward weakness" until they come to their first station and begin to go retrograde. From that first station until the Sun is opposed to them in a straight line, degree by degree, they are "oriental-retrograde." But after the Sun has transited past them by opposition, they are "occidental-retrograde" until they come to their second station and begin to go direct. And from thence until the Sun approaches them by 30°, they are said to be "occidental-strong." From that point until the Sun approaches them by 15°, they are called "occidental, going toward weakness." After that they are "occidental-weak" until they enter under the rays of the Sun. From that point they are "occidental-combust" until they are then united with the Sun in the same degree. And when they are in the opposition of the Sun, they are called "opposite." And when they have transited the opposition they are called "occidental-left." And it is a certain impediment for them, not a middling one, because they begin to fear coming again to combustion: just like a man who, when someone is following him, begins to get tired in his flight, and sees the one who is following him catching up to him, and sees that he is faster than himself, and is approaching him: for he fears that he cannot escape his grasp.

On Venus and Mercury when they are being separated from the Sun

Indeed Venus and Mercury, after they are being separated from the Sun, and are retrograde, are oriental until they come to their second[164] station, and begin to go direct. From their direct [motion] until they are elongated by as much as they were distant from him when they undertook to go retrograde, they are "oriental-strong." Then until they approach the Sun by 20° they are "oriental-weak" until they enter under the Sun's rays. After they are under the rays, they are "oriental-combust," until they are united with the Sun.

And Al-Qabīsī said,[165] then they are "combust, going toward appearance," wherever they are seen. And after they are being separated by the Sun in direct [motion], they are called "occidental strong" until they come to their retrogradation. And after they undertake to go retrograde, until they are united with the Sun again, they are called "occidental-weak." And he said when a planet goes out from under the rays of the Sun, and is joined to no planet, it is said that it is in its own light.[166] This is the condition of the planets with the luminaries.

Chapter 9: On the conjunction of the planets according to latitude

Mention was made in the preceding concerning the conjunction of the planets, and that mention was of their conjunction according to longitude, by considering the conjunction from the east toward the west or *vice versa*.[167] Now however it remains to speak about their conjunction according to latitude. And this is what comes to be between them from the south to the north or *vice versa*, or on either side.

---

[164] Reading *secundam* for *primam*.
[165] Al-Qabīsī, III.10.
[166] Again, this is version (b), a planet in its *"own* light." See above.
[167] In Ch. 4.

But it is a conjunction in latitude when one of the planets is conjoined to another according to its latitude, namely like when one planet is joining to the other by its body, and they would both be in one degree, it will be their conjunction by latitude and equal, whether the conjunction or application were northern or southern, because the latitude of both of them will be to one and the same area. And if their conjunction were by opposition, their latitudes will be equal, namely when the latitude of one is ascending in the north, and the other's is ascending in the south.

And even though this statement may seem hard to understand, still in itself it is easy: because when a planet goes toward a farther longitude, then it is ascending in the north. And it is necessary that in order for one to be joined to the other by opposition, that one be in one quarter of its epicycle, and the other be in its own epicycle, in the quarter opposite it. All the other conjunctions which come to be by another means than by this, are conjunctions in longitude and not latitude. And this way is like when one northern planet is ascending in the north, and the other southern one is descending in the south. This is the conjunction in latitude. But those wise in this art, and particularly those who use an almanac, do not bother very much about this conjunction in latitude in their judgments; which does not seem appropriate to me, especially in great matters (as are nativities, universal questions, revolutions of the year, and the like).

Chapter 10: On the voiding of the course of the planets

After one planet is joined to another, and their conjunction is perfected, and after the perfection is carried through, so that one of them is separated from the other, and after the separation it is joined to no other planet, it is said to be "void in course," because it then runs alone. And this being void in course will last until it is joined to another or it seeks [the other's] conjunction, just as was said elsewhere; and this is a certain impediment to it.

And al-Qabīsī said[168] that so long as any planet is alone in any sign, and another planet did not aspect that sign, it is said that it is feral or wild; and likewise this is a great impediment to it, and a very horrible thing.

---

[168] Al-Qabīsī, III.13.

Chapter 11: On the transfer of nature of the planets

It was the opinion of certain philosophers that one planet transfers the nature of one to another unconditionally. For they said that when a light planet is being separated from a heavier one, and is joined to another (whether it is heavier or lighter than it), that it transfers the nature of the first to the second.[169] Which seems to me obscure in a certain way, I freely confess. For it does not seem accurate that even though one planet is joined to another (unless it is joined to it from one of its dignities) that it would give it its own virtue, or commit its own nature or disposition to it, according to what the philosopher says. A planet does not give something in a place in which it promises nothing. Whence if a planet does not give its nature or virtue to it, it does not seem that it can carry the nature of one to another. And even if it gave or committed it to it, by the same reasoning it does not seem that it would give it to another unless it were joined to that same one from one of its own dignities. And I believe that this was their intention, even if they did not express it.

But if a light planet were joined to a heavier planet from some dignity of the heavier one, the heavier one would commit its nature and disposition to it, [and] it could carry it with itself until it were joined to another planet whom it finds in one of its own dignities,[170] and commit to it what it had accepted–unless perhaps the virtue were to lie hidden[171] from the conjunction of another, even if it did not commit it to it. For it does not seem accurate that one would give to an unknown person in a strange land what it had acquired for itself. However, because they were wiser than me, their statements ought to be upheld, whatever their intention was.

And they said a planet carries the nature of a planet to another, with such an example:

---

[169] This is Abū Ma'shar's first version of transfer (*an-naql*, النَّقْل), in *Abbr.* III.23.
[170] I believe this means the third planet would have to be in one of its own dignities, or in one of the dignities of the transferring planet's (or perhaps in a dignity of the original planet). In the example below, Venus commits disposition to the Moon because the Moon is in Venus's domicile; but the Moon commits what she receives from Venus to Mars, since Mars is in the Moon's exaltation. In other words, there must be reception to transfer nature or virtue.
[171] I do not know what Bonatti means by this.

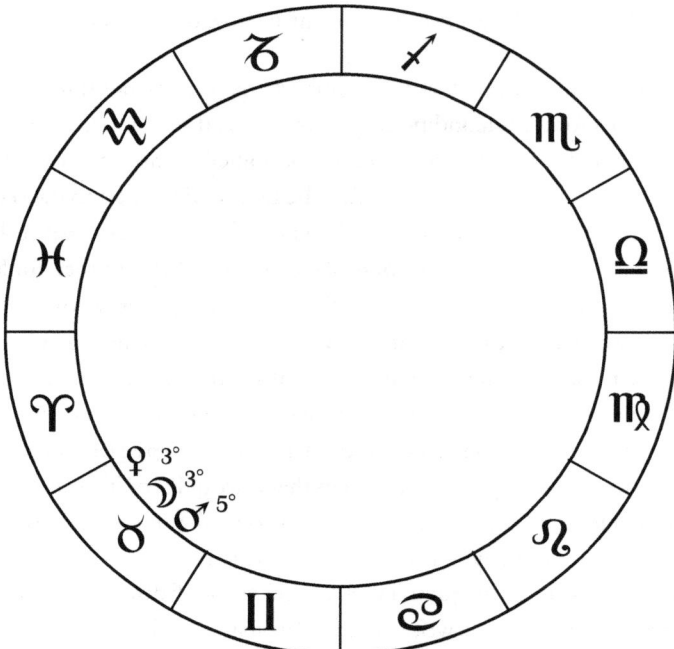

Figure 8: Transfer of Nature (a)

The Moon was joined to Venus in one sign, and in one degree (let her be put in the fourth degree of Taurus); and when she was separated from Venus (or Mercury, who is lighter than her), she was joined to Mars (in the sixth degree of Taurus, or in whatever other degree he was), who is heavier than Venus. Thus the Moon transfers the nature of Venus to Mars, or to another, whichever one she first encountered, or to whom she is first joined. For Venus committed her own disposition and nature to the Moon, and [the Moon] commited to him whom she first encountered, and to whom she was first joined, what she had been committed by Venus.

And they said that there is another method of the transferring of the nature of one planet to another, namely that a lighter planet is joined to a heavier one, and the heavier one is joined to another heavier than he: thus the heavy one who is in the middle between the light one and the heavier one, transfers the nature of the light one to the heavier one.[172] For example, Mercury was joined to Venus in the tenth degree of Pisces, or in any other [degree], and after the

---

[172] This is Abū Ma'shar's second version of transfer or *an-naql* (*Abbr.* III.23).

separation from Venus he was joined to the Sun in the twelfth degree of Pisces (or in any other [degree]), and the Sun again is joined to Mars in the fourteenth degree of the same Pisces (or in another other [degree]), provided that the degrees are correlated to each other: thus Mercury transfers the nature of Venus to the Sun, and the Sun transfers it to Mars.[173]

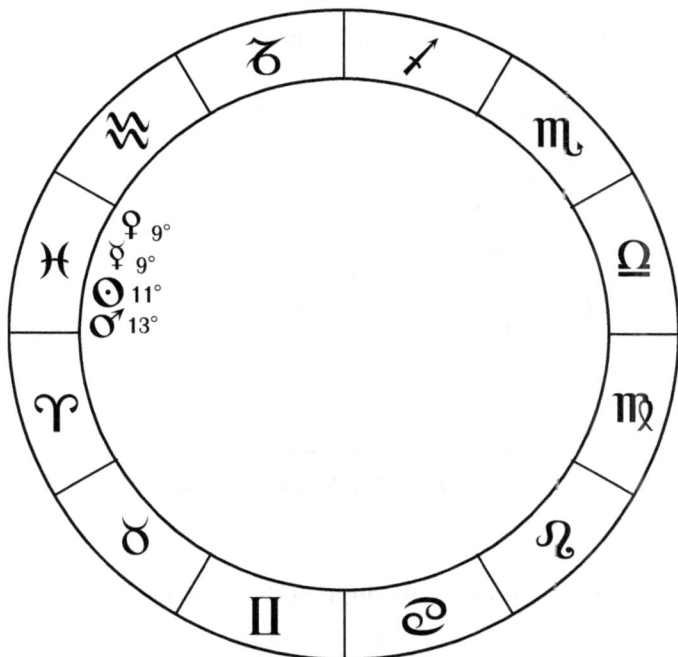

Figure 9: Transfer of Nature (b)

But if neither of those two heavier ones by itself is joined to another planet, but they both are joined at one and the same time to one planet, then that third planet is said to render[174] their light to the place of the circle which it aspects.[175] And this is called the "rendering of light," with such an example: Mercury was separated from Venus from the tenth degree of Pisces (or from any other [degree]), and after the separation from Venus, he was joined to the Sun and

---

[173] In this case, neither Mercury nor Mars nor the Sun are in one of their dignities, but by their being in the exaltation of Venus, the transfer has the effect of a reception (and commiting of disposition).
[174] *Redditio.* "Returning" is misleading, but "rendering" (another translation for *redditio*) at least is closer to Abū Ma'shar's "reflecting." See following footnote.
[175] This is Abū Ma'shar's "reflecting the light," or *ar-radd al-nūr* (Ar. الرد النور).

Mars in the twelfth degree of Pisces (or in any other [degree]), and they were joined again to Jupiter in the thirteenth degree of Pisces (or in any other [degree]). But Jupiter is joined to no other planet: thus Jupiter transfers the light of Venus to that place in the circle which he aspects, namely to the thirteenth degree of Taurus in front of him (by a sextile aspect); and to the thirteenth degree of Gemini (by a square aspect); and to the thirteenth degree of Cancer (by a trine aspect); and to the thirteenth degree of Capricorn behind him (by a sextile aspect), and to the thirteenth degree of Sagittarius (by a square aspect), and to the thirteenth degree of Scorpio (by a trine aspect).[176]

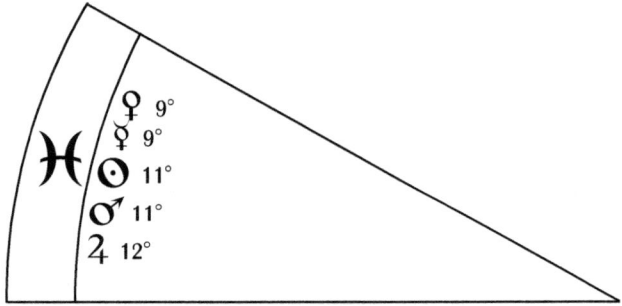

Figure 10: Rendering of Light

Chapter 12: On the return of the light of the planets, and its cutting-off

Having spoken of the transfer of the nature of the planets, it remains to speak of the return of their light and its cutting-off.[177] And this is when one planet seeks the conjunction of the other, but they are not joined together thus far, and another planet besides them is joined beforehand to the one whose conjunction the first [planet] was seeking, and that third one returns the light of the first[178] to the first: it is called the "return of light," and it is called its "cutting-off."

---

[176] But not to the thirteenth degree of Cancer by a trine, or to Virgo by an opposition? Perhaps Bonatti accidentally omitted these.

[177] This entire example seems to be Abū Ma'shar's second version of "cutting the light" or *al-qaT' al-nūr* (Ar. القطع النور) in *Abbrev.* III.46.

[178] Reading *primi* for *tertii* ("of the third").

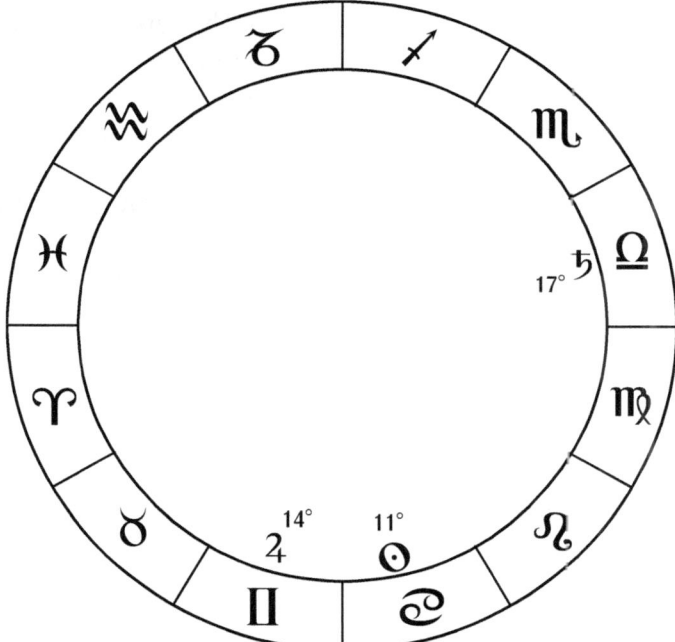

Figure 11: Return and Cutting-Off of Light

For example, let it be put that the Sun is in the twelfth degree of Cancer, and Saturn is in the eighteenth degree of Libra, and Jupiter in the fifteenth degree of Gemini: thus it is the Sun seeking the conjunction of Saturn by a square aspect. But Jupiter, who is closer to the conjunction of Saturn than the Sun, is [already] joined to him by a trine aspect, and cuts off the light of the Sun from Saturn: and this is called the "cutting-off of light."

And likewise it is called a return of light:[179] because Saturn returns the light to the Sun which he had undertook to receive from him, and [Saturn] receives [instead] the light of Jupiter, who is more close: because [Jupiter] is in the fifteenth degree of the sign in which he is, and the Sun is only in the twelfth degree of the sign in which he is, and thus the matter about which the question came about (or hope was had), can be destroyed. And this comes to be by a method which some merchants use, or anyone else, who are wont to sell and buy things: for one seeks someone else in order to buy[180] some thing for

---

[179] "Returning" the light is not supported by the definition of *ar-radd* in Abū Ma'shar's text (or Sahl's), but it could be Bonatti's way of describing what results from the cutting.
[180] Reading *emat* for *vendat*.

himself, and he who seeks the thing hopes he will have it for himself, through the means by which he seeks it; nor does he believe that someone else would interpose himself in it; and then another [person] comes from the side, and gives something more to the seller than the first one had promised him, and he accepts the thing: [thus] he frustrates the matter, or makes someone else interpose himself so that he frustrates it from the first person, and he acquires the thing for himself.[181]

And this is a matter very much to be considered in questions, because often matters are frustrated even after they seem to be arranged. And you ought to know that the return of light is considered[182] according to aspect. Indeed the transferring of light or virtue is considered according to corporal conjunction and according to aspect, but more often according to corporal conjunction.

Chapter 13: On the prohibition of conjunction and why sometimes matters are not perfected

The prohibition of conjunction, and that matters sometimes are not perfected, comes to be in two ways. Of which one is when three planets are in one sign, in different degrees, and the more heavy one is in more degrees than the others, and one of the other two seeks the conjunction of the heavier one. And between him and the one whose conjunction he seeks, there is another in the middle. He who is in the middle will prohibit the one who is in fewer degrees so that he is not joined to the [the heavier one] who is in more degrees than them both. Nor is he joined to him until the middle one transits the conjunction of the heavier one, and leaves him behind him.[183]

---

[181] The point here is simply to say that Saturn returns an offer of light made to him by the Sun. Bonatti's mercantile logic suggests that the Sun is *paying* for something Saturn promises, i.e., the perfection of the matter which the Sun (representing the querent) seeks.

[182] Reading *consideratur* for *considerantur*.

[183] This is Abū Ma'shar's first version of "prohibition" or *al-man'* (لمَنْع) in *Abbr.* III.28. In both of the examples below, Bonatti is implying that the corporal conjunction does not need to be in the same degree–the orbs of the two planets must only be touching, which seems to be sufficient.

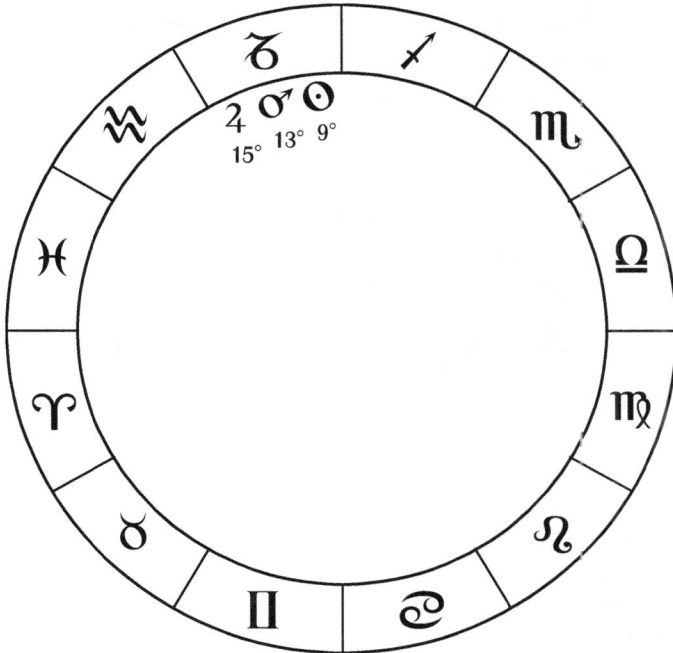

Figure 12: Prohibition of Conjunction (a)

For example, the Sun was in the tenth degree of Capricorn, and Mars was in the fourteenth degree of Capricorn, and Jupiter was in the sixteenth degree of the same sign. Now the Sun was seeking to be joined with Jupiter, but Mars (who was between them, namely closer to Jupiter than the Sun was), prohibited the Sun from being joined to Jupiter, and Mars himself was joined to him. And so Mars did not cease prohibiting the conjunction of the Sun with Jupiter until [Mars] had transited [Jupiter], and left him behind him—and then the Sun was joined to Jupiter after Mars had transited him. Whence if the matter about which it had been sought were not wholly destroyed, it could have been perfected then when they (namely the Sun and Jupiter) were conjoined.[184]

The second way is when two planets are in one sign, and the lighter is joined to the heavier by body, and another is also joined to the heavy one by aspect,

---

[184] This example is somewhat ambiguous. What does Bonatti mean by the matter perfecting "when" the Sun and Jupiter are conjoined? Suppose the querent and the quaesited were represented by the Sun and Jupiter, and the querent asked, "Will action X be successful?" Is Bonatti saying, "No, it will not be perfected for four days until the Sun and Jupiter are conjoined?" Because if the question were about a matter in the distant future, such a response would not make sense.

from a similar degree from which the one who is with him (namely with the heavy one) in the same sign, is joined to him: thus he who is joined to him in the same sign, annuls the conjunction of the one aspecting, and prohibits him from it (namely from the conjunction of the heavy one): because a corporal conjunction is stronger than an aspectual one.[185]

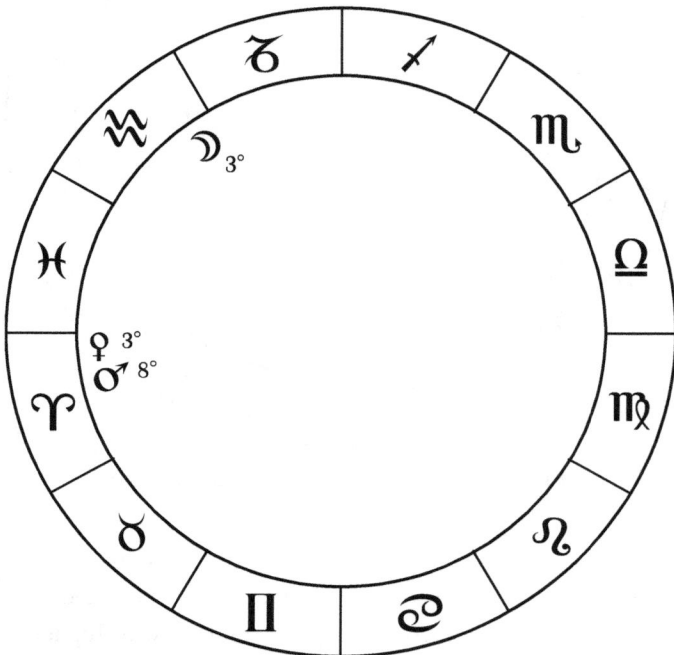

Figure 13: Prohibition of Conjunction (b)

For example, Venus was in the fourth degree of Aries, and Mars in the ninth degree of Aries, and the Moon in the fourth degree of Aquarius, wanting to join herself to Mars by aspect. And she would be joined with him unless something else were to impede. But Venus, who was joined to Mars corporally, was prohibiting the conjunction of the Moon to Mars for the aforesaid reason, namely that the corporal conjunction destroys an aspect. Indeed an aspect does not annul a corporal conjunction. It would be different if the one aspecting were in more degrees in its sign than he who is joined by body: because then it would be a conjunction of the aspecting one, and not the one conjoined by

---

[185] This is Abū Ma'shar's second version of prohibition or *al-man'*.

body, by this example: Venus was (as I said) in the fourth degree of Aries, and Mars in the ninth degree of Aries, and the Moon in the sixth degree of Aquarius. Thus the Moon is joined to Mars, and annuls the conjunction of Venus to Mars, because she aspects him from a nearer degree than Venus was joined to him.

[Reception and Commission of Disposition]

And it is said that if some planet is joined with the Lord of the sign in which it is (or with the Lord of the exaltation of the same sign, or with the Lord of the bound or triplicity, or face), whether by body or by aspect, that the planet who is the Lord of the sign (or some dignity of it), commits and gives its own disposition and nature and virtue to it.

It is for instance true, if it is joined with the Lord of the domicile or exaltation or with the Lord of two of the other lesser dignities (namely with the Lord of the bound and triplicity, or with the Lord of the bound and the face, or with the Lord of the face and the triplicity). But if it is joined only with the Lord of the bound, or with the Lord of the triplicity, or with the Lord of the face, [then] the Lord of one of those dignities of bounds[186]–by only one–does not receive him, because they are not of so much virtue that one of them alone can make reception without the help of another. Whence a planet who receives another from these dignities, as I said, commits its own disposition to it, even if they were enemies, from whatever aspect or by conjunction.

---

[186] *Illarum dignitatum terminorum.* Perhaps "of bounds" is a misprint.

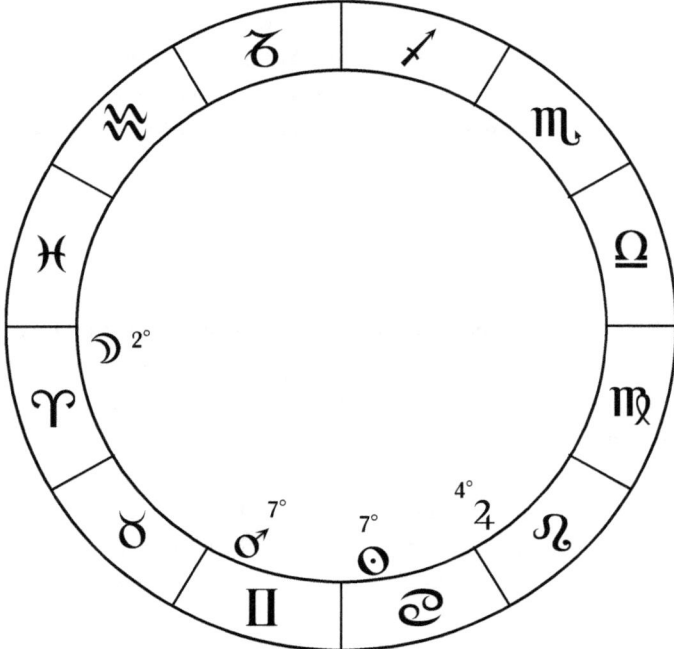

Figure 14: Reception and Commission of Disposition (a)

For example, the Moon was in the third degree of Aries, and Mars (who is the Lord of Aries) was in the eighth degree of Gemini (or Cancer or Leo in front of her; or Aquarius, or Capricorn, or Sagittarius behind her): so the Moon was being received by Mars by aspect, and he was receiving her from his own domicile, and committed to her his own virtue and disposition.

Or the Moon was in the said third degree of Aries, and the Sun (who is the Lord of the exaltation of Aries) was in the eighth or ninth degree of Gemini (or Cancer or Leo in front of her), or in the eighth or ninth degree of Aquarius (or Capricorn or Sagittarius behind her): so the Moon was being joined to the Sun by aspect, and he was receiving her from his own exaltation, and was committing his own strength to her.

Or the Moon was in the said third degree of Aries, and Jupiter (who is the Lord of the first bound of Aries, and is even the Lord of the triplicity of Aries), was in the fifth degree of Gemini[187] (or Cancer or Leo in front of her), or in the fifth degree of Aquarius (or Capricorn or Sagittarius behind her): so the Moon

---

[187] This suggests that Bonatti does allow the receiving planet to be in its own detriment– perhaps it is able to receive, even if the reception is not ultimately helpful (see Tr. 6).

was being joined to Jupiter by aspect, and he was receiving her from his own bound and triplicity, and committed his own virtue and disposition to her, just as if he received her by domicile or exaltation. This is the commission or giving of virtue and disposition of the planets.

But if the Moon had been joined to Saturn (who is the Lord of the triplicity of Aries, nor does he have any dignity there), he would not have received her: because he does not have but one of the lesser dignities there, from which perfect reception cannot come to be.

However, al-Qabīsī seemed to want to say[188] that a planet who is in the domicile or exaltation or in *any* dignity of some planet,[189] if it is joined with it, that he whose dignity it is, gives and commits his own nature to him—whose opinion I do not diminish, nor do I say it is to be thrown away, since he was an introducer [of these things]; whence it is better to uphold it than if another had said it, and since he most often was of value in an introduction.

And he said that when a planet is in one of its *own* dignities, and is conjoined to some planet by body, it will give it its own strength, and this is likewise explained by the aforesaid rationale.[190]

---

[188] This is al-Qabīsī's account of Abū Ma'shar's "pushing nature" or *daf' al-Tabii'a* (Ar. دفع الطبيعة) in al-Qabīsī (III.17).

[189] Emphasis mine. Bonatti's more stringent requirements (i.e., that if lesser dignities are involved there must be two of them) comes from Sahl (*Introduct.* §5.7).

[190] This is Abū Ma'shar's "pushing power" or *daf' al-quwwah* (Ar. دفع القوة) described in al-Qabīsī (III.18).

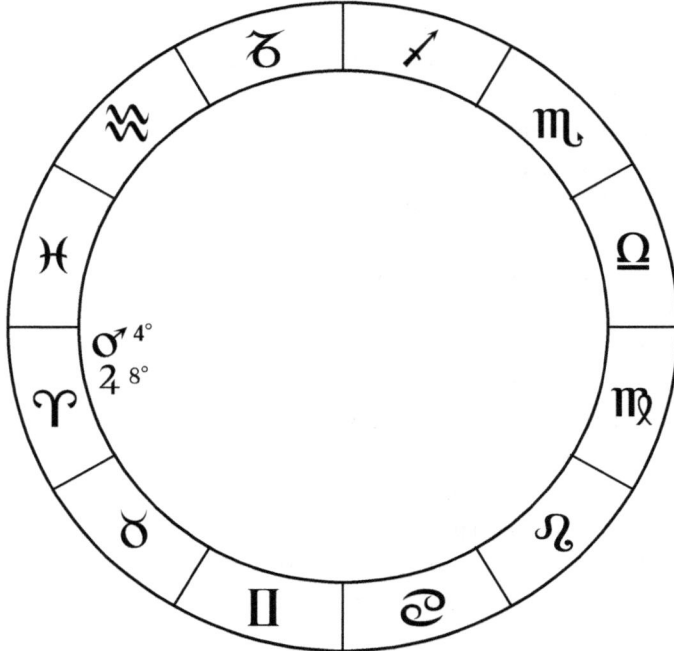

Figure 15: Reception and Commission of Disposition (b)

And if a planet were in such a dignity of its own that another planet had a dignity there, and were joined to him in it, he will give him his own strength, so that he to whom he is joined, has the strength or nature of both.[191] For example, Jupiter was in the ninth degree of Aries, and Mars was in the fifth degree of Aries: thus Mars is joined to Jupiter, and receives him from his own domicile, whence he commits his own strength or disposition and nature to him; and Jupiter has the dignity of triplicity there; whence he therefore has the dignity of both, namely the one he has there by triplicity, and the one which Mars gives him by domicile. And the mixture which Mars makes is said to be reception, which the philosophers called *al-qubūl*.[192]

---

[191] This seems to be Abū Ma'shar's first version of "pushing two natures," or *daf' al-Tabii'ain* (Ar. دفع الطبيعتين), in *Abbr.* III.32; see also al-Qabīsī III.19.
[192] See Tr. 5 (4th Consideration). This sentence is based on al-Qabīsī (III.19), who sums up the various forms of "pushing" derived from Abū Ma'shar, saying "All this pushing is called 'reception'."

Chapter 14: On the return of virtue, when a planet returns it to him who gave it to him

When some planet is joined to another, and gives or commits its own virtue or disposition to it, and he who whom the virtue or disposition is given, is retrograde or combust, he cannot retain the virtue—whence he returns it to him to gave it to him.[193] Because he cannot retain it on account of the weakness which he has from that retrogradation or combustion. Then, if they were both in angles, or in succeedents to the angles, the return will be good and useful, and with advantage. And even if he who is conjoined to the other were in an angle, and he to whom he is joined were to receive him, or were in an angle, or in a succeedent to an angle, the return will be with advantage and usefulness.

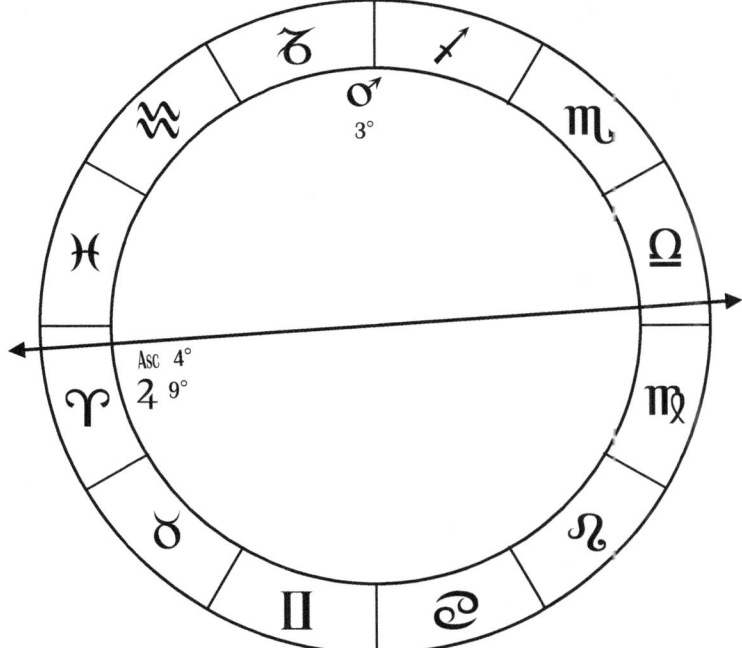

Figure 16: Return of Virtue (a)

---

[193] This definition, and the examples which follow, derive from Abū Ma'shar's "returning" or *ar-radd* (Ar.الرد), also described briefly in al-Qabīsī III.20. It is *not* the same as "returning/rendering the light" in Ch. 12.

For example, Jupiter was in Aries (let him be put in the tenth degree), but he was retrograde or combust, and he was in an angle. Let it be put that the fifth [degree] of Aries was ascending, and Mars was in the fourth degree of Capricorn, in the angle of the 10th house (or in Aquarius in the fourth degree, in the succeedent to the angle). Mars was joined to Jupiter by aspect, and was receiving him from his own domicile, and committed his own disposition and virtue to him. But Jupiter, because he was retrograde, could not retain the virtue, whence he returned it to him. And such a return was good and useful with advantage, because Mars was in an angle or a succeedent to the angle, so that he could well retain the virtue returned to him by Jupiter, and afterwards all of the virtue remained to Mars, so that the matter about the question was, proceeded well from his virtue and from his power.[194]

If indeed the planet who is joined (namely the light one), or he to whom the virtue is returned, were cadent from an angle, wherever the heavy one or he who returned the virtue was (whether in an angle or in a succeedent or a cadent), the return will be useless, and bad and with detriment.

---

[194] The suggestion seems to be that if Jupiter had been able to retain the virtue (and the reception were perfect), that Mars would *not* have perfected the matter, since he had given his disposition over to Jupiter.

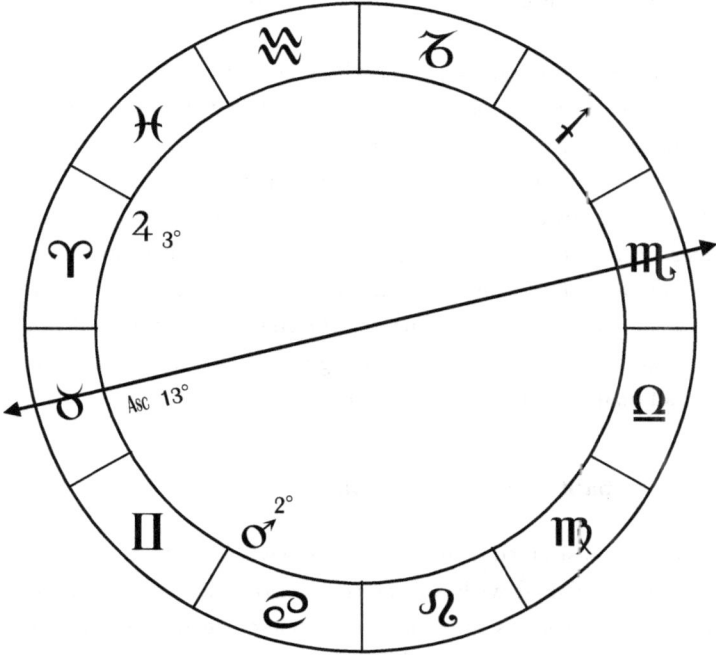

Figure 17: Return of Virtue (b)

For example, the Ascendant was the fourteenth degree of Taurus, and Jupiter was in the fourth degree of Aries, cadent from the angle, and Mars was in the third degree of Cancer, likewise cadent. And Mars received Jupiter, and committed his disposition to him; but Jupiter, because he was cadent from the angle, could not retain the virtue committed to him by Mars—whence he returned it to him. But Mars, because he was likewise cadent from an angle, nor could he retain the virtue returned to him by Jupiter (on account of the weakness of his falling from an angle), it was more harmful to him than useful—by way of the example of a certain man who had a bundle of sticks in his arms, which he could not carry: he gave it to another, and he returned it to him, not strong enough to carry it. What was returned was not useful to him, but harmful. And thus, if a question was made about some matter, the purpose about which the question was, was destroyed and was annulled on account of the weakness of Jupiter, who could not retain the virtue committed to him by Mars. However, with Mars weak, he could not retain what was returned by him

[Jupiter], nor could he lead the matter to its effecting, and the weakness of both did it.

I however have found some people who seemed to me different from others, and were of a certain opinion that they did not believe that the return of virtue or disposition was anything, such a one being the tyrant Ezzelino da Romano;[195] and there was a certain astrologer of his named Salio, whom I believe agreed with him more from fear than because he believed it to be so. And I believe it moreover, because Ezzelino had a certain brother of his in leg irons, concerning whom [Salio] feared [Ezzelino] would kill him. And he said that the Moon, and any light planet, would accept the nature of him to whom it was joined, and any heavy one would give his own virtue to a light one, whether it received it or not. And he had many other erroneous opinions.[196]

Chapter 15: On the restraining[197] of the planets

One planet is restrained from a conjunction with another in this way: namely when one of the planets wishes to be conjoined with another planet or to be applied to it, and believes the conjunction will perfect, and in the meantime before the conjunction is perfected, retrogradation happens to him, and so the conjunction which he sought (and which the planet believed it would perfect) is not perfected,–just like someone holding the reins restrains a horse wishing to run, and does not permit him to run where the horse intended. Whence a planet is said to be restrained from a conjunction with the other planet.

---

[195] See Introduction.

[196] One wonders whether Ezzelino was an amateur astrologer, and refused to believe bad news from his own professional astrologer–much as dictators (and their lackeys) twist reality so as to always present the prospect of success.

[197] *Refranatione.* From the time of Lilly this has been called "refranation," which is only a transliteration of the Latin. This derives from Abū Ma'shar's "restraint" or *al-intikāth* (الإنتكاث) in *Abbr.* III.43; also described in al-Qabīsī III.21. Burnett *et al.* follow tradition in translating this as "refranation."

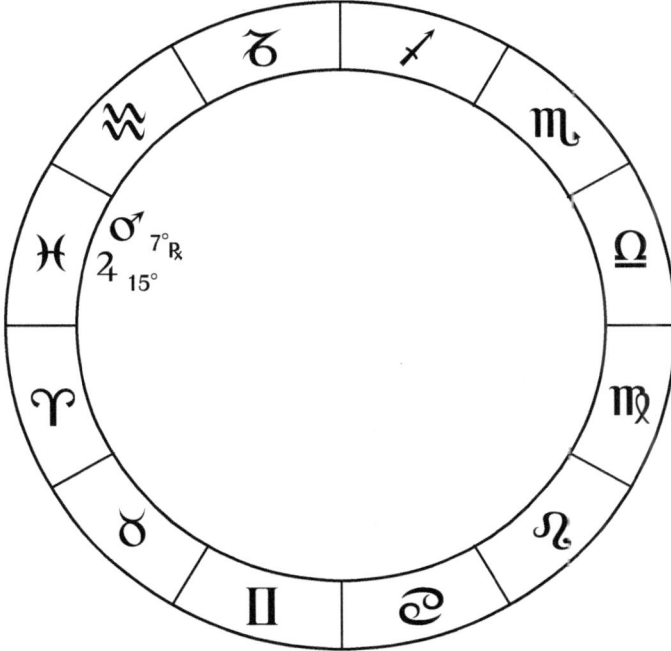

Figure 18: Restraining

For example, Jupiter was in the sixteenth degree of Pisces, and Mars was in the seventh degree of the same sign, wishing to be joined to Jupiter. But when Mars reached the fourteenth degree of Pisces, the retrogradation came about. Whence the retrogradation restrained him from Jupiter, so that he could not perfect the conjunction: and all of his signification was annulled, so that if a querent thought to perfect a matter, he would be in the hope of perfecting it until Mars went direct; but he would fear, and would always have a remorse of conscience, that the matter would not be perfected. However, hope would be greater that the matter would be perfected than the suspicion of it not being perfected. And so he would not cease in his hope of perfecting it while retrogradation was happening to Mars. For then he would despair that the matter he was thinking about would not be perfected. And this is called restraint proper, which al-Qabīsī called *al-intikāth*.[198]

---

[198] Lat. *alicichae*.

Chapter 16: On the contrariety of the planets

Sometimes contrariety[199] happens to the planets, and it comes to be in this way: namely when some light planet is in some sign in many degrees, and another heavier one is in fewer degrees than the lighter one; and a third planet who is lighter than the first, is in less degrees again than the heavy one, going toward the heavy one, wishing to be joined to him. But before he is joined to him, the other who was in more degrees than the rest is made retrograde, and in that retrogradation he is joined to the heavier one before the light one who sought his conjunction is joined to him. And after leaving the heavier one behind, by retrograding it is joined to the other light planet. Then he destroys the conjunction of the light, direct one who sought the conjunction of the heavier one, and destroys the matter that was signified by that conjunction, even if it were completed.[200]

---

[199] This derives from Abū Ma'shar's "resistance" or *al-i'tirād* (الإعتراض) in *Abbr.* III.44, also described in al-Qabīsī (III.22).
[200] I believe Bonatti means "even if *the conjunction* were completed [later]" (*destruit rem quae significabatur per illam coniunctionem, etiam si foret completa*), not "even if *the matter* were completed [later]."

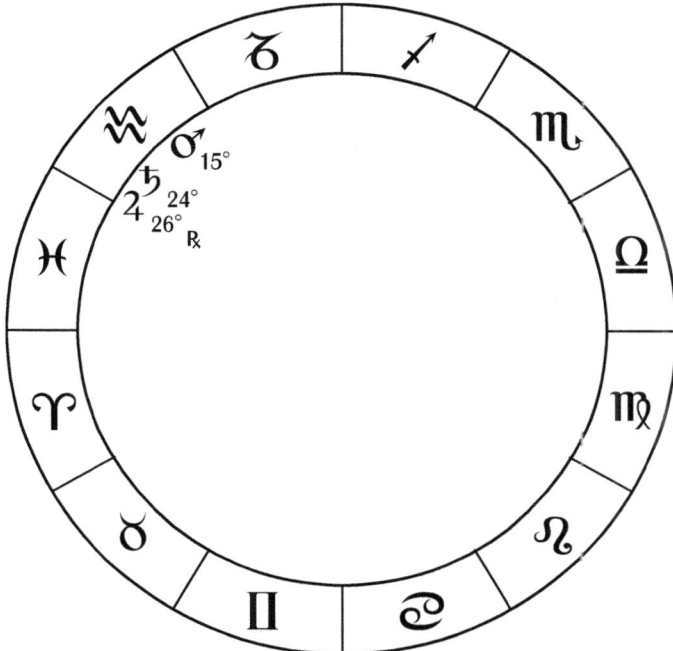

Figure 19: Contrariety

For example, Jupiter was in Aquarius by 26°, and Saturn in Aquarius by 24°, and Mars in the same sign by 15°, seeking the conjunction of Saturn, wishing to be joined to him; in the meantime Jupiter was made retrograde, and was joined to Saturn by his retrogradation, and transited him in that retrogradation, and left him behind himself, and by retrogradation was joined again to Mars, and did not permit Mars to be joined with Saturn. And this is called "contrariety," because what happened was the contrary of what ought to have happened: for Jupiter ought to have gone his own way and not to have been joined to him [Saturn], since he is less heavy than Saturn and had transited him; on the contrary, Mars, who pursued [Saturn], ought to have been joined to Saturn. For he was less heavy than him, and less heavy than Jupiter. Whence if a question had been made about some matter which it ought to have been signified that it would come to be or be perfected by the conjunction of Mars and Saturn, the matter would be destroyed on account of the retrogradation of Jupiter, who [was] joined to Saturn by retrograding before the conjunction of Mars with Saturn was completed, even after the querent had thought it to be in order, and ought to have been perfected. And al-Qabīsī called such contrariety *al-i'tirād*.[201]

Chapter 17: On the frustration[202] of the conjunction of the planets

Indeed the frustration of the conjunction of one planet by another comes to be in this way, namely when one planet wishes to be conjoined to another heavier than he, and seeks its conjunction in any sign, but he cannot be joined to it in it, but rather the heavier one is changed into the next sign, and a certain other planet aspects that sign,[203] so that he to whom the other wanted to be joined to first, encounters the rays of the one aspecting so that it is joined to him by aspect, before he who wanted to be joined to him first can be joined to the heavier one. Since the rays of the one who was aspecting were in the beginning of the sign, it was necessary that he whose conjunction the other sought, was first joined with the aspecting one, than that he be joined to the one who wanted to be joined with him by body. And thus the conjunction is destroyed and frustrated. And so you may understand more easily, I will give you an example of this situation, because the text is very difficult.

---

[201] Lat. *halintirad*.
[202] This derives from Abū Ma'shar's "evasion" or *fawt* (Ar. الفوت) in *Abbr.* III.45, also described in al-Qabīsī (III.23).
[203] This is another indication that Bonatti does not use out-of-sign aspects.

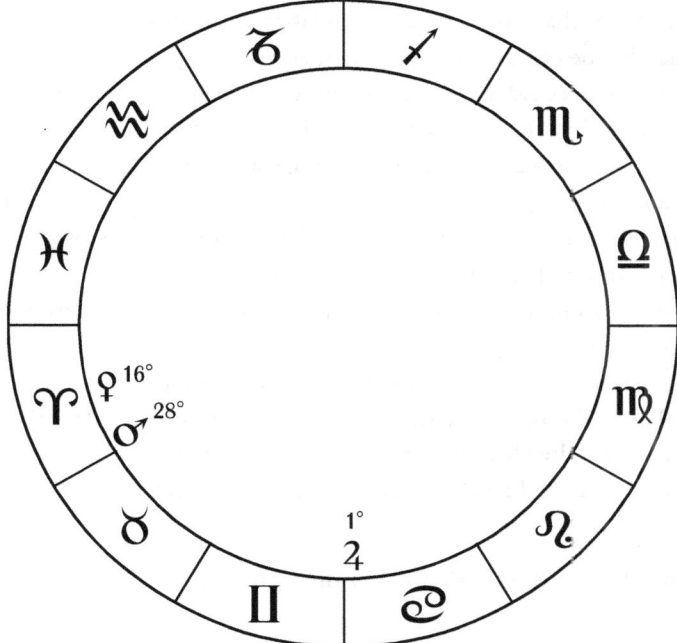

Figure 20: Frustration

For example, Mars was at 28° Aries, and Venus was in the seventeenth degree of Aries, seeking the conjunction of Mars, and Jupiter was in the second degree of Cancer. And the rays of Jupiter were in the beginning of Taurus, so that whenever Mars exited Aries and touched anything in Taurus, immediately he was joined to Jupiter by aspect[204]–namely before Venus could pursue Mars (whose conjunction she was seeking). And this frustrated the conjunction of Venus with Mars, so that Venus sought his conjunction in vain, because she could not perfect it on account of the hindering of Jupiter's rays and his conjunction with Mars: just as sometimes happens in the cases of hunters, when one of them is pursuing a wild beast, and has followed it in order to catch it; when, before he catches it, another person catches it, and thus his hunt is frustrated.

Whence if some question had been made about some matter which seemed ought to be perfected by the corporal conjunction of Venus with Mars, it will be frustrated and destroyed by the aspectual conjunction of Mars with Jupiter. And

---

[204] This is another indication that Bonatti does not use out-of-sign aspects.

it often happens that when someone has labored and has applied himself for a long time, that he can perfect the matter, and he always believed it and was in the hopes that he could perfect it–and in the meantime, unexpectedly, another comes and perfects it without labor, and takes it away, of which this is an example: a question was made about marriage, with Libra ascending, and Venus was in Aries, wishing to join herself to Mars (as was said), and it seemed that Mars ought to receive her from Aries. And he whose significator was Mars, gave a good intention to her (whose significatrix was Venus) of perfecting what he sought, and in good conscience proposing, and believing he would do what was sought from him. And after many long talks, a certain other matter appeared which he had not contrived, that perhaps seemed to him to be more useful to him; or that he did not know what to say, as often happens. And thus he left behind what had already been long considered [the marriage], and, undisturbed, he perfected what had newly happened to him unexpectedly.

Chapter 18: On the cutting-off of the light of one planet by another

The cutting-off of the light[205] of one planet by another comes to be in this way: namely when one wishes to be conjoined to another heavier than he, and another planet is in the following sign from the sign in which the heavier one is; and before the first is joined to him with whom he wished to be joined (who is heavier than he), the third one (who is heavier than all) is made retrograde, and by retrograding he is joined to the one to whom the first light one wanted to be joined. Thus this heavier one cuts off the light of the lighter one from the other who is less heavy than he; and he does not permit the conjunction to be perfected; and thus the matter about which the question was made, is destroyed.[206]

---

[205] The following definitions derive from Abū Ma'shar's "cutting the light" or *al-qaT' al-nūr* (Ar. القطع النور) in *Abbr.* III.46, also described in al-Qabīsī (III.24).

[206] This seems to be the same as contrariety, except that the retrograding planet starts out in the following sign.

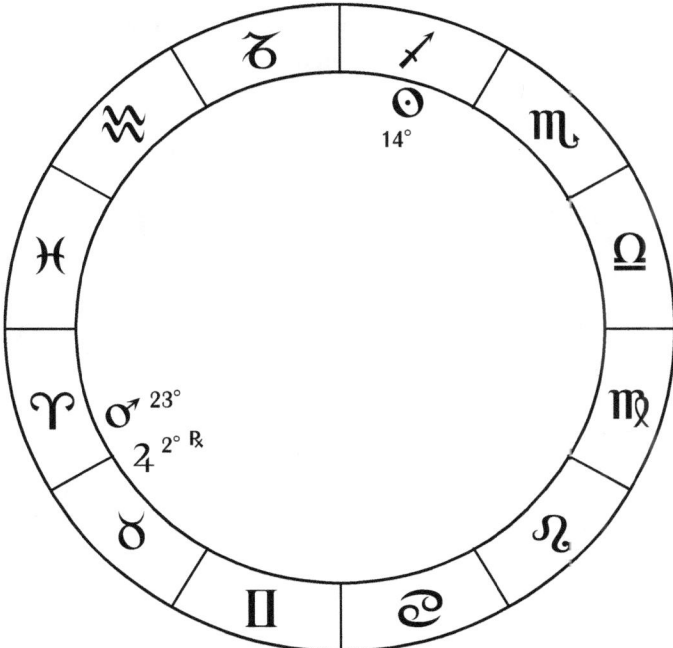

Figure 21: Cutting-Off of Light (a)

For example, Mars was in the twenty-fourth degree of Aries, and the Sun in the fifteenth degree of Sagittarius, seeking the conjunction of Mars, and wishing to be joined to him by aspect; and he projected his light upon the light[207] of Mars. And Jupiter was in the third degree of Taurus, and in the meantime he was made retrograde. And Jupiter was joined to Mars in that retrogradation before the Sun could perfect his own conjunction with Mars: and Jupiter cut off the light of the Sun from Mars, and so the conjunction was destroyed and annulled.[208] Whence if there were a question about some matter which seemed

---

[207] *Super lumen.*
[208] Bonatti has chosen a bad example because it could never have happened quite as he describes it. It would only have taken the Sun approximately 9 days to perfect the trine to Mars. It is impossible that Jupiter could have retrograded the required 2° to cross over into Aries and perfect a conjunction with Mars before that. Mars could have crossed into Taurus just before the Sun perfected the aspect, in which case he would be joined by orb to Jupiter, but the definition requires that Jupiter *by retrogradation* be joined to Mars. Mars's own direct motion could have carried him to Jupiter's orbs in the next sign regardless of Jupiter's retrogradation.

ought to be perfected by the conjunction of the Sun and Mars, it will be destroyed on account of the conjunction of Jupiter with Mars.

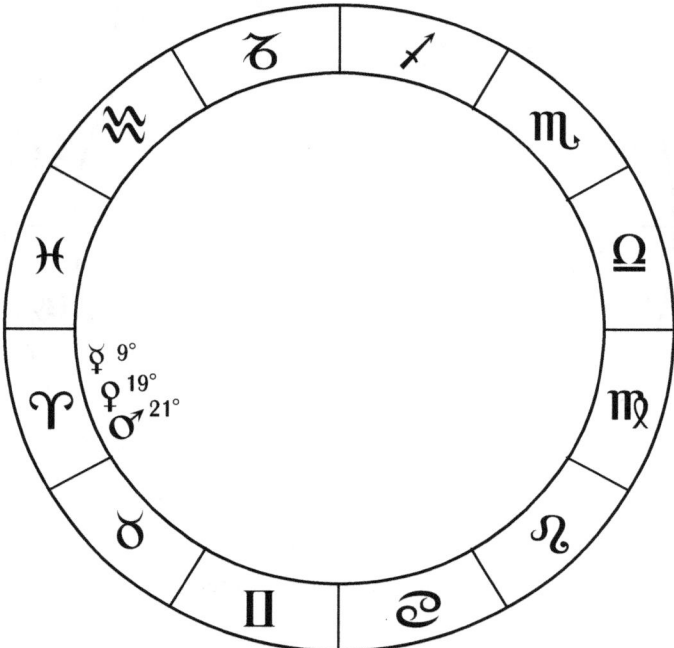

Figure 22: Cutting-Off of Light (b)

The cutting-off of the light of the planets (namely one from the other) even comes to be in another way: namely when one planet seeks the conjunction of another heavier than he, and the heavier one seeks the conjunction of another heavier than he again; and before the first light one is joined to the second heavier one, the heavy one is joined to the other (namely to the third one heavier than he). Thus the third one cuts off the light of the second from the first, lighter one. And thus the purpose that was signified by the conjunction is destroyed, as was said above. For example, Mercury was in the tenth degree of Aries (or of any other sign), seeking the conjunction of Venus, who was in the twentieth degree of the same sign, and Mars was in the twenty-second degree of the same sign–to whom Venus was joined first joined before[209] Mercury was

---

[209] Reading *antequam* for *quam*.

joined to her. Thus Mars cuts off the light of Venus from [the conjunction of] Mercury with Venus.

Chapter 19: In which places the planets become strong, and in which weak, and in which they become benefic, and in which malefic

There are certain places in which the planets are strengthened and become strong, and certain ones in which they become weak, and certain ones in which they become good and fortunate, and certain ones in which they become evil and unfortunate.

> For the places in which they become strong and fortunate are namely those when they are in the aspects of the good and fortunate planets (by trine or sextile or at least by square), and especially if the aspect were with reception: because then they are made fortunate, even if they are malefic.
>
> And when they are in places in which the malefic planets are cadent from them, so that they are not joined to them, nor [the malefics] to [the other planets].
>
> And when they are separated from benefics and are joined to benefics, or they are between two benefics, or they are between the rays of two benefic planets. For example, Jupiter was in the tenth degree of Aries, and Venus was in the twentieth degree of Sagittarius, and the Moon in the fifteenth degree of Leo: thus the Moon was being separated from Jupiter by a trine aspect which was from Aries and Leo, and she was being joined to Venus, likewise by a trine aspect, which was from Leo to Sagittarius.

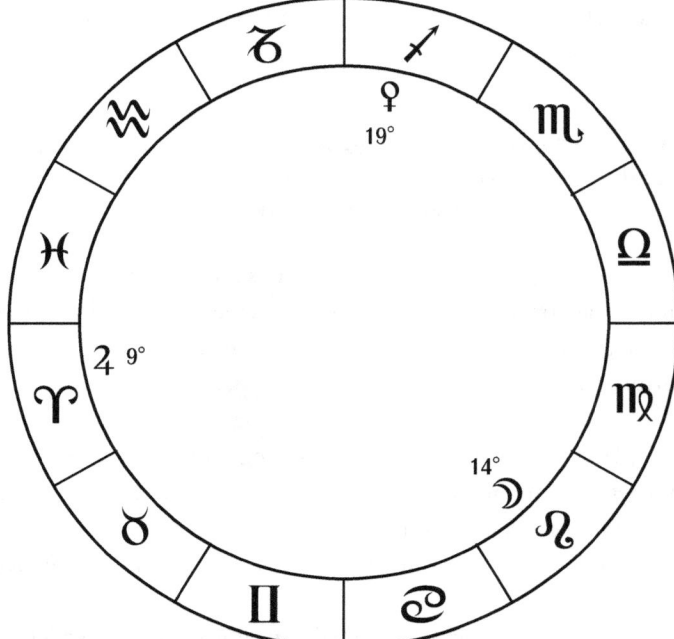

Figure 23: Besieging by benefics

Likewise when they are houses in which they rejoice (as was said elsewhere), namely Saturn in the 12th, Jupiter in the 11th, Mars in the 6th, the Sun in the 9th, Venus in the 5th, Mercury in the 1st, the Moon in the 3rd.

Likewise when they are in signs in which they rejoice when they enter [them]: namely Saturn in Aquarius, Jupiter in Sagittarius, Mars in Scorpio, Venus in Taurus, Mercury in Virgo.

And when they are [in] angles or the succeedents to angles.

And when they are united with the Sun as was said elsewhere–because a planet is not united unless it is next to the Sun by less than 16' in front and behind, to the right or the left. Because a planet is not said to be in the heart of the Sun unless it is as I said. Even if it were in the same minute with him according to longitude, and were distant from him by more than 16' in latitude, nevertheless it would be combust, nor could it therefore be called strong.

And when the planets are in the aspect of the Sun by a trine or a sextile, or by a trine or sextile to the Moon, and she is then fortunate.

And when they are fast in course, increasing in light and number.

And when they are in their own dignities: namely in domiciles, or exaltations, or bounds, or triplicities, or faces.

Or they are in their aforesaid likenesses: that is, a masculine one in a masculine sign, and a feminine one in a feminine sign, and a diurnal one in the day above the earth and in the night below the earth, and *vice versa*.

Or they are received, or are in the bright degrees.

And when they are ascending northerly, and are ascending in the circles of their *awj*es.

And when they are direct or in their second station (whichever one of them), when it wishes to go direct.

And when they are going out from under the rays of the Sun; or Saturn, Jupiter and Mars are oriental from the Sun, not far removed from him, so that they are not going toward weakness.

And masculine ones are in masculine quarters (which are from the Ascendant up to the 10th, and from the 7th up to the 4th), and feminine ones in feminine quarters (which are from the 10th up to the 7th, and from the 4th up to the Ascendant). And the Sun likewise rejoices in masculine quarters, unless he is in Libra (because his fall is there).

And when Venus and Mercury and the Moon are occidental from the Sun, so that they set in the evening after him. And when they are in feminine quarters, and the Moon below the earth in the day, and above the earth in the night. And when she is in a feminine sign and a feminine place, or the Moon is in the exaltation of the Sun.

These are the places in which the planets become strong, provided that they are otherwise free from impediments.

Chapter 20: When, and in what places the planets become weak

It was spoken of the strengths and fortunes: now we must discuss the weaknesses and misfortunes.

And this comes to be in many ways, namely when they are in the corporal conjunction of the malefics, or in one of their aspects without reception, or they were near the malefics or their rays—[but] less so if it is the bound of the planet: like if Jupiter is in Aries (and Saturn is near him or his rays) in less than the 6° which are the bound of Jupiter in Aries.[210] Or if Venus were there, and Saturn or his rays were near her in less than the 8° which is [in] the second bound of Venus in Aries; or Mercury were there, and there were, between himself and Saturn (or his rays) less than the 7° which namely is the third bound, of Mercury, in Aries. And you ought to understand this with any planet, and with any bound of any planet, and in any sign.

Or that the planets are in the bounds of the malefics, and when they are in [the malefics'] domiciles, not received; or the malefics are elevated above them, namely that they are northern from them, [or] from the 10th or from the 11th from their places (namely by a square or trine aspect, the hindmost which is from the back);[211] and worse than that is if the malefics did not receive them; indeed if they were to receive them, the reception decreases their malice.

Or if they were under the rays of the Sun (which are the degrees of combustion), or in his opposition; or in his square aspect without reception.

---

[210] I.e., if Jupiter were near Saturn but in his own bounds in Aries.
[211] By "from their places," Bonatti means "in the 10th or 11th house from the other planet by whole sign houses," i.e. if Mercury were in Libra and and Mars or Saturn were in Cancer or Leo. Yet none of these would be by a trine. This is a version of the Hellenistic doctrine of "overcoming," which has to do with being in the *tenth* sign from a given planet or Part. We will see below that "elevation" is often used in the Latin edition of *Tet.*, where Ptolemy *only* means this Hellenistic "overcoming." See Introduction.

Or if they were with the Head or Tail of the Dragon (or if they were in their own *jawzahirr*), so that there are between them and the Head or the Tail, or their *jawzahirr*, 12° or less before, or 10° or less after. And of those planets which are more impeded by their *jawzahirr*, are the Sun and the Moon, when there are between them and the Head or Tail of the Dragon 12° or less before them (because there they suffer eclipse, which is a great detriment to them).

Or if the planets are besieged by the malefics or by their rays.

And among the misfortunes of the planets is when a planet is retrograde or it is cadent from the Ascendant (so that it does not aspect it), or it is slow in course, or it is in its first station, namely so that it becomes retrograde; or it is in the dark degrees; or a masculine planet is in feminine degrees or in a feminine sign, or is below the earth during the day and above the earth at night; or a feminine planet is in masculine degrees or in a masculine sign, or it is above the earth in the day or below the earth by night;[212] or they are in opposition to their own domiciles or exaltations; or they are southern, or descending in the south; or they are cadent from the angles or their succeedents; or they are in houses cadent from the Ascendant; or they are in the *via combusta* (which is from the middle of Libra up to the middle of Scorpio); or one one of them is joined to a retrograde or combust planet (or impeded in some other way); or they are not received; or the three higher ones are occidental from the Sun, in feminine quarters; or the three inferiors are oriental from the Sun in masculine quarters. And when the Sun is in feminine signs or in feminine quarters (unless it is the 9th, which is the house of his joy, because he signifies religion just like the 9th house, according to the Philosopher).[213]

Or if the Moon is combust, or in the degrees of her descension; or is joined to planets who are in their own descension; or is in the opposition of the Sun; or she is joined to malefics, or in their opposition or square aspect, without reception; or she is besieged by the two malefics or their rays; or she is with the Head or Tail of the Dragon, as was said; or she is

---

[212] Here we see a medieval conflation of gender and sect.
[213] It is unclear who "the Philosopher" is, especially since the connection between the Sun, religion, and the 9th is a common enough one in the texts. Since Bonatti's list is heavily dependent on Sahl, perhaps he means Sahl.

in Gemini, not received by Mercury;[214] or she is in the bounds of the malefics; or she is cadent from the angles; or she is joined to a planet descending from them;[215] or she is in the *via combusta*; or she is slow in course; or is at the end of the lunar month, not received; or she is in the smoky or dark or welled or *azemene* degrees.

Whence the wise said that when the Moon is thus impeded, it is hardly possible but that she has one of the said impediments,[216] so that it is not good to begin a work from which good is hoped, nor any journey or pilgrimage; nor is it praised in nativities. Whence if someone were then born when the Moon is impeded by one of these impediments (which it rarely happens but that she is impeded by one of them),[217] if the nativity were good in itself, it subtracts from the native the good which is signified by the nativity according to the quantity or the quality of the impediment; and if it were bad [in itself], it increases evil for the native. And so with journeys or pilgrimages: if the journey were good, it decreases the goodness; if indeed it were bad, it increases the malice according to its impediment.

Chapter 21: On the besieging[218] of the planets and signs

Sometimes a planet is said to be "besieged": and this comes to be in two ways. By one [way] it is called called "veneration," and this besieging is said to be good in a good part [of the figure], namely when a planet is between two benefics or their rays, so that it has one benefic (or its rays) in front of it, and

---

[214] Undoubtedly because Gemini is the 12th from her own domicile of Cancer, by whole sign houses.
[215] I.e., cadent.
[216] This clause is oddly placed. As placed it is redundant (if she is impeded, she is impeded). But by itself it is true: since the Moon is in one of these impediments practically all the time, virtually no undertaking would be wise at *any* time. As it stands, Bonatti seems to be mixing two thoughts here.
[217] This is a better place for the clause mentioned above. Here the underlying message seems to be, "since the Moon is practically always impeded, a nativity rarely shows unimpeded distinction and glory: most people will not reach the highest levels of success and happiness."
[218] *Obsessione*. The derives from Abū Ma'shar's and al-Qabīsī's *al-hisāra*, "besiegement" or "containment" (Ar. الحصر), *Abbr.* IV.21*ff*, al-Qabīsī III.26. The Latin meaning of *obsessio* pertains from the besieging of cities or castles in war. But the equivalent Greek term can mean to "surround" or "distract." A besieged city is indeed surrounded, and since Bonatti (and Abū Ma'shar) describes both good and bad *obsessio*, "surrounding" or "containment" is perhaps more appropriate.

one (or its rays) behind it, so that it is separated from one (or its rays), and is joined to the other (or its rays).

A planet is said to be besieged in another way, and this besieging is evil, and in an evil part [of the figure], namely when a planet is between two planets or their rays, namely so that it has one malefic (or its rays) in front of it and the other malefic (or its rays) behind it.

Indeed just as a planet is said to be besieged, so a sign is said to be besieged, as al-Qabīsī says. And he said that if the Sun or another benefic were to aspect the besieged planet or sign by a trine or sextile aspect, so that there fall, between the planet and the Sun (or another benefic, or its rays or sign), less than 7°, that the malice or besieging is dissolved. And a sign is said to be besieged if one of the benefics or its rays were in front of it, and another benefic or its rays were behind it–and this besieging is good. And a sign is said to be besieged if one malefic or its rays were in front of it, and the other malefic or its rays were behind it–and this besieging is evil.

Chapter 22: How one planet loves another, and how it is loved by another, and how they hate one another

The ancient sages said that certain of planets love one another, and certain of them hate one another.

For they said that Jupiter loves all planets, and is naturally the friend of all; and all of them love him, and all are his friends except for Mars.

Venus loves all planets, and all love her except for Saturn.

Saturn loves Jupiter, the Sun, and the Moon, and they him; and he hates Mars and Venus, and they him. And Venus hates him more than Mars does. Mercury, when applied to by those loving Saturn, he loves [Saturn]; when he is applied to by those hating him, he hates him.

Mars loves only Venus, and she him; he hates the rest and they him, but Jupiter and the Sun hate him more than the rest do.

The Sun loves Jupiter and Venus with a perfect love, and they him; and he hates Mars, Mercury, and the Moon, and they him.

Mercury loves Jupiter, and Venus, and they him; and he hates Mars, the Sun, the Moon, and Saturn (as I said).

The Moon loves Saturn, Jupiter, and Venus, and they her; and she hates Mars, and the Sun, and Mercury.

The Head of the Dragon loves Jupiter and Venus, and they it; it does not care about the others. Its Tail loves Saturn and Mars, and they it; and it hates Jupiter, the Sun, and Venus, and the Moon, and they it.

Moreover, they said that there is a certain other kind of enmity, namely that two planets have opposing domiciles or exaltations, as do Saturn and the luminaries; Jupiter and Mercury; Mars and Venus (who [all] have their domiciles opposing). And so do Saturn and the Sun; Jupiter and Mars (who have their exaltations opposing). But such enmity is more by accident than by [planetary] nature.

Whence you ought to consider in judgments, or questions, or nativities, or whatever sort they are, that whatever was signified by one of the planets concerning those things which seem ought to happen to the native or querent, if what was signified were good, and it will be signified by a planet who is inimical to the Lord of the Ascendant of the nativity or question, that it will not freely give or do the thing which it ought to give or do; and always it will come to be with some decrease. But even though the planets are inimical to one another (as was said), still, if one of them were joined to another, or one found the other in its own domicile or exaltation, [and] it receives him, it looks on him with a good spirit, and with good will, and forgets all enmity, nor remembers anything about it. Just as if someone would find some enemy of his (who was not an enemy with ultimate or capital enmity), in his own house or in a place in which he had dignity or mastery (like an official power and the like), that he receives him and honors him with a cheerful face, fearing lest he be reprehended if he did otherwise—unless the man were of the forest, and very wild, whose mind was not socialized to men, nor suffered himself to associate with them, like that tyrant Ezzelino da Romano, whose tyranny none was found like, who spared no rank, spared no religion, spared no nobility, spared no age, spared no sex, spared no blood of his own or of a stranger, but rather without cause killed his own brother [and] his own nephew with his own hands. And I saw all of these things.

And such a reception as this, and show of good will, is said to be the "opening of the gates," because it opens the gates and entrances for him, and renders him secure; for one cannot say more clearly, "enter into [my] home," than by opening the doors for him.[219]

Chapter 23: On their friendship

Just as sometimes enmity falls between the planets, so friendship falls between them, namely when one planet agrees with another planet in nature, and quality, and substance, and power: as Mars and the Sun agree in heat and dryness, and Mars is the Lord of the exaltation of the Sun, in which his strength appears much. And stronger than all of these friendships is agreement in nature. Whence you ought always to consider in nativities or questions what may be signified by one of the planets (of those [accidents] which ought to happen to the native or querent): which if it were good, and it were signified by one of the planets who would be friendly to the Lord of the Ascendant of the nativity or question, he[220] who ought to give and perform it will give or perform the matter more freely and quickly and perfectly, and always without decrease: just as when someone divides certain things among various people, so that he strives to give to his friend the better part of the matter which he divides; and when he gives to someone who is not totally his friend, or who is inimical to him, even though he may give, still he strives to give him less of the good part of the thing which is divided. And as Venus and the Moon agree in coldness and moisture, and Venus is the Lady of the Moon's exaltation, so Jupiter and Venus agree in benevolence, and in the collecting of what is good, and of fortune, and in time.

---

[219] This is also referred to in Tr. 9, Part 3, 12th House, end of Ch. 5.
[220] Omitting *quia*.

BIBLIOGRAPHY

Abu Bakr, *Liber Genethliacus* (Nuremberg: Johannes Petreius, 1540)

Abū Ma'shar al-Balhi, *The Abbreviation of the Introduction to Astrology*, ed. and trans. Charles Burnett, K. Yamamoto, and Michio Yano (Leiden: E.J. Brill, 1994)

Abū Ma'shar al-Balhi, *Liber Introductorii Maioris ad Scientiam Iudiciorum Astrorum*, vols. VI, V, VI, IX, ed. Richard Lemay (Naples: Istituto Universitario Orientale, 1995)

Abū Ma'shar al-Balhi, *The Abbreviation of the Introduction to Astrology*, ed. and trans. Charles Burnett, annotated by Charles Burnett, G. Tobyn, G. Cornelius and V. Wells (ARHAT Publications, 1997)

Abū Ma'shar al-Balhi, *On Historical Astrology: The Book of Religions and Dynasties (On the Great Conjunctions)*, vols. I-II, eds. and trans. Keiji Yamamoto and Charles Burnett (Leiden: Brill, 2000)

Abū Ma'shar al-Balhi, *The Flowers of Abū Ma'shar*, trans. Benjamin Dykes (2nd ed., 2007)

Al-Biruni, Muhammad ibn Ahmad, *The Chronology of Ancient Nations*, trans. and ed. C. Edward Sachau (London: William H. Allen and Co., 1879)

Al-Biruni, Muhammad ibn Ahmad, *The Book of Instruction in the Elements of the Art of Astrology*, trans. R. Ramsay Wright (London: Luzac & Co., 1934)

Al-Fārābī, *De Ortu Scientiarum* (appearing as *"Alfarabi Über den Ursprung der Wissenschaften (De Ortu Scientiarum),"* ed. Clemens Baeumker, *Beiträge zur Geschichte der Philosophie des Mittelalters*, v. 19/3, 1916.

Al-Khayyat, Abu 'Ali, *The Judgments of Nativities*, trans. James H. Holden (Tempe, AZ: American Federation of Astrologers, Inc., 1988)

Al-Kindī, *The Forty Chapters (Iudicia Astrorum): The Two Latin Versions*, ed. Charles Burnett (London: The Warburg Institute, 1993)

Al-Mansur (attributed), *Capitula Almansoris*, ed. Plato of Tivoli (1136) (Basel: Johannes Hervagius, 1533)

Al-Qabīsī, *Isagoge*, trans. John of Spain, with commentary by John of Saxony (Paris: Simon Colinaeus, 1521)

Al-Qabīsī, *The Introduction to Astrology*, eds. Charles Burnett, Keiji Yamamoto, Michio Yano (London and Turin: The Warburg Institute, 2004)

Al-Rijāl, 'Alī, *In Iudiciis Astrorum* (Venice: Erhard Ratdolt, 1485)

Al-Rijāl, 'Alī, *Libri de Iudiciis Astrorum* (Basel: Henrichus Petrus, 1551)

Al-Tabarī, 'Umar, *De Nativitatibus* (Basel: Johannes Hervagius, 1533)

Al-Tabarī, 'Umar [Omar of Tiberias], *Three Books of Nativities*, ed. Robert Schmidt, trans. Robert Hand (Berkeley Springs, WV: The Golden Hind Press, 1997)

Alighieri, Dante, *Inferno*, trans. John Ciardi (New York, NY: Mentor, 1982)

Allen, Richard Hinckley, *Star Names: Their Lore and Meaning* (New York: Dover Publications Inc., 1963)

Aristotle, *The Complete Works of Aristotle* vols. I-II, ed. Jonathan Barnes (Princeton, NJ: Princeton University Press, 1984)

Bloch, Marc, *Feudal Society*, vols. I-II, trans. L.A. Manyon (Chicago: University of Chicago Press, 1961)

Bonatti, Guido, *Decem Tractatus Astronomiae* (Erhard Ratdolt: Venice, 1491)

Bonatti, Guido, *De Astronomia Tractatus X* (Basel, 1550)

Bonatti, Guido, *Liber Astronomiae: Books One, Two, and Three with Index*, trans. Robert Zoller and Robert Hand (Salisbury, Australia: Spica Publications, 1988)

Bonatti, Guido, *Liber Astronomiae Part IV: On Horary, First Part*, ed. Robert Schmidt, trans. Robert Hand (Berkeley Springs, WV: The Golden Hind Press, 1996)

Boncompagni, Baldassarre, *Della Vita e Della Opere di Guido Bonatti, Astrologo et Astronomo del Seculo Decimoterzo* (Rome: 1851)

Brady, Bernadette, *Brady's Book of Fixed Stars* (Boston: Weiser Books, 1998)

Burnett, Charles, ed., *Magic and Divination in the Middle Ages* (Aldershot, Great Britain: Ashgate Publishing Ltd., 1996)

Burnett, Charles and Gerrit Bos, *Scientific Weather Forecasting in the Middle Ages* (London and New York: Kegan Paul International, 2000)

Carmody, Francis, *Arabic Astronomical and Astrological Sciences in Latin Translation: A Critical Bibliography* (Berkeley and Los Angeles: University of California Press, 1956)

Carmody, Francis, *The Astronomical works of Thābit b. Qurra* (Berkeley and Los Angeles: University of California Press, 1960)

Dorotheus of Sidon, *Carmen Astrologicum*, trans. David Pingree (Abingdon, MD: The Astrology Center of America, 2005)

Grant, Edward, *Planets, Stars, and Orbs: The Medieval Cosmos, 1200–1687* (New York, NY: Cambridge University Press, 1994)

Haskins, Charles H., "Michael Scot and Frederick II," *Isis*, v. 4/2 (1921), pp. 250-75.

Haskins, Charles H., "Science at the Court of the Emperor Frederick II," *The American Historical Review*, v. 27/4 (1922), pp. 669-94.

Hermes Trismegistus, *Liber Hermetis*, ed. Robert Hand, trans. Robert Zoller (Salisbury, Australia: Spica Publications, 1998)

Holden, James H., *A History of Horoscopic Astrology* (Tempe, AZ: American Federation of Astrologers, Inc., 1996)

Ibn Labban, Kusyar, *Introduction to Astrology*, ed. and trans. Michio Yano (Tokyo: Institute for the Study of Languages and Cultures of Asia and Africa, 1997)

Ibn Sina (Avicenna), *The Canon of Medicine (al-Qanun fi'l tibb)*, ed. Laleh Bakhtiar (Great Books of the Islamic World, Inc., 1999)

Kennedy, Edward S., "The Sasanian Astronomical Handbook Zīj-I Shāh and the Astrological Doctrine of 'Transit' (Mamarr)," *Journal of the American Oriental Society*, v. 78/4 (1958), pp. 246-62.

Kunitzsch, Paul, "Mittelalterliche astronomisch-astrologische Glossare mit arabischen Fachausdrücken," *Bayerische Akademie der Wissenschaften Philosophisch-Historische Klasse*, 1977, v. 5

Kunitsch, Paul, trans. and ed., "Liber de Stellis Beibeniis," in *Hermetis Trismegisti: Astrologica et Divinatoria* (Turnhout: Brepols Publishers, 2001).

Kunitzsch, Paul and Tim Smart, *A Dictionary of Modern Star Names* (Cambridge, MA: New Track Media, 2006)

Latham, R.E., *Revised Medieval Latin Word-List from British and Irish Sources* (Oxford: Oxford University Press, 2004)

Lemay, Richard, *Abu Ma'shar and Latin Aristotelianism in the Twelfth Century* (Beirut: American University of Beirut, 1962)

Levy, Raphael, "A Note on the Latin Translators of Ibn Ezra," *Isis*, v. 37 nos. 3/4 (1947), pp. 153-55.

Lilly, William, *The Starry Messenger* (London: Company of Stationers and H. Blunden, 1652). Reprinted 2004 by Renaissance Astrology Facsimile Editions.

Lilly, William, *Anima Astrologiae*, trans. Henry Coley (London: B. Harris, 1676)

Lilly, William, *Christian Astrology*, vols. I-II, ed. David R. Roell (Abingdon, MD: Astrology Center of America, 2004)

Long, A.A. and D.N. Sedley, *The Hellenistic Philosophers*, vol. I (Cambridge: Cambridge University Press, 1987)

Māshā'allāh et al., *Liber Novem Iudicum in Iudiciis Astrorum* [Book of the Nine Judges], ed. Peter Liechtenstein (Venice: 1509)

Māshā'allāh, *De Receptione* [*On Reception*] and *De Revolutione Annorum Mundi* and *De Interpraetationibus*, in *Messahalae Antiquissimi ac Laudatissimi Inter Arabes Astrologi, Libri Tres*, ed. Joachim Heller (Nuremberg: Joannes Montanus and Ulrich Neuber, 1549)

Māshā'allāh, *On Reception*, ed. and trans. Robert Hand (ARHAT Publications, 1998)

Maternus, Firmicus Julius, *Matheseos Libri VIII*, eds. W. Kroll and F. Skutsch (Stuttgard: Teubner, 1968)

Michelsen, Neil F., *The Koch Book of Tables* (San Diego: ACS Publications, Inc., 1985)

Mantello, F.A.C. and A.G. Rigg, eds., *Medieval Latin: An Introduction and Bibliographical Guide* (Washington, DC: The Catholic University of America Press, 1996)

New Oxford Annotated Bible, ed. Bruce M. Metzger and Roland E. Murphy (New York: Oxford University Press, 1994)

Pingree, David, "Astronomy and Astrology in India and Iran," *Isis* v. 54/2 (1963), pp. 229-46.

Pingree, David, "Classical and Byzantine Astrology in Sassanian Persia," *Dumbarton Oaks Papers*, v. 43 (1989), pp. 227-239.

Pingree, David, *From Astral Omens to Astrology: From Babylon to Bīkīner* (Rome: Istituto italiano per L'Africa e L'Oriente, 1997)

Pseudo-Ptolemy, *Centiloquium*, ed. Georgius Trapezuntius, in Bonatti (1550)

Ptolemy, Claudius, *Tetrabiblos* vols. 1, 2, 4, trans. Robert Schmidt, ed. Robert Hand (Berkeley Springs, WV: The Golden Hind Press, 1994-98)

Ptolemy, Claudius, *Tetrabiblos*, trans. F.E. Robbins (Cambridge and London: Harvard University Press, 1940)

Ptolemy, Claudius, *Quadripartitum* [Tetrabiblos], trans. Plato of Tivoli (1138) (Basel: Johannes Hervagius, 1533)

Sahl ibn Bishr, *Introductorium* and *Praecipua Iudicia* [The Fifty Judgments] *De Interrogationibus* and *De Electionibus*, in *Tetrabiblos*, ed. Girolamo Salio (Venice: Bonetus Locatellus, 1493)

Sahl ibn Bishr, *De Electionibus* (Venice: Peter of Liechtenstein, 1509)

Selby, Talbot R., "Filippo Villani and his Vita of Guido Bonatti," *Renaissance News*, v. 11/4 (1958), pp. 243-48.

Seneca, *The Stoic Philosophy of Seneca*, ed. and trans. Moses Hadas (New York: The Norton Library, 1968)

Stegemann, Viktor, *Dorotheos von Sidon und das Sogenannte* Introductorium *des Sahl ibn Bišr* (Prague: Orientalisches Institut in Prag, 1942)

Thomson, S. Harrison, "The Text of Grosseteste's *De Cometis*," *Isis* v. 19/1 (1933), pp. 19-25.

Thorndike, Lynn, *A History of Magic and Experimental Science* (New York: The Macmillan Company, 1929)

Thorndike, Lynn, *The Sphere of Sacrobosco and Its Commentators* (Chicago: The University of Chicago Press, 1949)

Thorndike, Lynn, "A Third Translation by Salio," *Speculum*, v. 32/1 (1957), pp. 116-117.

Thorndike, Lynn, "John of Seville," *Speculum*, v. 34/1 (1959), pp. 20-38.

Utley, Francis Lee (review), "*The Legend of the Wandering Jew* by George K. Anderson," *Modern Philology*, v. 66/2 (1968), pp. 188-193.

Valens, Vettius, *The Anthology*, vols. I-VII, ed. Robert Hand, trans. Robert Schmidt (Berkeley Springs, WV: The Golden Hind Press, 1993-2001)

Van Cleve, Thomas Curtis, *The Emperor Frederick II of Hohenstaufen: Immutator Mundi* (London: Oxford University Press, 1972)

Weinstock, Stefan, "Lunar Mansions and Early Calendars," *The Journal of Hellenic Studies*, v. 69 (1949), pp. 48-69.

Zoller, Robert, *The Arabic Parts in Astrology: A Lost Key to Prediction* (Rochester, VT: Inner Traditions International, 1989)

Zoller, Robert, *Bonatti on War* (2nd ed., 2000)

INDEX

Aaydimon 26–28, 37, 39
Abraham 24
Absent persons
   banned persons 135
   exiles ... 121–22, 125, 127, 133, 135
   expelled persons ... 115, 121–23, 125, 127, 132-33, 135
   fugitives 107
   pilgrims 113
Abu Bakr 154, 162
Abū Ma'shar 26, 37, 46, 89, 149, 168, 179, 217, 218, 222, 225–27
   Abbr. ... 140, 215-16, 220, 226, 230, 232, 234, 236, 244
   Gr. Intr. ... 28, 39, 51–52, 55–58, 65, 86–87, 139, 167, 182, 219
ad-Dawla, Sayf 27, 46, 95, 97, 100, 102, 105, 107, 108–10, 112, 154, 163, 168, 173-74, 187
Afla 174
al-'ittisal (application) 206
al-Ahwaz 158
al-Andarzagar 27, 46, 72, 95, 97, 100, 102, 104–6, 108-12
al-Battani 107, 110
Albenait 26, 27
al-Bīrūnī 56, 198, 201-02
Albuaz 110, 151, 172, 176, 181
Alexandria 82
al-Fārābī 22-23
al-Farghānī 26, 200
al-hisāra (besieging) 244
'Ali (unknown 'Ali) 92
al-i'tirād (resistance) 232–34
al-intikāth (restraint) 230-31
al-kadukhadāh 174, 187
al-Khayyat, Abu 'Ali ... 26–27, 46, 104, 108, 162, 166
   JN 104, 108, 249
al-Kindī 26-27, 73, 110

al-man' (prohibition) 220, 222
al-Mansur, Caliph 26, 102
al-mawārīth (inheritance) 109
Almetus 26
al-mintaqah (zone, area, territory) 55
al-mubtazz
   over the nativity 169
   weighted-point 145-46
al-muwājahah .... See Facing
Alps 13
al-Qabīsī, Abd al-Aziz .. 27, 47–50, 55-56, 58, 62, 72–75, 77–81, 83, 85-89, 92, 95, 97, 99, 102-03, 105, 107, 109–12, 140-41, 149-51, 155, 159, 161, 163–68, 172–74, 176, 179, 181–84, 198, 202, 206-07, 209–11, 213-14, 225–27, 230–32, 234, 236, 244-45
al-Qalandar 185-87
al-qaT' al-nūr (cutting the light) 218, 236
al-qubūl (reception) 226
al-Rijāl, 'Ali ibn (Haly Abenragel) 26
al-Tabarī, 'Umar 26, 166, 172
   TBN 109
an-naql (transfer) 215-16
Aphetês 193
Apulia 13, 80
Arabia, Arabs 80, 173
Arabian peninsula 79
Arastellus 27-28, 37, 46
Aristotle 22, 26, 65
Armenia 78, 183
ar-radd (returning) 219, 227
ar-radd al-nūr (reflecting the light) 217
Arthephius 185-86
Asia 13, 251

Aspects
  defined 62
  in front/back 62
  out-of-sign 234-35
  related to planets 62
  whole-sign ... 52-54, 62, 214, 234, 235
as-Sawad 77
Astaphaz 26
Asthoatol 65
Astrology
  and theology 6
  causing distress 12, 17
  defined 20–23
  electing for enemies 18
  instruments 23
  its nobility 1, 9, 12
  knows individuals 7
  one of the sciences 4, 23, 25
  prediction beneficial 12, 17
  probability and necessity 8
Astronomy
  awj 198-201, 209, 241
  eccentric ... 158, 172, 177, 198-201, 208-09
  epicycle ... 163, 172, 177, 198-201, 208-09, 214
  equation 200
Atalanta 24
Atlas 24
at-tarīqah (course, journey) 56
Azemena 88
Azerbaijan 77-78
Babel 77
Babylon, Babylonia 77, 158, 165
Balkh 78, 80
Barqa 80
Ben 166
Besieging 243-45
Britain 171
Burnett, Charles 55, 77–79, 89, 166, 230
Byzantines 97

Cadence
  from the angles ... 23, 136, 141, 228-29, 243-44
  from the Ascendant ... 105, 138, 243
Cancaph 139, 158, 172
Census 96, 109, 131–33
Chaldeans 64-65
China 78
Climes and regions .. 13-14, 21, 48, 91, 182
Combustion/under the rays 75, 208-09, 211–13, 227-28, 240–43
  age analogies 185
  exhaustion/weakness analogies 213
  hiddenness analogies 183-84
  illness/death analogies 207, 212
Comes/comites 12, 69, 129
Committing disposition
  from own dignities 215-16
  with reception 223, 228-29
Contrariety of planets. *See al-i'tirād* (resistance)
Ctesiphon 158
Cutting-off of Light... *See al-qaT' al-nūr* (cutting the light)
daf' al-quwwah (pushing power) 225
daf' al-Tabii'a (pushing nature) 225
daf' al-Tabii'ain (pushing two natures) 226
dastūrīya 210
Daylam, Daylaman 81, 178, 183
Divination 22
Dorotheus .. 26, 56, 149, 154, 158, 163, 167, 172
Doruphoria (spear-bearing) 210
Ebrianus 176
Eclipses 22, 26, 139, 165, 243

Ecliptic
jawzahirr 201-02, 243
Egypt, Egyptians 24, 64, 78, 80, 82
Elections
    war..18
Elements............................2, 7, 28
    and sublunar qualities.............38
    and three principles of change
    .... 28, 37
    only four...................................38
Emilia-Romagna........................82
Empyrean heaven........................ 4
England......................................13
Ethiopia, Ethiopians......13, 80-81, 155
Euphrates..................................79
Ezzelino da Romano III..230, 246
Facing.................................. 202–6
fawt (evasion) 234
Firmicus Maternus 202
Fixed stars...............................150
    sphere of fixed stars 5, 199
Forlì..13
France....................................171
Fredona Girzavensis.................196
Frustration of planets 234
Garamaqa 79
God..... ...2, 6, 24, 27, 46, 75, 110, 153, 174, 180, 197
Gurgan 78, 82
Hamadan................................77
Hand, Robert.. ...4, 25, 56, 78-82, 97, 124-25, 130, 163, 168, 178, 181-82
Head/Tail of the Dragon...50, 57-59, 109, 123, 125, 127, 139, 187, 243, 246
    exaltations of 56, 58
Hejaz..................................80, 173
Hellenistic astrology..................242
Herat..80
Hermes Trismegistus.........27, 46, 190, 251

hīlāj 193
Hind.. 155
Hippocrates 14
Hours, masculine/feminine.... 192
Houses
    ascending/descending............93
    colors 139
    derived...96, 99, 101, 103-04, 106, 108, 114
    divided into quarters........91-92, 241, 243
    five-degree rule.......................91
    Lord of one in another 114
    Lords of angles in angles 142
    right/left of the Ascendant ...93
    right/left of the east 93
    right/left of the heaven 93
    significations 95
    strengths 94, 136, 141
    whole-sign............................ 101
    why numbered counterclockwise 135
ibn Ridwān, ʿAli..........................92
Idiots in tunics (friars) ...4, 13, 165
Ifriqiya.......................................80
Illness, disease, infirmity 15
India, Indians 65, 81, 139, 166, 178
Iraq.. 158
Isfahan...................................... 158
Italy, Italians..............................82
Jafar...............................26, 27, 177
Jerusalem................................... 163
Jesus Christ...................15, 24, 171
Jirjis 26, 27
John Duns Scotus 22
John of Seville/Spain...65, 79, 183
John of Vicenza..........................24
Judaism, Jews 24, 153
Jupiter
    bodily form 158
    general qualities 52, 156
    general significations 156
Kabul..80

Kankah................................. 139, 158
kasmīmī............................... 211, 240
Khorasan 78, 168
Kirman 80
Kufa..82
Kurds..77
Lilly, William 50, 230
Lombardy 13
Magnanimity 10, 194, 195
Mahan 77
Mahruban 81
Makran 178
Marche 82
Maria of Cremona 196
Mars
    bodily form............................163
    general qualities 53, 159
    general significations 159
Māshā'allāh 26-27, 62, 72, 110,
    145, 149, 153-54, 158, 163,
    167, 172, 178, 183, 207
    OR 207
Mauritania..................................79
Medicine 16
Mercury
    bodily form............................178
    general qualities 54, 173
    general significations 173
Moon
    bodily form............................183
    general qualities 52, 179
    general significations 179
    increased/decreased course..201
    increased/decreased light 3
    phase significations...... 183, 244
Nativities
    substance.................................97
    time *in utero* (Hermes)...........190
Opening of the gates 247
Orientality/occidentality . 202, 241
    defined.................207-08, 212-13
    occidental of the Moon 210
Own light
    version b (al-Qabīsī) 209, 213

Palestine 77
Parts
    Heavy Part (Saturn) 154
    of Blessedness and Aid (Jupiter)
   158
    of Blessing and Profit 158
    of Boldness (Mars) 163
    of Business............................178
    of Desire................................173
    of Divination 168
    of Fortune...19, 117, 134, 146,
    147
    of Love and Concord (Venus)
   173
    of Strength and Stability 154
    of Substance 146
    of Things to Be (Sun, Spirit)
    ....158, 168
Perfection
    transfer of light......................218
Persia, Persians 77, 79, 81, 158,
    168
Persian Gulf 81
Planets
    "overcoming"........................242
    above/below the earth...32, 92-
    93, 95, 136, 147, 210-11, 241,
    243
    action in inferior things...1-2, 5,
    7, 39
    assigned to bodily limbs 83
    average courses 201
    bounds...48-50, 64–67, 69, 154,
    158, 163, 167, 172, 176, 182,
    223, 241-42, 244
    conjunction by latitude 213
    descensions 57–59, 243
    detriment................................55
    dignity analogies....................72
    domiciles 50
    exaltation 50, 56–58
    faces 50, 70, 71
    fall..57
    feral 214

first station...177, 185, 209, 212, 243
in gestation..............................188
increased/decreased course 201
increased/decreased light....241
increased/decreased number 200, 201, 241
joys..50
joys, house-based........140, 240, 243
joys, sign-based 56, 240
loves and hates..............245, 247
planetary hours........................191
rejoicing, gender-based.........147
retrogradation..........................*See* Retrogradation
second station....177, 185-86, 212, 241
secondary motion.......135, 139, 155
stations (in general) 200
their motion.......................... 2, 21
their order 49, 164
their returns 50
triplicities.......................50, 59, 67
void in course..........................214
years of nourishing................190
Plato of Tivoli....................203, 206
Popes/Papacy.............................135
Prediction
directing through bounds.......69
firdārīah...154, 158, 162, 167, 172, 176, 182, 187-88
using planetary years...154, 158, 163, 167, 172, 176, 182
using triplicity rulers.......68, 95, 97, 100, 102, 104, 106, 108–12
Prohibition 220
Pseudo-Ptolemy..............................
Cent.......................................12, 92
Ptolemy.......26-27, 37, 43, 46, 57, 64, 67, 88, 190

Almagest..6
Tet....65, 91-92, 157, 182, 185, 202-03, 205-06, 242
Quadrivium.................................26
Questions
children.......................................74
conception..................................85
Reception
defined.................................. 223
perfect............106, 179, 183, 225
Rendering of light....*See ar-radd al-nūr* (reflecting the light)
Restraining of planets (refranation)...........*See al-intikāth* (restraint)
Retrogradation.........136, 139, 164, 185, 200, 208-09, 211–13, 236, 243
slowness............................ 177
and age............................177, 185
cannot sustain...................227-28
destruction 230–33, 236-37
dishonesty 177
slowness................................. 177
weakness................................ 227
Roman Church 126, 132
Romania..13
Rome, Romans ...80, 82, 163, 165, 168, 171
Roots 142, 193
Sacerdos...159, 168, 178, 183, 188
Sahl ibn Bishr.......95, 97, 100, 105, 107-12, 137, 243
Introduct....95, 97, 107, 110, 137, 219, 225
Salio of Padua 230
Samarkand 168
Sarcinator................................... 183
Saturn
bodily form 154
general qualities...............52, 149
general significations 149
Schmidt, Robert...................65, 254
Sect... 243

haym, likeness...147, 210-11, 241, 243
hayyiz..................................210
luminary rulers 210
rejoicing conditions................147
Seneca.............................. 11, 25
Sextus Empiricus........................12
Sigistan 80
Signs
  agreeing in journey/zone ...48, 55-56
  assigned to bodily limbs 76
  azemene degrees 88, 244
  beautiful voice 74
  bodily form 193
  bright degrees 86
  common 58, 60, 61
  crooked.......................................74
  dark degrees............86, 243, 244
  dark signs 75
  defective 74
  degrees having power together 89
  degrees increasing fortune 89
  direct/crooked 47
  domestic....................................74
  empty degrees..........................86
  fixed 61
  half-voiced 75
  masculine/feminine degrees 85
  movable.............. 52, 61, 89, 117
  mute..75
  northern/southern 47
  obeying/commanding 47
  of few children 75
  prolific 74
  quadrupedal.............................74
  rational......................................74
  smoky degrees 86, 244
  sterile...75
  very defective 75
  welled degrees 87, 244
  winged 74

Sind............................... 80-82, 155
Spain..13, 79
St. Augustine 25
Stoics, Stoicism............................29
Sublunar world, its corruption ...2, 7, 28
Sun
  and the seasons...13-14, 42-43, 61
  bodily form 167
  general qualities.............. 51, 164
  general significations 164
Syria 79, 82
Tabaristan...................... 80, 82
Thābit ibn Qurra 26-27, 46, 91
Thema Mundi 202
Toz the Greek............................181
Transfer of nature .... *See an-naql* (transfer)
Trivium 26
Troy 171
Trutanus.......................................73
Turks 79, 183
Vassals...73
Ven 107
Venice............... .... 82, 252-53
Venus
  bodily form.............................172
  general qualities.............. 53, 168
  general significations 168
Vettius Valens...103, 158, 166, 172, 176, 181
  Anth.................... 107, 158, 166
Via combusta.. .... 75, 243-44
Yemen...................... 80-81, 173
Zodiac
  and the seasons 29
  begins with Aries 41, 42
  divided into quarters 49
  elemental order 39-40
  hot/cold halves 49
  names of signs, why 43
  only 12 signs 27, 37, 38
  primary motion 135, 155

solar/lunar halves 48, 54

Zoller, Robert 4, 25, 56, 78–82, 97, 124-25, 130, 163, 168, 178, 181-82

www.ingramcontent.com/pod-product-compliance
Lightning Source LLC
Chambersburg PA
CBHW070546160426
43199CB00014B/2394